A Short History
of Archaeology

Glyn Daniel

A Short History of
Archaeology

WITH 146 ILLUSTRATIONS
10 IN COLOUR

THAMES AND HUDSON

THIS IS VOLUME ONE HUNDRED IN THE SERIES
Ancient Peoples and Places
GENERAL EDITOR: GLYN DANIEL

To Walter and Eva

Frontispiece: 'Digging the Barrow', from the
Gentleman's Magazine, 1852. Archaeology was for
long considered a dilettante pursuit for gentleman
amateurs.

Filmset and printed in Great Britain by
BAS Printers Limited, Over Wallop, Hampshire
Colour illustrations separated by D. S. Colour, London,
printed by Balding + Mansell, Wisbech, Cambridgeshire
Bound by Western Book Company Limited, Maesteg, Glamorgan

Contents

Preface

The first volume in the Ancient Peoples and Places series, *Peru*, by Geoffrey Bushnell, was published in 1956.

Now, 25 years, 5,000,000 words and 15,000 illustrations later we reach the hundredth volume. The series originated in a tentative way in a conversation between me and my former pupil, Simon Young, then on the staff of Thames and Hudson and for long a Director of John Murray. But the imaginative decision to launch the series, and support it vigorously, was that of Walter Neurath, who contributed so much to British publishing, and whose death in 1967 was a very great loss to all. The designing of the first volume was the work of his wife, Eva, and I am happy to dedicate this book to Walter and Eva, without whom this series would never have existed.

Its aims were simple: to summarize in an authoritative but readable way what was known about an ancient people (the Scythians, the Etruscans, the Phoenicians, the Maya) or an ancient place (Babylon, Constantinople, Mexico, New Grange, Brittany). We wanted the books to meet the needs of the student or the general reader who looked for an up-to-date summary of what was known of a people, a place or a topic in antiquity: but also to enable a serious specialist to go on from there by providing careful bibliographical notes and lists of books for further reading. And it was always our intention to save archaeology from falling back into its own dust by reproducing the artistic achievements of ancient peoples in the form of as many illustrations as possible. We succeeded from time to time, and Cyril Connolly once, generously, described the series as 'the ideal bridge between highbrow and lowbrow'.

For this centenary volume the publishers requested me to celebrate the occasion by writing a short history of archaeology. I had thought that I had already said what I had to say on the subject in my *The Three Ages*, *A Hundred Years of Archaeology*, *The Idea of Prehistory*, *Man Discovers His Past*, *The Origins and Growth of Archaeology*, and *A Hundred and Fifty Years of Archaeology*, but I found it a good exercise to concentrate my ideas into a long essay. It is inevitably selective and personal. I have tried to emphasize matters that seemed important to me, not only in the history of archaeological discovery, but also in the history of man's ideas about his ancient past.

I early realized the impossibility of dealing fully, in a short book, with the long history of a scientifically pursued humanistic discipline now practised widely all over the world. I have therefore given

I, II Palaeolithic cave paintings of bison from Altamira, Spain.

Overleaf:
III Gold mask of *c.*1550 BC found by Schliemann in the Shaft Graves at Mycenae and thought by him to represent Agamemnon. Ht 26 cm.

IV Bull's head of gold leaf and lapis lazuli over a wooden core, mounted on a lyre. Part of the great funerary treasure of *c.* 2500 BC excavated by Sir Leonard Woolley from the Royal Cemetery at Ur.

references throughout the text to other books where more extensive and more authoritative treatment can be found. I have broken up the story in the first five main chapters into five periods: first, from the beginnings to 1797 – when John Frere wrote his famous letter; second, from 1797 to 1867 – the date of the Exposition Universelle in Paris, eight years after the *annus mirabilis* of 1859 and the publication of Darwin's *Origin of Species*; third, from 1867 to the First World War; then fourth, the quarter-century between the two World Wars, with its quickening interest in archaeology all over the world; finally, the period from 1939 to the present, naturally the most difficult to deal with adequately, or at all, in a small book. Within each of these chapters, except chapter 5, I have dealt with topics and areas separately. The sixth chapter is a very personal statement of what I consider to be the great themes in the historical development of archaeology.

In 1978 the first conference on the history of archaeology was held in Aarhus, organized by Ole Klindt-Jensen (who died last year) and myself. The papers read then are being published in a volume entitled, *Towards a History of Archaeology*. I much benefited from that conference and from the papers in the book, particularly those on the development of the three-age system, Dilip Chakrabarti on the history of Indian archaeology, and K. Slenář on the history of Czechoslovak archaeology.

In the editing of this series, Ancient Peoples and Places, I have had the constant encouragement of Walter and Eva Neurath and, since Walter's death, of my old pupil and friend, Thomas Neurath, who is now Managing Director of the firm. And over a quarter of a century I have been firmly guided, advised and helped by that most kindly, but critical and exacting member of the Thames and Hudson editorial staff, Eric Peters, to whom so many modern authors on ancient matters owe so much. He and his younger colleague, Colin Ridler, have edited this book, and I have benefited from their generous advice and criticism. They wanted it to contain more, as may many of its potential readers, but then it would not have been a *short* history. It is already perhaps too long to justify its title and yet, short or long, it may sometimes achieve its purpose – namely, to stimulate anyone interested in the ancient past of man to think how archaeology developed, and to go and read more detailed books. This is what the series is for, to get the lowbrow over the bridge into the highbrow regions of specialization. This is the real and exciting fascination of being, or trying to be, an archaeologist – to know what is known at present about an ancient people or place. But always we must remember that our present state of knowledge is merely, like the present, a moment in time. We can be sure of only one thing in archaeology: that what is now said about the Sumerians or megaliths is not what was said a quarter of a century ago when the series began, and certainly not what will be said in a quarter of a century's time when a new General Editor will, I hope, be celebrating the two-hundredth volume.

Zouafques
Pas-de-Calais
1 October 1980

I

II

III

IV

The Birth of Archaeology

Introduction

Archaeology is that branch of the study of history which deals with the material remains of man's past. The study of history in its widest sense deals with all sources: literary, epigraphic and material and the historian aims to create as complete and true a picture of the human past as it is reasonably possible to do. The archaeologist deals with man's artifacts: his tools and weapons, his houses, tombs, temples. Written sources existed for the first time about five thousand years ago, and so there are, very broadly speaking, two kinds of archaeology. There is the archaeology that deals with human history before writing and this is called prehistory. It goes back to the first hominids in East Africa which are now dated to two and a half million years ago and more. The other archaeology deals with the material remains of societies that are documented by writing: at first the material remains are as important as or more important than the written sources: this is the time generally referred to as protohistory. Then as the written sources become common and important we move out of protohistory into history *sensu stricto*, and the study of man's material remains becomes, as has often been said, 'the handmaiden of history'.

The *Oxford English Dictionary* tells us the origin of the word archaeology: it comes from a Greek word *arkhaiologia* meaning 'discourse about ancient things'; and also tells us how it has been used first to mean ancient history generally, secondly to mean a systematic description or study of antiquities, and thirdly 'the scientific study of the remains and monuments of the prehistoric period'. The first usage is no longer in common parlance, and the third is a restricted use of the term – prehistory and prehistoric archaeology are very important aspects of our study of the past but prehistory, though much the longest period studied by the archaeologist, is only a part of archaeology which, in the correct second statement, is the 'systematic description or study of antiquities'.

What the *OED* definition does not make clear is that this 'systematic description or study' is not primarily concerned with the antiquities themselves but with using them to explain and illumine man's prehistoric, protohistoric and historic past.

Georges Daux, in his admirable short history of archaeology entitled *Les Étapes de l'Archéologie* (1942) in the *Que-sais-je?* series, tells us that the term archaeology was re-created in the modern world of scholarship in the seventeenth century by Jacques Spon (1647–85), a

V Gold mask of Tutankhamun, *c.* 1325 BC. Found in his tomb in the Valley of the Kings by Howard Carter. Ht 54 cm.

German doctor in Lyons who was forced to leave France by the revocation of the Edict of Nantes. He travelled widely accompanied by a Sir George Wheeler (d. 1723) who published in 1682 *A Journey into Greece . . . in the company of Dr Spon*. Spon himself published his *Voyage d'Italie, de Dalmatie, de Grèce et du Levant fait aux années 1675–1676* in Amsterdam in 1689 and his *Miscellanea eruditae antiquitatis* in Lyons between 1689 and 1713.

So when did archaeology begin? And who was the first archaeologist? The last native kings of Babylon carried out very active building schemes in several of the ancient cities of Sumer and Akkad. Both Nebuchadrezzar and Nabonidus, the last king of Babylon, dug and restored Ur. Nabonidus was delighted to find at Ur 'the inscriptions of former ancient kings', and his daughter En-nigaldi-Nanna (her name was formerly transcribed incorrectly as Belshalti-Nanner) had dug for years at the temple of Agade. When a heavy downpour of rain opened a great gallery revealing the temple it is recorded that this discovery 'made the king's heart glad and caused his countenance to brighten'. The princess seemed to have a room in her house for her collection of local antiquities. For an account of these early Babylonian archaeological activities see Joan Oates, *Babylon* (1979, 162).

But of course these early activities were not archaeology properly speaking and in the classical world of Greece and Rome there was no archaeology as a deliberate way of finding man's early history by studying his material remains. Herodotus and other Greeks made remarkable ethnographical observations and came into contact with surviving prehistoric barbarians: they were ethnologists or anthropologists but not archaeologists, although they saw ancient people whose remains were later rediscovered by archaeology.

The Greeks and Romans had ideas about man's past but they were not based on archaeology. The Greeks knew of their Mycenaean past when iron was not in use: and both Greeks and Romans speculated on the technological evolution of man. They had ages of stone, bronze and iron just as they had golden ages. And there were speculations about the origins of civilization and the spread of culture. In the time of Diodorus Siculus some Egyptians or Graeco-Egyptians maintained that mankind spread from Egypt, and, in later ages, all civilization as well. This was probably local pride and not an anticipation of the Egyptocentric hyperdiffusionist doctrines of the early twentieth century.

Curiously enough a Chinese compilation of AD 52 set out a sequence of the past of man based on an age of stone, then bronze, then iron. Professor R. H. Lowie, in his *The History of Ethnological Theory* (1937), said 'this is not a case of genius forestalling science by two thousand years: an alert intelligence is simply juggling possibilities without any basis of facts or any attempt to test them': but I think that the Chinese scheme probably preserved a folk memory of the technological succession of stone, bronze and iron which was to be established as historical fact and the cornerstone of modern archaeology in the early nineteenth century.

The Chinese compilation and the Greek and Roman speculations did not affect thought in Western Europe in post-Roman times.

Archaeology did not exist and the past was invented in terms of the Bible and classical writers. In *A History of the Kings of Britain* (1508) Geoffrey of Monmouth brought Brutus, son of Aeneas, to England in 1125 BC to start British history. This was the invented past – a past of myth and legend, but it was all people could do before the nature of archaeological evidence was appreciated.

The Mediterranean World and Egypt

The decay of the ancient world of Greece and Rome meant the loss of the notions about early man that the classical world had set out. The schemes of Hesiod and Lucretius were replaced by the story of the creation of the world and man and of a Universal Flood as set out in Genesis. The renaissance of learning in the fifteenth and sixteenth centuries, however, brought back an interest in the classical period: Lucretius, Aristotle, Hesiod and Herodotus were read again and so were Caesar's *Commentaries on the Gallic War* and Tacitus's *Agricola* and the *Germania*. Here was a description of the barbarians of central and northern Europe – the Celts, Gauls, Germans, Britons, and Goths – and a description of that remarkable class in Celtic society – the Druids, who were teachers, priests and judges.

The classical civilization of the ancient world survived to the sixteenth century in its material remains. Scholars in Italy and travellers from other countries to Italy, Greece, Asia Minor and Egypt began to discover, describe and admire classical and Near Eastern antiquities. Popes and cardinals began collecting antiquities and made their villas into private museums. It was this age in Italy that produced the word *dilettanti* – those who delighted in the arts.

In England the Society of Dilettanti was founded by learned men in 1732: it met in London to bring together those who had done Italy and the Grand Tour. In the preface to his *Ionian Antiquities* Richard Chandler wrote of the origin of the Dilettanti, 'Some Gentlemen who had travelled in Italy, desirous of encouraging, at home, a taste for those objects which had contributed so much to their entertainment abroad, formed themselves into a Society under the name of the DILETTANTI.'

It was during the period 1750–1880, the second renaissance of Greek scholarship, that the antiquities of the classical world were discovered by French, English and German scholars. The great age of English collectors began with the travels of the painter James Stuart (1712–86) and the architect Nicholas Revett (1720–1804) in Athens in the three years 1751–53. They spent those years measuring, drawing, recording. Their great work, *The Antiquities of Athens*, was long delayed: the first 1 volume appeared in 1762 but the fourth not until 1816. The Society of Dilettanti had financed the publication of *The Antiquities of Athens*: in 1764 they financed their 'first Ionic expedition' consisting of Revett, Chandler and William Pars. The results were published between 1769 and 1797 in the volumes entitled *The Antiquities of Ionia*. At the same 2 time as Stuart and Revett were working in Athens, two other Englishmen, Robert Wood and James Dawkins, toured Asia Minor and the Near East publishing their results in two volumes by Robert Wood, *Ruins of Palmyra* (1753) and *Ruins of Baalbec* (1757).

1, 2 (*Above*) Engraving of the Temple of Artemis from Stuart and Revett, *The Antiquities of Athens.* (*Right*) Capitals and pilasters from the Temple of Apollo at Didyma, from *The Antiquities of Ionia* by Chandler, Revett and Pars. The sketches and studies of English travellers in Greece and Turkey during the mid-eighteenth century brought about a revival of interest in ancient Greek civilization.

3 Portrait of J. J.
Winckelmann (1717–68).

3

During the eighteenth century the collecting zeal of Italians was
waning and much of the Roman collections had been dispersed to Paris,
Madrid, Munich and Prague. Yet when Joachim Winckelmann, in the
middle of the eighteenth century, wrote his famous *History of Art*
(1763–68), it was Rome that provided him with his main material.
Winckelmann has been called 'the father of archaeology': he was
certainly the first scholar to study ancient art historically – but art
history is only one facet of archaeology.

Excavation in classical lands had begun early together with
collecting and describing. The ancient cities of Pompeii and
Herculaneum, south-east of Naples, owe their fame in history and in
the history of archaeology to their sudden destruction when Vesuvius
erupted on 24 August AD 79. When the eruption ceased the next day,
Pompeii was covered with lapilli and ashes to a depth of twenty feet (six
metres). At Herculaneum the volcanic material was carried along by
torrents of water and mud which solidified into lava that covered the
city with a hard tufa up to sixty-five feet (twenty metres) thick. An eye-
witness account of these strange happenings is given in letters by Pliny
the Younger to Tacitus.

4 Excavations at Herculaneum from *Voyages pittoresques de Naples et de Sicile* (1782).

The ruins of Pompeii were discovered in the late sixteenth century during tunnelling to build a conduit. Excavation of these buried cities began in 1709 at Herculaneum during the Austrian occupation. Workmen found three marble statues of young women and these excited the imagination of the wife of King Charles IV of Naples. In 1738 the king began excavations at Herculaneum: ten years later excavation began at Pompeii and in 1763 an inscription *rei publicae Pompeianorum* was found which identified the site as Pompeii.

Excavations at Herculaneum were carried on by sinking shafts and driving tunnels until 1765 by which time the theatre, the Basilica and the Villa of the Papyri were found and a plan of the city made. In the neighbourhood of Stabia and Gragnano, excavations between 1749 and 1782, organized by King Charles IV of Naples (later Charles III of Spain), uncovered a dozen villas.

The discovery and appreciation of classical antiquity had an effect on taste and design in eighteenth-century Europe. An important collection of painted Greek vases formed by Sir William Hamilton, the man who was cuckolded by Nelson, British ambassador at Naples in

1772, was acquired by the British Museum and his *Antiquités Etrusques, Grecques et Romaines* (1766–67) inspired Josiah Wedgwood to fashion Greek, Etruscan and Pompeian vases. The Wedgwood Works at Staffordshire in England still bear the name Etruria in recognition of this inspiration.

Many of the dramatic surface antiquities of Egypt were known to early Greek and Arab travellers. Herodotus, 'the Father of History' as he has been called, travelled in Egypt as far south as Aswan and wrote about mummification and the pyramids. Diodorus Siculus, Strabo, Pausanias and Pliny the Elder all visited Egypt. The great seated statues of Amenhotep III at Thebes were mistakenly named the Colossi of Memnon after the Homeric hero Memnon. The Greeks also called the mortuary temple of Ramesses II the Memnonium: but Diodorus called it the tomb of Ozymandias (the Greek for the real name of Ramesses) and quotes an inscription found on one of the statues, 'My name is Ozymandias, king of kings: if any would know how great I am and where I lie, let him surpass me in any of my works.' (This is probably the source of Shelley's poem *Ozymandias*.)

5 Engraving of the Temple of Isis at Pompeii by Piranesi the Younger. The discovery and excavation of Pompeii and Herculaneum had a profound impact on taste in eighteenth-century Europe.

Overleaf:
6 The pyramids at Giza caught the imagination of travellers from Herodotus onwards, and were often fancifully interpreted as in this engraving by Fischer von Erlach of 1721.

19

A. Die Gröſte Pyramide, worun 360000 Menſchen 20 Jahr gearbeitet *Plin:* B. Die ande
welche etwas weniger im Umfange hat C. Die kleineſte, in welche, wie in die andere g
kein Eingang iſt D. Das überbliebene von dem *Coloſſaliſchen Sphynx* E. Deſſen ſon
vollkomne Geſtalt. *Auſan:*.

J. B. Fiſchers v: E: delin.

C. P. S. C

La plus grande des Pyramides, qui a eté l'ouvrage de 360000 hommes
endant 20 Ans. Plin. B. La seconde, qui a un peu moins de circonference
a plus petite, qui a nulle ouverture, comme la Seconde. D. Le reste du
hynx Colossal. E. Le Sphynx dans sa forme entiere. Ausone.

the First PYRAMID. 659

A Description of the Inside of the first PYRAMID.

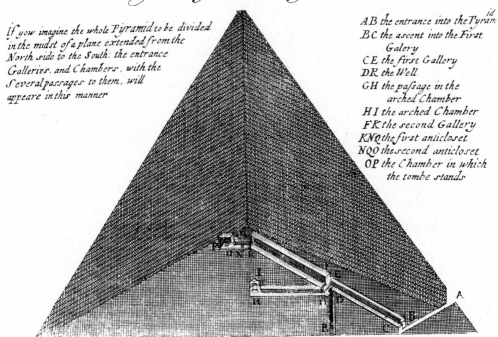

The inside of the first and fairest Pyramid

If you imagine the whole Pyramid to be divided in the midst of a plane extended from the North side to the South: the entrance Galleries, and Chambers, with the Several passages to them, will appeare in this manner

AB the entrance into the Pyram.id
BC the ascent into the First Galery
CE the first Gallery
DR the Well
GH the passage in the arched Chamber
HI the arched Chamber
FK the second Gallery
KNQ the first anticloset
NQO the second anticloset
OP the Chamber in which the tombe stands

7 John Greaves of Oxford visited the Egyptian pyramids in 1638. This drawing from his *Pyramidographia* is the first accurate one of the Great Pyramid.

8 (*Opposite*) The Rosetta Stone, now in the British Museum, was discovered in the Nile Delta near Alexandria in 1799.

Arab travellers exploring Egypt in the Middle Ages were mainly concerned with the pyramids at Giza: they were interested above all in finding treasure. European travellers in the sixteenth, seventeenth and eighteenth centuries seldom travelled further from Cairo than the Giza pyramids. In 1610 an Englishman called Sandys, in his *Travels*, described how he entered the First pyramid and declared it was not a treasure store but a king's tomb. John Greaves of Oxford was in Egypt in 1638 and later wrote *Pyramidographia*. He produced the first true measurements of the Great Pyramid, argued that its purpose was to act as a royal tomb and a symbol of immortality, and produced the first accurate drawing of the interior entitled 'The Inside of the First and Fairest Pyramid.'

Richard Pococke, whose *Travels in Egypt* appeared in 1755, went beyond Giza: he described the pyramids at Sakkara and Dahshur, gave probably the earliest account of the stepped pyramid of Zoser and described the mastabas at Giza which he correctly said were the tombs of princes and nobles.

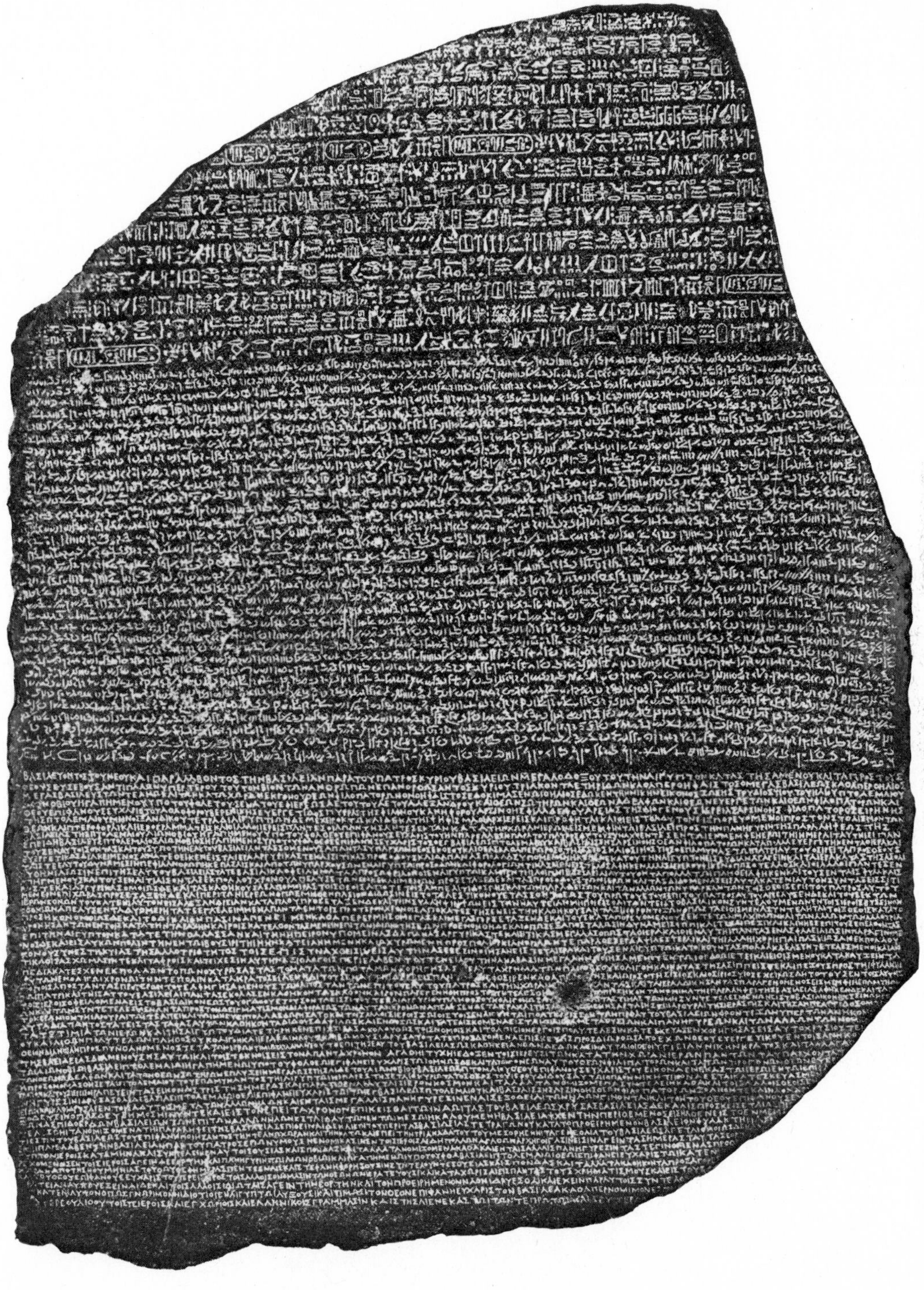

Napoleon Bonaparte deliberately equipped his great expeditionary force to Egypt, that left Toulon on 19 May 1798, with skilled draftsmen and scientists to investigate the geography, resources and antiquities of Egypt. These savants – the 'donkeys' as they were called by the soldiers – included Dolomieu, the mineralogist, and Dominique Vivant, Baron Denon (1747–1825) (see p. 64). It is said that Napoleon even used the pyramids for a pep talk to his troops, and he is supposed to have addressed them with these words: 'Soldiers: forty centuries of history look down upon you from the top of the Pyramids.' Despite the destruction of the French fleet in Aboukir Bay by Admiral Nelson, the army lasted on for a while until in August 1799 Napoleon sailed back to France. Meanwhile the French Egyptian Institute was set up, and it continued through to the twentieth century. The archaeological work of the Institute did not involve excavation; it was concerned with the recording of field monuments and the collection of portable antiquities.

8 Among these was the famous Rosetta Stone. In 1799 a French soldier found quite by chance, while digging for a fort near Alexandria, a black basalt slab 3 feet 9 inches (114 centimetres) in height, 2 feet 4½ inches (72 centimetres) in width, and 11 inches (28 centimetres) thick bearing an inscription in three different scripts. An officer named Boussard or Bouchard thought this stone might be of great importance and had it taken to Cairo. Plaster casts were made of the Rosetta Stone and sent to Paris. In 1802, when the British took possession of Egypt, all the antiquities collected by the French were taken over by the British including, after some difficulty, the Rosetta Stone. This is why this priceless antiquity is in the British Museum – one of the spoils of war!

European travellers from the sixteenth century onwards journeyed in Mesopotamia: they visited the two large tells near Hillah in Babylonia and near Mosul in Assyria which were described, correctly, in Jewish and Arab traditions as the sites of Babylon and Nineveh, and they collected potsherds, brickbats and fragments of tablets covered with cuneiform writing such as was found in old Persian monuments. In 1765 the Danish scholar, Carsten Niebuhr, visited the ruins of Persepolis and made copies of many cuneiform inscriptions: he observed that the inscriptions seemed to be of three different kinds and these were later deciphered as Old Persian, Elamite and Babylonian.

9 Carsten Niebuhr visited Persepolis in 1765 and recorded the carvings and Persian cuneiform inscriptions there.

verschiedene Buchstaben der ältesten persischen Schrift.

10 One of the earliest illustrations of British antiquities. Roman coins from the 1600 edition of Camden's *Britannia*.

Antiquarianism in Northern and Western Europe

But not all European antiquaries could find time and money to take themselves to study the antiquities of classical lands and Egypt. Dr William Borlase, who published his *Antiquities of Cornwall* in 1754, says that he conducted his Cornish researches as a substitute for foreign travels.

A brief survey of British antiquaries may serve to illustrate what was going on. John Leland (1506?–52) was appointed, in 1533, King's Antiquary by Henry VIII, and toured Britain describing things of antiquarian interest, mainly libraries, monasteries and buildings.

William Camden (1551–1623), first a master of Westminster School, then Clarenceux King of Arms in the College of Heralds, travelled extensively studying the visible antiquities of Britain. He defended the study of antiquities which he called 'the back-looking curiosity'; he recognized that there were some 'which wholly contemne and avile this Study of Antiquity' but he was of quite another view: he wrote, 'In the Study of Antiquity (which is always accompanied with dignity and hathe a certaine resemblance with eternity) there is a sweet food of the mind well befitting such as are of honest and noble disposition.' When he was only 35, in 1586, he produced his *Britannia*, the first general guide to the antiquities of Britain. It went through several editions, being reproduced and revised during two hundred years. In the original edition there appeared the first illustration in an English antiquarian book: it was of a re-used Saxon chancel arch in a church at Lewes in Sussex. In 1600, when he produced a new edition of the *Britannia*, he added illustrations of Stonehenge and of Roman coins. Camden was a very careful observer and noted what we now call cropmarks, which are most easily picked up by air photography. Writing of the Roman city of Richborough he said: 'By now age has eras'd the very tracks of it: and to teach us that cities dye as well as men, it is at this day a corn-field, whereas when the corn is grown up, one may observe the draughts of streets crossing one another for where they have gone the corn is thinner.'

Robert Plot and Edward Lhwyd, among others in Britain, carried on the traditions of Leland and Camden. Plot (1640–96) was the first curator of the Ashmolean Museum in Oxford. His *Natural History of Staffordshire* and of *Oxfordshire* were published in the 1670s: he was a topographer as well as a historian and antiquary. He, like his contemporaries, worked by field visits and by questionnaires addressed to the landed gentry, clergy and schoolmasters. One of Plot's questions was, 'Are there any ancient sepulchres hereabout of Men of Gigantic Stature, Roman Generals, and others of ancient times?' and a

11 New Grange, a great chambered tomb north of Dublin in Ireland, was discovered in 1699. Edward Lhwyd visited it soon afterwards and had this drawing made.

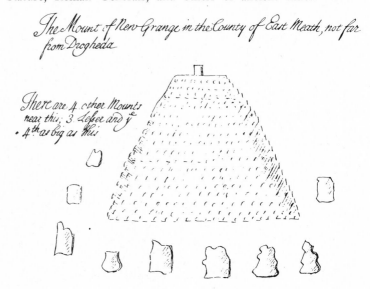

contemporary, Machell, in his questionnaire asks for answers to these questions: 'What memorable places where Battles have been fought? Round heaps of stone or earth cast up in Hills, trench'd round about or otherwise? What fortifications, camps?'

Edward Lhwyd (1660–1708) succeeded his old tutor Plot as Keeper of the Ashmolean. A polymath, he wrote about geology, Celtic languages and antiquities. He travelled extensively in England, Wales, Scotland, Ireland and briefly in Brittany. The great chambered tomb of New Grange, north of Dublin, was discovered by accident in 1699 and Lhwyd visited it and was most impressed by it and the carved stones. A Roman coin was found near the top of the barrow which he said 'might bespeak it Roman: but that the rude carving at the entry and in the cave seems to denote it a barbarous monument. So, the coin proving it ancienter than any Invasion of the Ostmans or Danes: and the carving and rude sculpture barbarous: it should follow that it was some place of sacrifice or burial of the ancient Irish ... the monument was never Roman, not to mention that we want History to prove that ever the Romans were at all in Ireland.' This is one of the earliest and clearest examples of good archaeological reasoning: Lhwyd was arguing from material remains and not from classical writers.

12

11

John Aubrey (1626–97), author of the famous *Brief Lives*, was a friend of Lhwyd's and a keen field archaeologist. His great *Monumenta Britannica* lay unpublished till recently (1980) in the Bodleian Library at Oxford. Writing of North Wiltshire in the 1660s he says,

> Let us imagine then what kind of countrie this was in the time of the Ancient Britons. . . . a shady dismal wood and the inhabitants almost as savage as the Beasts whose skins were their only rayment. . . . Their religion is at large described by Caesar. Their priests were Druids some of their temples I pretend to have restored, as Avebury, Stonehenge etc as also British sepulchres. Their way of fighting is lively sett down by Caesar. . . . They knew the use of iron.

12 (*Below, left*) Portrait of Edward Lhwyd (1660–1708), from a decorated initial capital in the Ashmolean Book of Benefactors, Ashmolean Museum, Oxford.

13 (*Below, right*) Portrait of John Aubrey (1626–97), from John Britton's *Memoir of Aubrey*.

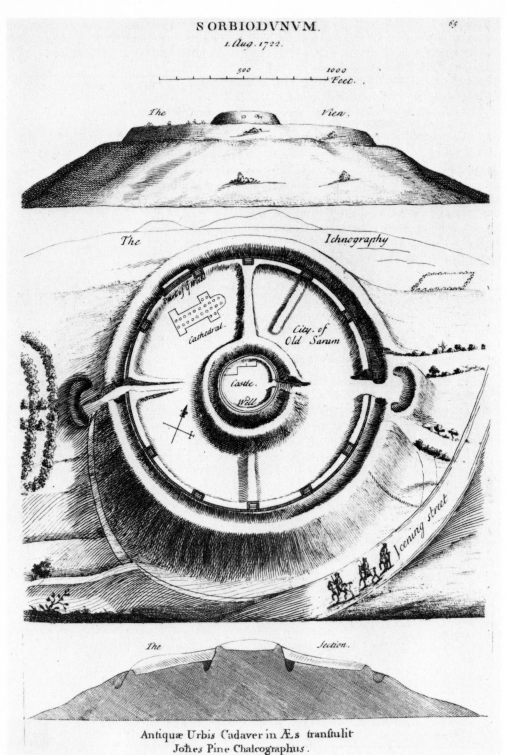

SORBIODVNVM.

1. Aug. 1722.

500   1000
Feet.

The   View.

The   Ichnography

Port of the Wall.

Cathedral.   City. of
                       Old Sarum

              Castle.
              Wall.

                                    Iceaning street

The   Section.

Antiquæ Urbis Cadaver in Æs transtulit
Johes Pine Chalcographus.

Stukeley designavit

14 (*Opposite*) Plan and section of Old Sarum, near Salisbury, by William Stukeley, from his *Itinerarium Curiosum*, Centuria I (1725).

15 Stukeley's drawing of Stonehenge, from his *Stonehenge, a Temple Restored to the British Druids* (1740).

... They were two or three degrees I suppose less savage than the Americans. ... The Romans subdued and civilized them.

Aubrey was using classical writers to interpret antiquities. He it was who first attributed stone circles to the Druids. The literary movement known as the Romantic Revolt, with its interest in the picturesque in the landscape, made it easy to make the Ancient Britons and their Druids attractive.

The finest example of the romantic British archaeologist was William Stukeley (1687–1765), who is sometimes mainly remembered for his Druidomania, but he was a good and careful field archaeologist and his *Itinerarium Curiosum* (1725), *Abury* (1743) and *Stonehenge* (1740) are very fine for their time. His intentions were clear: he says his purpose was 'to oblige the curious in the Antiquities of Britain: [to give] an account of places and things from inspection, not complete from others' labours, or travels in one's study.'

14, 15

The eighteenth century saw not only field archaeologists but those who speculated philosophically about the early past of man. Such was Thomas Pownall (1722–1805), who was Governor of Massachusetts from 1757 to 1760: 'The face of the earth', he wrote in 1733,

> being originally everywhere covered with wood, except where water prevailed, the first human beings of it were *Woodland-Men* living on the fruits, fish and game of the forest. To these the land-worker succeeded. He *settled* on the land, became a fixed inhabitant and increased and multiplied. Where-ever the land-worker came, he, as at this day, ate out the thinly scattered race of Wood-Men.

Here was a different way of looking at the past: it looks forward, in a way, to economic prehistory and is akin to the views of the Scottish primitivists of the eighteenth century like Thomas Blackwell and James Burnett, later Lord Monboddo (1714–99), who took their ideas from the medieval notion of an ordained universe of purposeful and unfolding plan: the concept of the Great Chain of Being in which everything from the lowliest object to man had a place in the framework. Monboddo's great work *On the Origin and Progress of Language* was published in six volumes between 1773 and 1792, and his *Ancient Metaphysics* in another six volumes between 1779 and 1799. He argued that the orang-utan was a variety of man and its want of speech accidental; man was born with a tail and it was the work of midwives that had prevented this fact from being generally known.

Dr Samuel Johnson (1709–84) did not approve of Monboddo's speculations. 'Other people have strange notions,' he wrote, 'but they conceal them. If they have tails, they hide them: Lord Monboddo is as jealous of his tail as a squirrel.' Neither did Johnson approve of antiquarian speculations based on field monuments and surface antiquities. 'All that is really known of the ancient state of Britain is contained in a few pages.' he wrote. 'We can know no more than what old writers have told us.' This negative attitude to archaeology was very widespread in the late eighteenth century.

The development of archaeology in Renaissance Scandinavia presents a pattern parallel to that of Britain, but there was some early excavation. In 1588 the long 'dolmen' north of Roskilde, known as the Langben Rises Høj, was excavated in the hope of proving that these tombs were the tombs of giants and warriors as folklore alleged: but there were only meagre finds of pottery and other artifacts. During the late sixteenth century the famous field monuments of Jelling in Jutland were depicted on the orders of the governor of Holstein and some other runic inscriptions were copied and deciphered. King Gustavus Adolphus II of Sweden and King Christian IV of Denmark encouraged the study of antiquities. John Bure, or Johannes Bureus as he was known in his latinized form (1568–1652), was for a time tutor to Gustavus Adolphus. He studied rune-stones, travelling all round Sweden and publishing his results in *Monumenta Sveo-Gothica Hactemus Exsculpta* and an unpublished corpus entitled *Monumenta Runica*. The king established the post of Riksantikvariat or Royal Antiquary to which Bure was appointed.

16

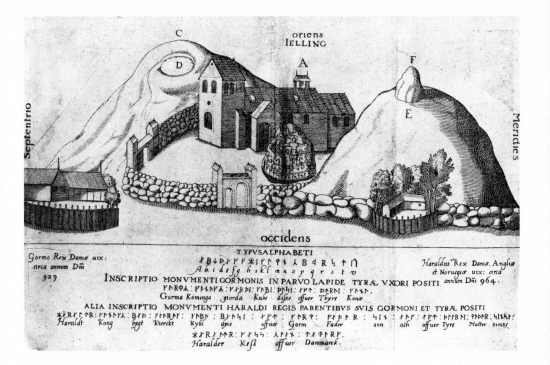

Ole Worm, or Olaus Wormius to give him his latinized name (1588–1654), was the son of the mayor of Aarhus but came of a family of refugees from religious persecution in Holland. Trained as a doctor he was a true polymath, being successively professor of humanities, then Greek, then medicine at the University of Copenhagen. He collected many types of objects, especially flora and fauna and human artifacts, which he very carefully arranged and classified according to a rigorous system he had invented. He prepared a detailed catalogue which was published as *Museum Wormianum* in 1655 after his death by his son William. His museum, which was a great attraction in Copenhagen, included an assortment of bizarre and exotic objects, antiques and stuffed animals. Worm was very interested in Danish antiquities, particularly runic monuments, and published *Monumenta Danica* and *Fasti Danici* (1643). In 1626 he organized a royal circular to be sent round to all clergy to report on all rune-stones, burial sites and other historical remains in their parishes. In 1639 a gold horn was found at Gallehus in south Jutland, and Worm, with his great knowledge of runes and antiquities, was asked to describe it, which he did in *De aureo cornu* in 1641. This gold horn, and another discovered a hundred years later, were stolen from the royal collections in 1802 and destroyed. Worm's account of the horn and the runes and designs on it are therefore of great importance still, over three hundred years later.

Thomas Bartholin, a professor of history, was appointed Danish Royal Antiquary in 1684. In 1689 he published, together with his assistant, the Icelander Arni Magnusson, a three-volume work entitled *Antiquitatum Danicarum de causis contemptae a Danis adhuc gentilibus*

16 In Denmark, the recording of field monuments began as early as the late sixteenth century. This drawing of the two royal tumuli and large rune stone (with transcription) at Jelling, East Jutland, was published in 1591.

23, 24

17

31

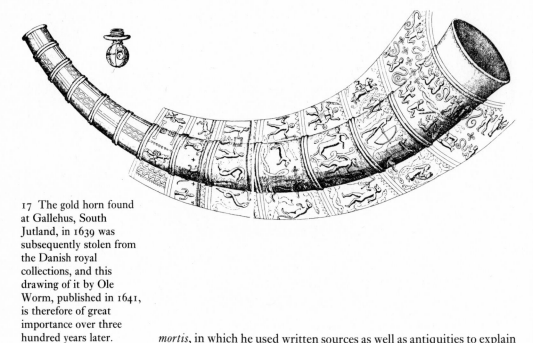

17 The gold horn found at Gallehus, South Jutland, in 1639 was subsequently stolen from the Danish royal collections, and this drawing of it by Ole Worm, published in 1641, is therefore of great importance over three hundred years later.

mortis, in which he used written sources as well as antiquities to explain the scornful attitude of the heathen Danes to death.

In 1662 in Sweden a Chair of Antiquities was created in the University of Uppsala: Olof Verelius was the first holder. In 1666 he was appointed Royal Antiquary and an Antiquities College was created affiliated to the University of Uppsala. The College was the brain child of Johan Hadorph, Secretary of the Museum. He also drafted a royal proclamation protecting the ancient monuments of the Kingdom of Sweden and Finland: a few years later a second royal proclamation added protection to portable antiquities. With its Antiquities College and these royal proclamations, Sweden led all Europe in pioneering archaeological studies. In 1692 the College was transferred to Stockholm and called the Antiquities Archive.

In Denmark Erik Pontoppidan (1698–1764), then court chaplain, and the crown prince, later Frederik V, excavated a megalithic passage-grave at Jaegerspris in 1744. It was perhaps the first such excavation properly carried out; the report was published in the first (1744) issue of the proceedings of the Danish Royal Society. Pontoppidan argued that this monument was the burial place of ordinary human beings not giants as had been thought previously: 'built', he said, 'by our pious, though heathen, forefathers at least 1,800 years ago.' In 1763 he summarized his researches on Danish antiquity in his great work *Den*

18 The Neolithic chambered tomb at Cocherel, near Dreux, in northern France, found by chance in 1685 and excavated. It was one of the earliest excavations to be published in Western Europe.

danske Atlas I. The achievements of the antiquaries of Denmark and Sweden in the seventeenth and eighteenth centuries are truly remarkable.

In France a megalithic tomb was discovered and excavated in 1685 at Cocherel near Dreux in the Eure. It was obviously a good example of what we would now call an *allée couverte*. The records present one of the earliest accounts of the excavation of a chambered tomb in Western Europe: they were published in Bernard de Montfaucon's *L'Antiquité expliquée et représentée en figures* (1719) and Le Brasseur's *Histoire Civile et Ecclésiastique du Comté d'Évreux* (1722).

Southern Brittany with its great number and variety of megalithic monuments was bound to attract the early attention of antiquaries. In the decade 1727–37 de Robien described the megalithic monuments of Carnac and Locmariaquer and employed an artist to record them. The Comte de Caylus (1692–1765) in the last volume of his *Recueil d'antiquités égyptiennes, Etrusques, grecques et gauloises* (1767) illustrates many prehistoric monuments. Legrand d'Aussy (1738–1800) was elected a member of the Institut in 1795 and read a paper called 'Les anciennes sépultures nationales': he quoted with approval the book of La Tour-d'Auvergne-Coret *Origines gauloises celles des plus anciens peuples de l'Europe* (1796), who correctly assigned Breton megaliths to the pre-Roman Gauls.

18

33

The Age of Man and Stone Tools

We have seen that the antiquaries of the seventeenth centuries had at their disposal four sources: folk memories, myths and legends, the antiquities themselves, classical writers, and the Bible. It was only the Bible that seemed to give any evidence of the chronology of man, in the list in Genesis of how long Old Testament characters lived – and they seemed to have been very long-lived! The early fathers had attempted to translate these dates into a hard absolute chronology. Jerome, who translated Eusebius into Latin, counted 2,242 years from Adam to the Flood and 942 years from the Flood to Abraham – though later he revised these figures to 1,656 and 292. With Jerome's additions the chronology of Eusebius provided the numerical time-scale from which Western historians founded their dating system and the idea that the world was six thousand years old.

Luther took 4000 BC as the date of creation, but while he liked a round figure there was support for other dates such as 4032, 4004, 3949 and 3946. The astronomer Kepler declared that he had found an error of four years in the chronology of the Christian era and it was the acceptance of this that produced the date of 4004 BC in the margin of the Authorized Version of the Bible published in 1611.

This date was argued for by seventeenth-century English divines. Archbishop Ussher's work appeared in English in 1658 under the title *The Annals of the World Deduced from the Origins of Time and continued to the beginning of the Emperor Vespasian's Reign, and the total Destruction and Abolition of the Temple and Commonwealth of the Jews*, in which he says: 'I incline to this opinion that from the evening ushering in the first day of the world, to that midnight which began that first day of the Christian era, there were 4003 years, seventy days, and six temporarie howers', and he decided that man was created on the sixth day, a Friday, and October the 28th.

In 1642 Dr John Lightfoot, Master of St Catharine's College and Vice-Chancellor of the University of Cambridge, published *A Few and New Observations on the Book of Genesis, the most of them certain, the rest probable, all harmless, strange and rarely heard of before*, in which he wrote:

> Our bodies, Heaven and Earth, Centre and circumference were created together in the same instant, and clouds full of water, not such as we can see made by evaporation but such as are called the Windowes or Cataracts of *Heaven* ... Man was created by the *Trinity* about the third houre of the day, or nine of the clocke in the morning on 23 October 4004 BC.

These views were held in general by most people. William Shakespeare in *As You Like It* (1600) makes Rosalind say (Act IV, Scene 1): 'The poor world is almost six thousand years old, and in all this time there was not any man died in his own person, *videlicet*, in a love-cause.' This was the sort of world that enabled Sir Thomas Browne in his *Religio Medici* (1643) to say: 'Time we may comprehend. 'Tis but five days elder than ourselves, and hath the same horoscope with the world.' And this notion of the shortness and comprehensibility of time lasted well into the eighteenth and nineteenth century. Samuel Rogers in his poem *Italy, A Farewell* (1822–28) has a line 'By many a temple half as old as Time', and this phrase was borrowed by his friend Burgon in his Newdigate Prize poem *Petra* (Oxford, 1845) when he described that astonishing and beautiful Nabataean capital as 'A rose-red city – half as old as Time.'

The notion of this short six-thousand-year span of man and the Earth was destroyed by the development of fluvial geology based on the doctrine of uniformitarianism in the second quarter of the nineteenth century, and by the finding of human artifacts with extinct animals in contexts that must be, according to the new geology, well over six thousand years old. But our first stone tools had to be recognized for what they were, namely artifacts made and fashioned by man.

This recognition took a considerable time. For a long time stone tools were explained away as thunderbolts, fairy arrows, elfshot. Ulysses Aldrovandi in the mid-seventeenth century described stone tools as 'due to an admixture of a certain exhalation of thunder and lightning with metallic matter, chiefly in dark clouds, which is coagulated by the circumfused moisture and conglutinated into a mass (like flour with water) and subsequently indurated by heat, like a brick.' Tollius, at about the same time, claimed chipped flints to be 'generated in the sky by a fulgurous exhalation conglobed in a cloud by the circumposed humour'.

The discovery of America produced living people who were using stone tools. Unless one assumed that these were backward people, 19 people who were impoverished descendants of metal-users, they posed a simple question: if such stone-using people existed in America, could there not have been similar people, not knowing the use of metal, living in the most ancient past of ancient Europe? Columbus discovered America in 1492: the impact was immediate and Peter Martyr (Pietro Martire d'Anghiera), whose books were published between 1504 and 1530, and Ferrante Imperato in his *Dell' Historia Naturale* (1599), discussed this problem of the nature of stone-using Americans.

Michele Mercati (1541–93) was one of the first people to accept prehistoric stone tools for what they were. He was appointed Superintendent of the Vatican Botanical Gardens by Pope Pius V and was retained in this office by his successors Gregory XIII and Sixtus V. A medical man, he was polymathic in his interests and expert knowledge: a good mineralogist, he was also one of the founders of palaeontology. He collected fossils, minerals and artifacts and wrote about them in his *Metallotheca* which remained in manuscript in the Vatican Library until its publication in 1717. In this work he illustrated stone artifacts and said they were weapons of war used before metal was known. In declaring the human artifactual nature of these stone tools he drew on classical writers and the Bible, but was impressed by the collection of native American Indian artifacts which were accumulating in the Vatican as presents from Spanish, Portuguese and Italian explorers.

In 1655 Isaac de la Peyrère of Bordeaux published in Amsterdam and London his *A Theological System upon that Pre-supposition that Men were before Adam*. In this he said that the 'thunderbolts' were in fact the artifacts of a primitive and ancient pre-Adamitic race of human beings. His theological views and particularly his theory of pre-Adamites were fiercely criticized: he and his books were seized by the Inquisition. He was forced to recant and his book was publicly burnt in Paris. Is this the only statement of man's origins and his stone artifacts that has been so treated in the history of antiquarian and archaeological literature?

In the year following the publication of de la Peyrère's book, Sir William Dugdale (1605–86) in *The Antiquities of Warwickshire* (1658) describes and illustrates a stone axe and refers to the finding of several of them 'curiously wrought by grinding or some such way . . . being at first made by the native Britons . . . were made use of for weapons, inasmuch as they had not then attained to the knowledge of working iron or brass to such uses.' Dr Robert Plot had no doubt of the true nature of stone implements, and Sir Robert Sibbald and Edward Lhwyd were of the same view. Lhwyd emphasized the American evidence and wrote in a letter dated 17 December 1699:

I doubt not but you have often seen these Arrow-heads they ascribe to elfs or fairies: they are just the same chip'd flints the natives of New England head their arrows with at this day: and there are also several stone hatchets found in this kingdom, not unlike those of the Americans. . . . they were not invented for charms, but were once used in shooting here, as they are still in America. The most curious, as well as the vulgar throughout this country, are satisfied they often drop out of the air, being shot by fairies and relate many instances of it, but for my part I must crave leave to suspend my faith until I see one of them descend.

At the end of the seventeenth century a flint hand-axe was found near Gray's Inn Lane, London by a Mr Conyers. It was associated with the skeleton of an 'elephant', presumably a mammoth. John Bagford, who described this find in a letter dated 1715, accepts the association of a human artifact with an extinct animal but thinks the 'elephant' a Roman import.

18   The 1685 excavations in the megalithic tomb at Cocherel, to which we have already referred, produced polished axes, including one of jade. The Abbé of Cocherel writing in 1722 noted that these axes were like those used by American Indians and went so far as to suggest the Scythians as possible links between America and the tomb-builders of Cocherel. Dom Bernard de Montfaucon in his 1719 account of the Cocherel excavations concludes, very wisely and properly, that from the evidence of the stone implements the tomb was built by 'some barbarous nation, that knew not yet the use either of Iron or any other metal'. Here is one of the first examples of the ascription of prehistoric monuments, as distinct from stone axes and arrowheads, to a stone age.

19 Watercolour of an American Indian by John White, 1585. The discovery of such peoples in America posed the question: had there been a similar folk, not knowing the use of metal, in the ancient past of Europe?

In France in the eighteenth century, particularly after the publication of Mercati's *Metallotheca* in 1717, many scholars such as de Jussieu, Lafitau, Mahudel and Goguet argued in favour of the authenticity of stone implements and the existence of a stone age. Père Lafitau's *Moeurs des Sauvages Amériquains Comparée aux Moeurs des Premiers Temps* – a fascinating and revealing title – was published in

The manner of their attire and
painting them selues when
they goe to their generall
huntings or at theire
Solemne feasts.

1724. He insists on the value of ethnographic parallels for studying the past of western man. 'I was not content with knowing the nature of the savages and with learning of their customs and practices,' he wrote. 'I sought to find in these practices and customs vestiges of the most *remote* antiquity.'

Antoine Yves Goguet (1716–58) published in 1738 a book translated into English three years later entitled *The Origin of Laws, Arts and Sciences and their Progress among the most Ancient Nations.* He declared that we can guess at the state of the ancient past of man in Europe 'by the condition of the greater part of the New World when it was first discovered', and went on, 'the use of bronze preceded that of iron . . . formerly stones, flint pebbles, bones, horn, fish-bones, shells, reeds and thorns were used for everything for which civilized people use metal today. Primitive peoples give us a faithful picture of ancient societies.'

Clearly in the eighteenth century in France some were prepared to accept a stone age and even to accept a three-age system of stone, bronze and iron. In England a few scholars were prepared to follow Dugdale, Sibbald and Plot. In 1765 Lyttelton, Bishop of Carlisle, wrote a paper published in the second volume of *Archaeologia* in 1773, in which he said:

> I entirely agree with Dugdale that they were British instruments of war, and used by them, before they had the art of making arms of brass or iron; but I go farther and am persuaded that when they fabricated these stone weapons they had no knowledge at all of these metals. . . . I am of the opinion that these stone axes are by far the most antient remains existing at this day of our British ancestors and probably coeval with the first inhabitants of this land.

At about this time the authentic association of human bones and stone tools with extinct animals was being reported by Johann Friedrich Esper in the Gaylenreuth Cave near Bamberg in the German Jura. Esper published his finds in 1774 in his *Detailed Report on Recently Discovered Zooliths of Unknown Quadrupeds and the Caves containing them . . . in the upper mountainous countries of the Margravate of Bayreuth.* He asked himself the question: 'Did they belong to a Druid or to an Antediluvian or to a Mortal Man of more recent times?', and, sadly, answers his own question: 'I dare not presume without any sufficient reason these human members to be of the same age as the other animal petrifactions. They must have got there by chance together with them.'

20 John Frere (1740–1807) by J. Hoppner.

There was an English country gentleman in East Anglia, by name
20 John Frere (1740–1807), who made the right deductions from what he observed in a gravel pit at Hoxne near Diss in Suffolk. In 1797 he wrote to the Secretary of the Society of Antiquaries of London enclosing
21 some flint implements which, he said, 'if not particularly objects of curiosity in themselves, must, I think, be considered in that light, from the situation in which they were found.' They were Palaeolithic hand-axes and were found twelve feet (three-and-a-half metres) below the surface of the ground in the bottom layer of some undisturbed strata and they were associated with the bones of extinct animals. Frere very

Flint Weapon found at Hoxne in Suffolk

21 Acheulian handaxes
found at Hoxne in
Suffolk. They were sent in
1797 to the Society of
Antiquaries in London by
John Frere and reproduced
in *Archaeologia*, XII (1800).

correctly described them as 'Weapons of war, fabricated and used by a
people who had not the use of metals'. So far he was not in advance of
the long line of antiquaries we have listed from Mercati to Bishop
Lyttelton who believed in stone artifacts and a stone age; but his ideas
were in advance of them because he realized that the twelve feet of
gravel above the axes must have taken a long time to accumulate if one
believed in the new geology. He wrote:

> The situation in which these weapons were found may tempt us to
> refer them to a very remote period indeed, even beyond that of the
> present world; but, whatever our conjectures on that head may be, it
> will be difficult to account for the stratum in which they lie being
> covered with another stratum which, on that supposition, may be
> conjectured to have been once the bottom, or at least the shore, of
> the sea.

Here was the crux of the matter, in that one phrase 'beyond that of the present world' – by which he meant of course the short world of six thousand years, the comfortable world that began in 4004 BC and which Sir Thomas Browne could comprehend. Petra might be described as half-as-old as time: the Hoxne flints were many hundreds of times older than 'Time' – the time of Eusebius, Ussher and Lightfoot. Frere's fascinating and percipient letter presaged the acceptance of the great antiquity of man which is one of the basic beliefs of archaeology. But no one paid any attention to him: his letter was printed in *Archaeologia* for 1800 and forgotten by most people for sixty years.

America

From the discovery of the New World by Columbus in 1492, the Old World began to speculate on the origins of the American Indians and of archaeological remains observed there. At first speculations were entirely theoretical: archaeological sources were not used until the mid-nineteenth century. Fancy ran free, deriving the Americans from the Egyptians, the Phoenicians, the Lost Tribes of Israel or from a supposed sunken continent called Atlantis.

The mounds of the mid- and south-west of North America soon attracted attention and the question 'Who were the mound-builders?', was an early one frequently asked by students of American antiquities. 22 General Samuel Parsons sent an account of the mounds at Marietta, Ohio, to Ezra Stiles, President of Yale, who in an address in 1783 said they were built by 'the Canaanites of the expulsion of Joshua'. Stiles consulted Benjamin Franklin who replied that he had no explanation for them but thought they might have been built by the soldiers of Hernando de Soto who made a journey from Tampa in Florida to New Orleans 1539–42.

The Ohio Company floated by Brigadier General Rufus Putnam developed tracts of land in Ohio from 1787–8 onwards, close to Marietta. Putnam surveyed the earthworks with very great care. Brian Fagan writes, 'His accurate survey, with its precise dimensions, is a landmark of serious inquiry into America's past' (*Elusive Treasure*, 1976, 91) and Henry Shetrone in 1930 described Putnam's map as 'the genesis of the science of archaeology in the Americas'. The Company set the mounds aside as historical monuments, preserving them in public squares.

Putnam's agent at Marietta was the Reverend Manasseh Cutler, a priest from Massachusetts. Cutler found workmen cutting down trees and began counting the growth rings of the felled trees. One yielded 463 rings: he assumed that each ring represented one year's growth and therefore that the mound on which the tree grew had been built before AD 1300.

B. S. Barton argued in 1787 that the mound-builders were Danes who later moved on to Mexico and turned into the Toltecs. William Bartram on the other hand declared that while the mounds were not built by living Indians they were built by older unspecified Indians. General William Henry Harrison, later ninth President of the United States, came down in 1839 on the side of the anti-Indian or 'lost race' explanation of the Ohio mounds.

In 1784 the famous Thomas Jefferson, subsequently third President of the United States, retired temporarily from politics to his estate at Monticello and wrote his *Notes on the State of Virginia*. Among many other things he was interested in the origin of the mound-builders and to satisfy his curiosity conducted excavations to discover the true nature of the mounds on his property. He trenched one mound and recognized successive strata. He discovered a large quantity of bones and noted that the bones placed in the mound were covered over and then more bones added and then those covered over and the process repeated until the mound was twelve feet high. He observed six 'peculiar circumstances' as follows: '1. the number of bones, 2. their confused position, 3. their being in different strata, 4. the strata in one part having no correspondence with those in another, 5. the difference in the time of inhumation and 6. the existence of infant bones among them.' Lehmann-Hartleben said that Jefferson's excavation 'anticipates the fundamental approach and the methods of modern archaeology by about a full century', and Sir Mortimer Wheeler said of his work that it was 'the first scientific excavation in the history of archaeology . . . unique not only in its age but for long afterwards'.

But Jefferson's work had not solved the matter of the date of the mounds: 'that they were repositories of the dead, has been obvious to all', he wrote, 'but on what particular occasion constructed, was a matter of doubt.' He would not comment himself as regards the general mound-builder problem.

22 The mounds of the American mid-west, such as this one at Marietta, Ohio, aroused interest from an early date. In the eighteenth century they were attributed to, amongst others, the Canaanites, Danes, Spaniards and – more accurately – American Indians of a bygone era.

In 1799, when he was President of the American Philosophical Society in Philadelphia, Jefferson sent round a circular to correspondents which began by stating that the Society had 'always considered the antiquity, changes and present state of their own country as primary objects of their research'. The recipients of the circular were urged

> to obtain accurate plans, drawings and descriptions of whatever is interesting . . . and especially of ancient Fortifications, Tumuli, and other Indian works of art. . . . Cuts in various directions may be made into many of the Tumuli, to ascertain their contents; while the diameter of the largest tree growing thereon, the number of its annulars and the species of the tree, may tend to give some idea of their antiquity.

Jefferson and Manasseh Cutler were pioneers in dendrochronology, the technique of tree-ring dating.

Jefferson has been called 'the father of American archaeology': but as Willey and Sabloff point out, he had no immediate intellectual offspring (*A History of American Archaeology*, 1974, 36). What we most remember about Jefferson's work is not only that he excavated, and excavated well, observing stratigraphy, but that he dug for a purpose – not to find treasure, but to find the answer to a problem.

Museums and Societies

The first museums grew out of the private collections of kings, dukes and cardinals and of humbler people. Ulysses Aldrovandi's (1527–1603) collection became the basis of the museum at Bologna. The collections of Thomas Howard, Earl of Arundel (1586–1646), whom Horace Walpole called 'the Father of Vertu in England', found their way eventually into museums. John Tradescant (d. 1638) and his son John (d. 1662) were two of the earliest English collectors and naturalists. The Tradescant Closet of Curiosities, a remarkable collection of 'varieties and oddities', popularly known as Tradescant's Ark, at Lambeth, was well-known and much visited. The younger Tradescant published the *Musaeum Tradescantianum; or a Collection of Rarities preserved at South Lambeth near London* in 1656. The collection was acquired by Elias Ashmole in 1659 and added to his own collections and the whole presented to the University of Oxford in 1682. It formed the basis of the Ashmolean Museum which was opened by James II, then Duke of York, in that year. The first curator was, as we have said, Robert Plot with Edward Lhwyd as his assistant, and the collections were open to the public.

23
124 One of the most famous private collections was that of Ole Worm: we know what it looked like from the drawing in *Museum Wormianum*, the catalogue that came out after his death in 1655. On his death Worm's collection passed to the King of Denmark, Frederik III, who planned a new building opposite his castle of Christiansborg to house his collections and library. The second storey, housing the museum, was completed only after the King's death: this museum, the *Kunstkammer*, had some seventy-five prehistoric exhibits at the end of

23 Portrait of Ole Worm (1588–1654) at the age of thirty-eight, by Simon de Pas.

the seventeenth century; it was open to the public on payment of an admission charge which went to the curator.

Peter the Great in his Western European travels was interested in museums and private collections as well as industry, ship-building and government. One of the very largest private museums of the seventeenth century was that of Albert Seba (1665–1736), who began life as a druggist in Amsterdam, was then employed by the Dutch East India Company, became very wealthy and poured his money into a collection of all interesting objects in the animal, vegetable and mineral kingdoms. When Peter the Great was in Amsterdam in 1716 he bought Seba's museum (Seba immediately started another one) and had it removed to St Petersburg; it formed the basis of the museum (open to the public in 1719) which eventually developed into the Hermitage, officially founded by Catherine the Great as a Court Museum in 1764 and opened to the public in 1852. Peter himself, although he got his ambassadors to collect objects for his St Petersburg Museum from not only Amsterdam but Paris and Vienna, was most interested in curiosities and freaks and accumulated a very large collection of

24 The first museums grew out of the private collections of men like the polymath Ole Worm, physician to King Christian IV of Denmark. His famous Museum Wormianum contained exotic antiquities, stuffed animals, geological specimens and much else besides. On his death in 1654 Worm's collection passed to King Frederik III, who installed it in the old castle at Copenhagen.

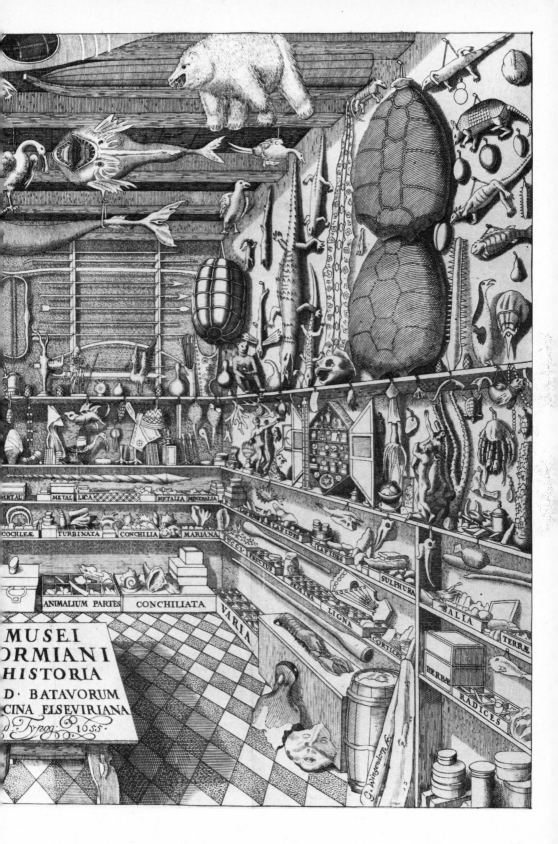

monsters pickled in alcohol, which were displayed in his *Kunstkamera*. But, freaks and monsters apart, he did pass the Decree of February 1718 which directed everyone who had discovered some unusual or ancient object to turn it over to the government.

One of the greatest collectors of all time was Sir Hans Sloane (1660–1753), the famous English physician who was President of the College of Physicians and the Royal Society. His library and collections, valued at £80,000 when he died, he bequeathed to the nation: his gift was accepted and in 1753 an Act was passed for the purchase of the Sloane library and museum and of the Harley manuscripts, to unite them with the Cotton library and to provide one 'general repository' for these and later additions. This repository, opened to the public in January 1759, became the British Museum in Montagu House, Bloomsbury, London.

There had been two remarkable French collections: the first that of N. Fabri de Peiresc (1580–1637) of Aix, often referred to as the founder of the study of antiquity in France. The second was by M. le Comte Caylus, the eighteenth-century scholar and traveller. The illustration reproduced here shows the general arrangement of his collection, and is 25 the frontispiece of his *Recueil d'Antiquitiés* (1752, vol. I). Many of his specimens of classical archaeology were excavated by him in Asia Minor.

The seventeenth century saw the formation of the first learned societies. The Accademia dei Lincei in Rome, to which Galileo belonged, flourished from 1603 to 1630. The Accademia del Cimento was founded by the Medici family in Florence in 1650 and the Accademia Secretorum Naturae had been founded in Naples as early as 1560. The Royal Society of London was founded in 1660 and the Académie des Sciences in Paris in 1666.

As long ago as 1572 a society was formed in England for the preservation of national antiquities. The prime movers in the foundation of the society were Archbishop Matthew Parker, John Stow, William Camden and his pupil Sir Robert Cotton. Application was made to Queen Elizabeth I for the grant of a Royal Charter to this society; but after her death the scheme was opposed by James I and the new society was abolished as being political in aim. In 1707 a group of young men interested in antiquities and history formed themselves into a club. They used to meet in the Young Devil and Bear Taverns in the Strand and out of this was formed an Association on the same lines as the Elizabethan Society. This was formally constituted as the Society of Antiquaries of London in 1718 and received its Royal Charter in 1751.

The French *Journal des Scavans* was published in 1665, the *Miscellanea Curiosa* of the German Academy in 1670. The journal of the London Society of Antiquaries, *Archaeologia*, was first published in 1770 with the avowed purpose 'to explode what rested upon only the vanity of the inventors and propagators of fantasies'. But all were not happy about what was published in *Archaeologia*. Horace Walpole castigated those members of the Society of Antiquaries who had no aesthetic feeling and no taste. 'Mercy on us', he wrote on reading through the second volume of *Archaeologia*, 'what a cartload of bricks

RECUEIL
D'ANTIQUITÉS
EGYPTIENNES,
ETRUSQUES, GRECQUES
ET ROMAINES.

A PARIS,
Chez DESAINT & SAILLANT, rue S. Jean de Beauvais,
vis-à-vis le Collége.

M. DCC. LII.

25 Title page of Caylus'
Recueil d'Antiquités
(1752), with an engraving
of his antiquarian
collection.

and rubbish and Roman ruins they have piled together.' And elsewhere
he added:

> The antiquaries will be as ridiculous as they used to be; and since it
> is impossible to infuse taste in them, they will be as dry and dull as
> their predecessors. One may revive what perished, but it will perish
> again, if more life is not breathed into it than it enjoyed
> originally. . . . I have no curiosity to know how awkward and clumsy
> men have been in the dawn of arts or in their decay.

It would be a long time before the work of archaeologists was
generally recognized as a serious discipline.

2

Antiquaries and Archaeologists (1797–1867)

The New Geology and the Antiquity of Man

In 1851 Daniel Wilson wrote a book entitled *The Archaeology and Prehistoric Annals of Scotland*, believing, as did many others, that he had invented the word 'prehistoric'. In the preface to his second edition of 1863 he says, 'the application of the term prehistoric introduced – if I mistake not – for the first time in this work'. But he was mistaken: the word *préhistoire* was being used by Tournal, the Curator of the Narbonne Museum, as early as 1833.

Five years earlier Tournal published in the *Annales des Sciences naturelles* (XV, 348) the results of his work in the Grotte de Bize (Aude), where he had found human bones and pottery associated with bones of animals, some still surviving, but many extinct. Marcel de Sèvres insisted that the human bones were in the same state of preservation as the bones of extinct animals and in 1829, again in the *Annales des Sciences naturelles* (XVIII, 244), Tournal announced the finding of bones of extinct animals which bore the marks of cutting tools. The next year de Christol of Montpellier published in a pamphlet entitled *Notice sur les Ossements Humains des Cavernes du Gard* (1830) his discovery in a rockshelter near Montpellier of human bones associated with bones of hyena and rhinoceros.

Excited and encouraged by this work in the south of France, Dr P. C. Schmerling began work in several caves at Engihoul, near Liège, in Belgium, of which the most famous was Engis. His discoveries included seven human skulls, many artifacts, some associated with the skeletons of rhinoceros and mammoth. His results were published in *Recherches sur les Ossements Fossiles découverts dans les Cavernes de la Province de Liège* (1833), in which he said, 'There can be no doubt that the human bones were buried at the same time and by the same cause as the other extinct species.' But his work was not considered seriously by his contemporaries. As Charles Lyell wrote in 1863 in *The Geological Evidences for the Antiquity of Man*, 'a quarter of a century . . . elapsed before even the neighbouring professors of the University of Liège came forth to vindicate the truthfulness of their indefatigable and clear-sighted countryman.'

The same neglect befell the work of Father J. MacEnery, a Roman Catholic priest, who carried out excavations in Kent's Cavern, Torquay, from 1824 to 1829. During these years he found flint implements associated with the remains of extinct animals such as rhinoceros, stratified and sealed under the undisturbed floor of stalagmite in the cave. These discoveries suggested to MacEnery that his finds belonged, in John Frere's phrase, 'to a very remote period indeed; even beyond that of the present world'. MacEnery consulted Dean Buckland, the Oxford geologist, who refused to accept MacEnery's inference, arguing that the 'Ancient Britons' whose artifacts he had found had scooped ovens in the stalagmite at Kent's Cavern and that their implements had penetrated under the stalagmite through these holes: their alleged 'association' with the bones of extinct animals was 'fortuitous'. MacEnery protested that there were no such ovens; Buckland, who refused to travel from Oxford to Torquay to inspect the cave, urged MacEnery to go on looking, assuring him he would eventually find them. Disheartened and disenchanted, MacEnery refrained from insisting on the evidence of his eyes and declaring the contemporaneity of implements and rhinoceros bones, and, though he went on working at Kent's Cavern until his death in 1841, he abandoned his intention of publishing his discoveries. They therefore passed unnoticed at the time and like Schmerling he had to wait a quarter of a century for recognition.

26 William Buckland (1784–1856), first professor of geology at Oxford and later Dean of Westminster.

At about the same time Ami Boué dug in the quaternary deposits of south Austria and found the remains of fossil man in association with extinct animals. Later, in 1835, an ancient skull that had been found at Cannstadt in 1700 and had lain in the Stuttgart Museum ever since, was described scientifically, but no attention was paid to what was the first skull of ancient man ever found. In 1848 a skull of the type now known as Neanderthal Man was found at Gibraltar: the find attracted no attention at all, and indeed was not properly described until as late as 1907.

The evidence was gradually accumulating. Why did it take so long for the antiquity of man to be established and the idea of the six-thousand-year past to be discarded? Because, in the first place, men did not want to believe in man's great antiquity with all the implications that the chronology based on Genesis was wrong, and its apparent undermining of Christian faith. So that all sorts of alternative explanations and false arguments were used. Desnoyers advanced an archaeological argument declaring that some artifacts found in caves were the same as those found in megalithic monuments (indeed some were, but *not* those associated with the bones of extinct animals), and were therefore no older than the fringe of recorded history.

Then it was a commonplace of knowledge that caves had been occupied by a succession of inhabitants, that they were sometimes used for burials and that their deposits could be and were altered by burrowing animals, floods and rivers. Dean Buckland went down to South Wales, in 1823, to explore the Goat's Hole Cave at Paviland on the Gower coast and found what we know now to be the skeleton of a young man of Upper Palaeolithic date – the 'Red Lady of Paviland', so called because the bones were stained with red ochre – associated with Palaeolithic flint implements and the bones of extinct animals. He declared the skeleton to be 'clearly not co-eval with the antediluvian bones of the extinct species', and explained away the presence of the skeleton as being that of an intrusive Romano-British burial. He had to find another explanation for the occurrence of human bones encrusted with stalactite in a cave at Burringdon in the Mendips: he said the cave had 'either been used as a place of sepulture in early times or resorted to for refuge by the wretches that perished in it, when the country was suffering under one of our numerous military operations.' Then Buckland went on to admit that the state of the bones 'affords indication of very high antiquity', but added, 'there is no reason for not considering them post-diluvian'.

There was every reason, and every reason for daring to presume, as Esper had not the courage so to do. The very slow acceptance of the evidence from the French, Belgian and British caves, and its deliberate rebuttal, was because most geologists were still catastrophists in their interpretation of sedimentary deposits.

The development of geological thinking in Western Europe as a whole is a long and gradual one and it is a mistake, often made, to suppose that all changed dramatically when Charles Lyell (1797–1875) published his *The Principles of Geology* in 1830–33. There was a gradual change and an awareness of what strata meant and what stratigraphical geology was about: much the same as the gradual change which, as we shall see in the next section, led to the adoption of the technological model of stone, bronze and iron. The French scientist Georges Cuvier (1769–1832) held that the record of the rocks could be interpreted in only one way, namely, by supposing that there had been a series of great catastrophes in the history of the earth and that the Noachian flood of Genesis preserved an historical account of the most recent of these many catastrophes. Cuvier has been very properly called 'the founder of vertebrate palaeontology'; but he denied the existence of fossil man in antiquity, saying that such things *could* not be. He was nicknamed 'the pope of bones' and had a European reputation for the study of fossils – 'the medals of creation' as he called them. Cuvier's disciples and pupils carried on his work: Brongniaert and d'Orbigny drew up a remarkable system of twenty-seven successive and separate acts of creation and catastrophes!

In England the Reverend W. D. Conybeare (1787–1857), a geologist who became Dean of Llandaff, settled for three deluges before that of Noah. Adam Sedgwick (1785–1857), who became Woodwardian Professor of Geology at Cambridge in 1818, was also in favour of the Flood and so of course was William Buckland (1784–1856), whom we have already met at Paviland, Burringdon and Kent's Cavern. Buckland was appointed Reader in Mineralogy at Oxford in 1813: his courses attracted the attention and admiration of the university, and very largely contributed to the public recognition of geology as a science by the endowment of a professorship in the subject in 1819. But by then he had left Oxford to be Dean of Westminster. In 1823 he published his *Reliquiae Diluvianae: or Observations on the Organic Remains Contained in Caves, Fissures and Diluvial Graves and on other Geological Phenomena Attesting the Action of an Universal Deluge*, and, thirteen years later, his *Geology and Mineralogy Considered in Relation to Natural Theology*. He insisted on a Universal Deluge and argued that the record of the rocks proved it.

But, gradually, opposition was growing to the catastrophists: the Universal Deluge became less convincing as a careful appraisal of the record of the rocks replaced a literal belief in Genesis. The concept of strata was known in the late seventeenth century. John Michell (1724–93), who was elected Woodwardian Professor of Geology in the University of Cambridge in 1762, showed a remarkable knowledge of the strata in various parts of England and abroad, and set out a very clear definition of stratification. 'The earth is not composed of heaps of matter casually thrown together,' he wrote, 'but of regular and uniform strata – these strata, though they frequently do not exceed a few feet, or a few inches, in thickness, yet often extend in length and breadth for many miles.' In 1785 James Hutton (1726–97) published his *Theory of the Earth : or an Investigation of the Laws Observable in the Composition, Dissolution, and Restoration of Land Upon the Globe.* He saw the deposits of sand, gravel, clay and limestone as the results of the ordinary deposition of sediments together with organic remains under water, that is, in the rivers or in the seas in the same way as happens at the present. He recognized that the greater part of the land had once been beneath the sea but had formed in a gradual and ordinary way; a non-catastrophic way. 'No processes are to be employed', he said, 'that are not natural to the globe: no action to be admitted except those of which we know the principle.' William Smith (1769–1839), 'Strata Smith' as he was often called, drew up a table of thirty-two different strata and found different fossils in them. Fossils were to him not 'medals of creation' but 'the antiquities of Nature'. The first part of his *Strata Identified by Organized Fossils* was published in 1816. He not only assigned relative ages to the rocks by noting their fossil contents but himself argued for the orderly deposition of strata over a very long period of time.

The doctrines of stratigraphic geology and uniformitarianism were well to the forefront before the publication of Charles Lyell's *The Principles of Geology.* The full title of the book is itself a good definition of the principle of uniformitarianism: *The Principles of Geology, being an attempt to explain the former changes of the Earth's surface by reference to causes now in action.* Dean Conybeare, himself a catastrophist and diluvialist, claimed that Lyell's work was 'in itself sufficiently important to mark a new era in the progress of our science'. Like Darwin's *Origin of Species* – and Darwin was much influenced by Lyell's *Principles* – it was not that the ideas were new, but they were set out clearly and cogently, for all who could read, to understand. Lyell's sister-in-law, in her account of his life and work, describes him in 1894 as having a mission 'to free science from Moses'. This is what he did: his work sealed the case of the fluvialists against the catastrophic diluvialists. From now on, in archaeology as well as geology, Moses and the Flood were dead. The archaeologists who were working in the post-Lyell years were no longer cabined in their interpretations by diluvial catastrophes.

Jacques Boucher de Crèvecoeur de Perthes (1788–1868) was a minor customs official at Abbeville, in the north of France. He became interested in what he called 'Celtic' remains thrown out by dredgers cleaning the Somme canal. These were, in fact, chipped flints, Neolithic polished axes and broken prehistoric bones. He became more interested in what he called the pre-Celtic or diluvial remains of man, in

27

INDUSTRIE PRIMITIVE, TOME 2. CHAP. XXIV.   PL. VIII.

Quart de grandeur.

Suite des haches diverses en pierre. Celtiques.

27, 28 Boucher de Perthes (1788–1868) (*below*), a customs official at Abbeville, who discovered Palaeolithic handaxes in the Somme gravels. His finds were not at first believed in, because (*right*) he uncritically published genuine artifacts together with naturally formed objects.

the form of roughly chipped flints, and the bones of extinct animals found in quarries near Abbeville. He exhibited these flint artifacts in Abbeville in 1838 and to the Institut in Paris the following year, and they were published in his five-volume work *De la Création: essai sur l'origine et la progression des êtres* (1838–41). His finds were at first not believed in and he was regarded as a crank. 'At the very mention of the words "axe" and "diluvium",' he once said, 'I observe a smile on the face of those to whom I speak.' But he went on collecting and in 1847 published the first volume of a three-volume work entitled *Antiquités*

Celtiques et Antédiluviennes. This title indicated the progress of his   28
researches: the *haches diluviennes*, as he had first named them, were
now *haches antédiluviennes* and the association of human artifacts and
extinct animals in the Somme gravels was no longer to be explained by
the diluvial theory.

Most of the contemporary French geologists were still catastrophists
and many did not even believe in the human nature of what Boucher de
Perthes claimed as artifacts. Indeed he often did poor service to his
cause by including with the chipped Palaeolithic implements objects
which were *lusus naturae*. Dr Rigollot of Amiens, a noted geologist,
himself excavated in gravel pits at Saint-Acheul with the avowed
intention of disproving the claims of Boucher de Perthes; but he
became converted, and in his memoir, published in 1854, entitled
Mémoires sur les Instruments en Silex trouvées à Saint-Acheul, he
provided new evidence of the contemporaneity of early man and extinct
animals. A young French palaeontologist, Albert Gaudry, also
conducted his own excavations at Amiens and Saint-Acheul and was
convinced Boucher de Perthes was correct. The tide was turning.

In England in 1846 a committee was set up, by the newly founded
Torquay Natural History Society, to explore Kent's Cavern; the work
was directed by a local schoolmaster, William Pengelly, who had an
overmastering passion for geological research. Pengelly proved that
MacEnery's findings were correct. In 1858, in quarrying the rock
which overlooks Brixham Harbour, across the bay from Torquay, a
new cave was found. Pengelly carried out excavations there from the
summer of 1858 to the summer of 1859: they revealed indisputable
proof of the association of flint tools with the bones of extinct animals in
the cave earth 'in which', wrote Pengelly, 'lay a sheet of stalagmite from
three to eight inches thick: and having within it and on it relics of lion,
hyaena, bear, mammoth, rhinoceros and reindeer.'

These Brixham discoveries convinced many people. Both Prestwich
and Lyell accepted the evidence: Lyell said in 1859, 'The facts recently
brought to light during the systematic investigation . . . of the Brixham
Cave must, I think, have prepared you to admit that scepticism in
regard to the cave evidence in favour of the antiquity of man had
previously been pushed to an extreme.'

But meanwhile English geologists and archaeologists had visited the
Somme gravels and found the claims of Boucher de Perthes
convincing. Prestwich and John Evans visited Abbeville in 1859. Evans
wrote after his visit, 'the flint axes and implements found among the
beds of gravel' were 'evidently deposited at the same time with them –
in fact the remains of a race of men who existed at the time when the
deluge or whatever was the origin of these gravels took place.' On
returning to England Prestwich read a paper to the Royal Society on 26
May 1859 entitled, 'On the Occurrence of Flint Implements associated
with the Remains of Animals of Extinct Species in beds of a late
Geological Period at Amiens and Abbeville and in England at Hoxne.'
The tide had turned: the antiquity of man was established and it was
pleasant that Prestwich and Evans had not forgotten the 1797 letter of
John Frere. In the same year Professor Ramsay said: 'the flint hatchets
of Amiens and Abbeville seem to me as clearly works of art as any

29 Sir John Evans
(1823–1908), who wrote
about stone implements
and bronze implements
from pre-Roman Britain,
and confirmed the
authenticity of Boucher de
Perthes' discoveries at
Abbeville.

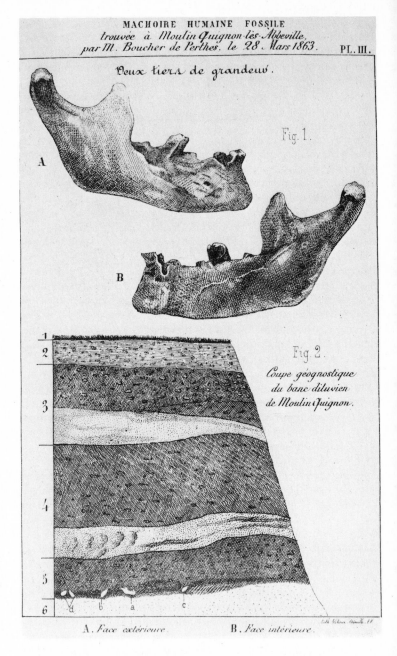

MACHOIRE HUMAINE FOSSILE
*trouvée à Moulin Quignon-les-Abbeville,
par M. Boucher de Perthes. le 28. Mars 1863.* PL. III.

Deux tiers de grandeur.

Fig. 1.

A

B

Fig. 2.

*Coupe géognostique
du banc diluvien
de Moulin Quignon.*

A. *Face extérieure.* B. *Face intérieure.*

30 The Moulin Quignon jaw, 'found' by Boucher de Perthes' workmen in 1863, but later proved to be a forgery.

Sheffield whittle.' The hatchets and their makers were now clearly seen as belonging to a time beyond the present world of the short six-thousand-year chronology.

Hatchets, yes, but where were the bones of their makers? In 1857 the skull and long bones of a man-like creature were found in a cave at Neanderthal on the River Düssel in Rhenish Prussia. Schaaffhausen first described these remains and noted the large size, low forehead and enormous brow-ridges of the skull-cap, features we now list as typical of Neanderthal man. He believed the remains were those of a man belonging 'to a barbarous and savage race' and he regarded them 'as the most ancient memorial of the early inhabitants of Europe'. There was naturally a dispute, Virchow declaring the remains those of a pathological idiot. Huxley accepted Schaaffhausen's diagnosis, saying that they were those of the most ape-like human being yet found. He placed it below the Australian aborigines in physical type and declared it 'most nearly allied to the higher apes than the latter are to the lower.'

In France scholars seemed unhappy that no human bones had been found by Boucher de Perthes and he was himself anxious that physical remains should confirm his discovery of the cultural remains of early man. The first finds of human bones from the Moulin-Quignon pit at Abbeville were declared by anatomists to be too badly preserved for certain diagnosis. Boucher de Perthes then offered a reward of two hundred francs to the finder of the first definite fossil remains of man. Shortly after this announcement a complete jawbone and some teeth 30 were found together with hand-axes in the pit in March 1863. 'The certainty of the find was absolute', declared de Perthes: Quatrefages in Paris and Lyell in London accepted its authenticity. Prestwich and Evans were doubtful and, alas, the find was unmasked as a forgery. Boucher de Perthes had been swindled by his workmen. He had been the victim of his own over-enthusiasm and the cupidity and skill of his workmen. 'The implements and jaw . . . at Moulin Quignon are recent manufactures', wrote Evans, and he was right. But many Frenchmen believed in them, passionately wanting anatomical as well as artifactual proof of early man. And Boucher de Perthes died still believing in Moulin-Quignon man.

The Three Ages of Stone, Bronze and Iron

The three technological stages of stone, bronze and iron had been clearly suggested by Goguet in 1738 but they were not immediately or widely accepted. Archaeology demanded excavation: the field monuments did not speak for themselves and classical writers and the Bible told nothing about them. Excavations had taken place in Scandinavia and France of prehistoric monuments, chiefly megalithic tombs, in the seventeenth and eighteenth centuries, but the results of the excavations were not interpreted in terms of these three successive ages because this technological model of the past had not as yet been accepted.

In England serious excavations began in the second half of the eighteenth century with the work of men like the Reverend Bryan Faussett in Kent and the Reverend James Douglas. Faussett's work on the Kentish Anglo-Saxon barrows was carried out between 1757 and 1773. Douglas's *Nenia Britannica, or a History of British Tumuli* was published in 1793.

William Cunnington and Sir Richard Colt Hoare, however, may be properly called the fathers of archaeological excavation in England. Colt Hoare declared in his *History of Ancient Wiltshire* (1810–21), 'we speak from facts not theory. I shall not seek among the fanciful regions of Romance an origin of our Wiltshire barrows'; and William Cunnington describes himself digging barrows on Salisbury Plain in 1803, 'in the hopes of meeting something which might supersede conjecture'. They together dug too many barrows and too quickly. Colt Hoare records the excavation of 379 barrows: but he does give careful accounts of his work and distinguished between different forms of barrows, different types of interments and between primary and secondary interments. He abandoned terminology relating to the Druids, and distinguished between long barrows and round barrows; he classified the round barrows into four categories, but he was not entirely free of the romantic approach: he called one of his round barrow types the 'Druid' barrow, and the title page of *Ancient Wiltshire* 31 is romantic enough, with its archaic spelling and border of arrowheads.

Colt Hoare set out as his aim, 'to ascertain to which of the successive inhabitants of this island they [i.e. the prehistoric antiquities] are to be ascribed, or whether, in fact, they are the work of more than one people', but after ten years of hard and devoted labour he was forced to confess 'total ignorance as to the authors of these sepulchral memorials: we have evidence of the very high antiquity of our Wiltshire barrows, but none respecting the tribes to whom they appertained, that can rest on solid foundations.'

The same problem faced the study of French and Danish antiquities. In France in 1818 a commission was set up to investigate 'all the national monuments . . . the Gallic, Greek and Roman antiquities', but the commission could see no way of resolving the problem of the apparent contemporaneity of prehistoric remains. In Denmark, in 1806, Professor Rasmus Nyerup published *Oversyn over foedrelandets mindesmaerker fra oldtiden*, in which he recommended the formation of a National Danish Museum of Antiquities, and the following year the Danish Government set up a Royal Committee for the Preservation and Collection of National Antiquities with Nyerup as Secretary. For many years he had been privately collecting antiquities and had formed them into a small museum at the University of Copenhagen of which he was librarian. But he was quite unable to classify them in any significant or meaningful way and confessed that 'everything which has come down to us from heathendom is wrapped in a thick fog: it belongs to a space of time which we cannot measure. We know that it is older than Christendom, but whether by a couple of years or a couple of centuries, or even by more than a millennium we can do no more than guess.' There is a despairing note in these words as there was in the writings of Colt Hoare. Yet the answer was there: it had been given by Goguet and ought to have been arrived at when Colt Hoare and Cunnington distinguished between primary and secondary interments. The fog could be dispelled and the ignorance dispersed. It was two Danes, Thomsen and Worsaae who did so.

Actually from the beginning of the last quarter of the eighteenth century the three-age idea had been set out as a fact by Danish historians. P. F. Suhm, in his *History of Denmark, Norway and Holstein* (1776), stated that in those areas weapons were first of stone, then of copper and then of iron. In *Concerning Thor and his Hammer and the earliest Weapons that are related to it* (1802) Skuli Thorlacius refers

31 (*Opposite*) The title page of Colt Hoare's *Ancient Wiltshire*, published in 1820–21.

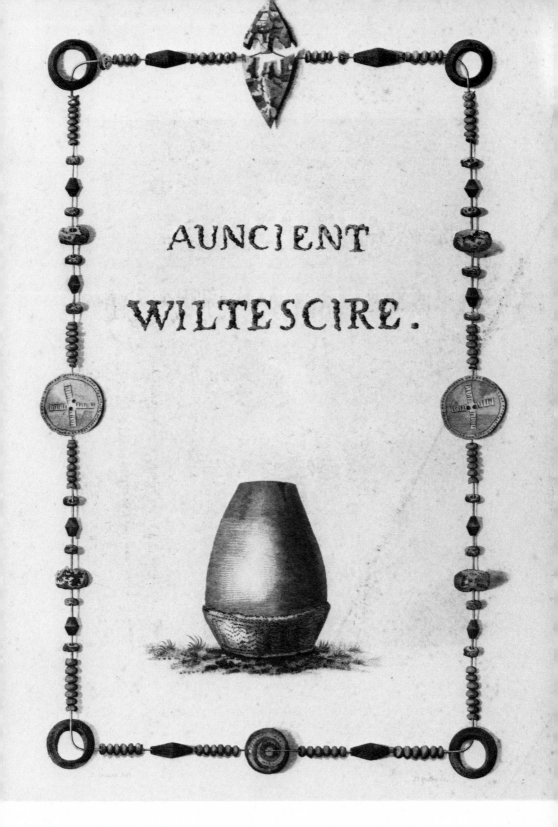

AUNCIENT

WILTESCIRE.

throughout to three successive ages of stone, copper and iron, and L. S. Vedel Simonsen wrote in *Udsigt over Nationalhistoriens aeldste og maerkeligste Perioder* (1813–16):

> At first the tools and weapons of the earliest inhabitants of Scandinavia were made of stone or wood. Then the Scandinavians learnt to work copper and then to smelt it and harden it . . . and then latterly to work iron. From this point of view the development of their culture can be divided *into a Stone Age, a Copper Age and an Iron Age*. These three ages cannot be separated from each other by exact limits, for they encroach on each other. Without any doubt the use of stone implements continued among the more impoverished groups after the introduction of copper, and similarly objects of copper were used after the introduction of iron . . . Artifacts of wood have naturally decomposed, those of iron are rusted in the ground: it is those of stone and copper which are the best preserved.

There it is: and I have italicized the words which set out without question the three successive ages of stone, copper and iron. But these were the speculations of a historian: they needed archaeological support and proof and these were supplied by Thomsen and Worsaae.

32, 33 Christian Jurgensen Thomsen (1788–1865) (*above*), who opened the Danish National Museum to the public in 1819 (*right*) and was more than anyone responsible for the introduction of the three-age system into archaeology.

Christian Jurgensen Thomsen (1788–1865) succeeded Nyerup as secretary of the Danish Committee in 1816 and at the same time was appointed the first curator of the National Museum, a post which he held until his death. Thomsen was the son of a Copenhagen merchant and continued working in the family firm part-time while he was in the Museum. From his early youth he had taken a great interest first in coins and then in all kinds of antiquities. He set about arranging in some kind of order the growing collections that came under his care. At that time the collection of antiquities was mixed up with all sorts of non-archaeological curiosities in a small room in the library of Copenhagen University. Thomsen classified the archaeological collections into three groups based on the material used in making weapons and tools which he claimed represented three chronologically successive ages of stone, bronze and iron. In 1819 the Museum opened to the public. A few years later he was allotted rooms in the royal palace of Christiansborg and there Thomsen fully carried out his new plan of arranging and classifying the pagan antiquities of Denmark: he created separate rooms for the Stone Age, the Age of 'Brass' or Bronze, and the Age of Iron.

The first clear statement of this new concept of *Museum-ordning* as it was called – and Thomsen's work was essentially an ordering or arrangement of a Museum – appeared in a guidebook to the Danish National Museum entitled *Ledetraad til Nordisk Oldkyndighed* published in Copenhagen in 1836. An English translation by Lord Ellesmere appeared in 1848 entitled *A Guide to Northern Antiquities*. Thomsen edited the *Guide* and was himself responsible for the section in the guide on the early monuments and antiquities of the north.

This is what Thomsen wrote in the *Ledetraad*:

> Our collections are . . . still too recent and our facts too few for the drawing of conclusions with full degree of confidence . . . The remarks which we now proceed to offer must therefore be viewed merely in the light of conjectures, destined to be confirmed or rectified in proportion as a more general attention is directed to the subject . . .

And then he lists his three periods:

34 J. J. A. Worsaae (1821–85), author of *Danmarks Oldtid* (1843) and successor to Thomsen as Director of the Danish National Museum.

> *The Age of Stone*, or that period when weapons and implements were made of stone, wood, bone, or some other material, and during which very little or nothing at all was known of metals. . . .
>
> *The Age of Bronze*, in which weapons and cutting implements were made of copper or bronze, and nothing at all, or very little was known of iron or silver. . . .
>
> *The Age of Iron* is the third and last period of the heathen time, in which iron was used for those articles to which that metal is eminently suited, and in the fabrication of which it came to be employed as a substitute for bronze.

Thomsen was helped in the museum by a young law student from the University of Copenhagen. Jens Jacob Asmussen Worsaae (1821–85) came from Jutland where, from his youth, he had been collecting antiquities and excavating barrows. In due course he

32

33

34

59

Kong Frederik den 7de lader bore i Gorm den Gamles Höi i Jellinge, den 9de August 1861.

35 Soldiers drilling down to find the royal grave at Jelling, East Jutland, in 1861. Worsaae explains the procedure to King Frederik VII of Denmark.

succeeded Thomsen as Director of the National Museum, was Inspector-General of Antiquities in Denmark, Riksantiqvariet and Professor of Archaeology in the University of Copenhagen. His twentieth-century successor, Johannes Brønsted has very appropriately called him 'the first professional archaeologist'. When he was only twenty-two, he published *Danmarks Oldtid oplyst ved Oldsager og Gravhöje* (1843) which was published in English in 1849 as *The Primeval Antiquities of Denmark*.

Danmarks Oldtid was a remarkable work. It took the three-age system out of the Copenhagen Museum and applied it to field monuments and proved empirically the stratigraphical succession of these three ages by excavations in barrows and peat bogs. Between 1829 and 1843 the three-age system had been established as a fact, *the* fact of prehistory. The fog and the gloom of Colt Hoare and Nyerup had been dispelled: a clear light now shone over prehistoric antiquities. It was very right that Déchelette in 1908 should refer to the three-age system as 'the basis of prehistory' and Macalister in 1921 call it 'the corner stone of modern archaeology'.

Worsaae had 'confirmed' in the field the three-age system. Further empirical proof was provided by the excavation of the Swiss lake-dwellings.

During the very dry winter of 1853–5 the low lake levels of Lake Zurich at Obermeilen revealed the remains of wooden piles as well as stone axes, horn implements, pottery and charred wood. Dr Ferdinand Keller of Zurich examined the finds and diagnosed them as the remains of a lake-dwelling. There had been reports from fishermen for years of

36 Neolithic lake-dwelling at Lüscherz-Locras, in the canton of Berne, Switzerland. Originally, following Keller's interpretation, the double lines of piles would have been regarded as the remains of a foot-bridge, but the modern view that the dwellings were lake-shore settlements suggests this was once part of a track leading to a palisaded enclosure.

'submerged forests' off the shores of the Swiss lakes but it was not until Keller's work on Lake Zurich that the now archaeologically famous Swiss lake-dwellings became known to archaeology. Following the discovery at Obermeilen other lake villages were discovered, such as those at Morges on Lake Geneva, Cortaillod, Auvernier, Concise and Corcelettes on Lake Neuchâtel, and Robenhausen on Lake Pfaffikon. By 1863 Colonel Schwab could list 46 lakeside sites on Lake Neuchâtel, and by 1875 it was possible to list over 200 such sites in Switzerland. Keller's findings, first published in a series of memoirs in Zurich, were translated into English under the title of *The Lake Dwellings of Switzerland and other Parts of Europe* (1866). This book included memoirs by Dr Rutimeyer on the fauna and Heer on the flora of the lake-dwellings – among the first examples of such surveys of archaeological sites. At the time the lake-dwellings were thought of as built on platforms in the lake approached by a built causeway, and a reconstruction on these lines can be seen on Lake Constance. Present-day opinion inclines to the view that these reconstructions are wrong 36 and that the dwellings were built on the shores of the lakes.

It soon became clear that the lake-dwellings in Switzerland did not all belong to one period. Troyon divided them into three periods corresponding to the three ages of stone, bronze, and iron.

As the Scandinavian three-age system spread to other countries it became evident that the Stone Age of the Danish peat bogs, shell-mounds and barrows was only the later part of the Stone Age and that there was an earlier part represented by the implements of chipped flint found by John Frere in the Hoxne gravels, by Boucher de Perthes in the

37 Sir John Lubbock (1834–1913), banker, politician, scientist and writer, whose *Prehistoric Times* (1865) introduced the words Palaeolithic and Neolithic into the languages of the world.

Somme gravels, and by MacEnery, Schmerling and Pengelly in their cave explorations in Belgium and Britain. French archaeologists proposed to distinguish two ages of stone, the earlier to be called the *période de la pierre taillée* and the later the *période de la pierre polie*.

Sir John Lubbock (1834–1913), who later became Lord Avebury, published in 1865 his *Prehistoric Times* and accepted the French division, but coined the words Palaeolithic and Neolithic for these two Stone Ages. The Palaeolithic or Old Stone Age period was 'that of the Drift, when man shared the possession of Europe with the Mammoth, the Cave Bear, the Woolly-haired rhinoceros and other extinct animals.' The Neolithic or New Stone Age was 'the later or polished stone age, a period characterized by beautiful weapons and instruments of flint and other kinds of stone, in which, however, we find no traces of the knowledge of any metal excepting gold, which seems to have been sometimes used for ornament.' The Danish three-age system had now become a four-age system and Palaeolithic, Neolithic, Bronze and Iron Ages became the framework into which archaeological discoveries were fitted in the sixties of the last century.

But it soon became clear that the Palaeolithic itself must be subdivided: that there was a Lower Palaeolithic characterized by the chipped stone axes of Hoxne and the Somme gravels, and an Upper Palaeolithic characterized by finds from the rockshelters of southern France. The discovery of Upper Palaeolithic man will always be associated with the name of Edouard Lartet (1801–71), a magistrate in the district of Gers, who abandoned law for palaeontology. In 1852 a road-mender of Aurignac in the Haute-Garonne put his hand into a rabbit-hole and drew out a human bone. Curious, he dug down and found a rockshelter closed by a stone slab and, buried in it, seventeen human skeletons together with the remains of extinct animals, flint and ivory tools, and engravings on bones. The human skeletons were re-buried in the Christian cemetery nearby and went unnoticed until Lartet learnt of the find. At first he thought the discovery was that of a Neolithic collective burial, then changed his view and declared them to be pre-Neolithic.

In 1860 Lartet explored another Pyrenean site, Massat in Ariège, where he found hearths with reindeer bones and worked flints, barbed harpoons of stagshorn, bone needles, and a bear's head engraved on the point of a broken stagshorn tine. This discovery was published in 1861, by Lartet, together with an engraving of two deer on a reindeer bone which had been found between 1834 and 1845 by Brouillet in the cave of Chaffaud in the Vienne. Brouillet and others had thought the engraving to be Celtic, but Lartet declared it to be much earlier: his appreciation of the significance and true date of the finds from Chaffaud, Aurignac and Massat was the first clear statement of what we now call Franco-Cantabrian Upper Palaeolithic art.

38

38 Engravings of two deer on a reindeer bone found in the cave of Chaffaud near Sévigné in the Vienne in the 1830s.

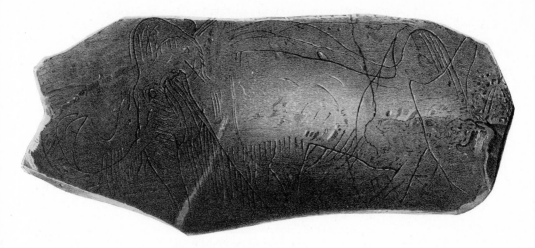

While working on the Pyrenean caves Lartet was sent a box of flint and bone splinters from a rockshelter at Les Eyzies in the Dordogne and told that the caves of Périgord abounded in such finds. He moved to Les Eyzies, and from 1863 began a series of excavations at sites such as Gorge d'Enfer, Laugerie Haute, La Madeleine and Le Moustier – names now famous in archaeology. He was helped, financially and personally, by an English banker, Henry Christy. The first results of their collaboration were published in 1864. A larger work was planned but delayed by Christy's death in 1865 and Lartet's in 1871. The full publication was edited by Rupert Jones and John Evans and published between 1865 and 1875 under the title *Reliquiae Aquitanicae: being contributions to the Archaeology and Palaeontology of Périgord and the adjoining provinces of Southern France*. It was a landmark in the development of Palaeolithic archaeology.

There were others working in different parts of France on the Upper Palaeolithic: the Vicomte de Lastic-Saint-Jal and Victor Brun at Bruniquel, Garrigou and Martin at Lourdes, Ferry and Arcelin at Solutré. Dupont was excavating caves in Belgium and published in 1872 his *Les Temps antéhistoriques en Belgique: L'Homme pendant les Ages de la Pierre dans les Environs de Dinant-sur-Meuse*, and the Englishman Boyd Dawkins summarized his exploration of caves and rockshelters in *Cave-Hunting: Researches on the Evidence of Caves respecting the Early Inhabitants of Europe* (1874).

In *Reliquiae Aquitanicae* Lartet argued that the sites of Le Moustier, Laugerie Haute and La Madeleine, 'although within the chronological divisions of the age of simply worked stone without the accompaniment of domestic animals, do not possess a uniformity in the production of human industry collected there.' The Upper Palaeolithic had to be divided: Lartet suggested periods based on associated fauna, viz. 1. The Cave Bear period, 2. The Woolly Mammoth and Rhinoceros period, 3. The Reindeer period, and 4. The Aurochs or Bison period. Garrigou prefaced this with a Warm Elephant/Hippopotamus period which was pre-cave and included the axes of Saint-Acheul and Abbeville, when man was living mainly in open sites. The

39 Engraved mammoth tusk found in Dordogne, from Lartet and Christy's *Reliquiae Aquitanicae* (1865–75).

39

63

Lartet/Garrigou classification was entirely on zoological and palaeontological grounds: Lartet then introduced three divisions of the Palaeolithic, viz. Lower (Hippopotamus), Middle (Cave Bear and Mammoth) and Upper (Reindeer) ages.

This was a revolutionary suggestion which introduced an entirely new principle – the classification of archaeological remains on the basis of non-archaeological data. But through the second half of the nineteenth century archaeologists preferred to classify the material remains they were studying in terms of that material. Gabriel de Mortillet re-interpreted Lartet's classification in archaeological terms: Lartet's Hippopotamus Age became the Chellean, a great deal of the Cave Bear/Mammoth Age became the Mousterian, after the rockshelter of Le Moustier, and there were Solutrean, Aurignacian and Magdalenian periods as well. Lartet argued that we should base our divisions of the past on fauna: he saw his as a classification of periods, but interpreted those periods as the work of people such as in historic times produced the periods of the Greeks, Etruscans and Romans. The de Mortillet system, ultimately based on stratigraphical geology, and its subsequent extension, became orthodox prehistory and continued so well into the twentieth century.

Egypt and Mesopotamia

The 167 savants – nicknamed the 'Donkeys' – who formed the scientific and artistic commission which Napoleon brought with him to Egypt, started work soon after he reached Cairo on 21 July 1798. (Incidentally, it is interesting to note that Napoleon took to Egypt a copy of Carsten Niebuhr's *Description of Travels in Arabia*.) The French Egyptian Institute was set up in a palace in Cairo and in three years achieved an astonishing amount of work. The publication of the *Description de L'Egypte* by Jomard (1777–1862) was the beginning of the serious study of Egyptian antiquities. The first volume of the *Description* appeared in 1809 and it was completed in twenty-four sumptuous and wonderfully illustrated folio volumes between then and 1813.

One member of this remarkable team was Dominique Vivant, Baron de Denon (1747–1825), who was Director-General of Museums in France from 1804 to 1815 and accompanied Napoleon to Austria, Spain and Portugal – in the words of the entry in the fourteenth edition of the *Encyclopaedia Britannica*, 'advising the conqueror in his choice of spoils of art from the various cities he pillaged'. The account of Denon's journeys in Egypt, first published in France in 1802, later the same year came out in English as *Travels in Upper and Lower Egypt during the campaigns of General Bonaparte*.

Although the Rosetta Stone had been seized by the British and taken to London, one of Napoleon's generals, himself a scholar, had already translated the bottom inscription which was in Greek. He deciphered the inscription to say that it was made in 196 BC by priests from Memphis and contained praise for King Ptolemy Epiphanes for his many benefactions and granting him divine honours. The upper inscription was in hieroglyphic, a script previously noted by travellers in Egypt, but totally unread. The middle inscription was in Demotic, a

form of writing derived from the Hieratic, itself a cursive form of hieroglyphs. It was assumed, correctly as it turned out, that this was a trilingual inscription and that the Demotic and hieroglyphic writing could be deciphered with the aid of the lower Greek inscription.

So scholars in England, France, Germany and Italy addressed themselves to the problem of decipherment, aided by other inscriptions such as that on an obelisk found in 1822 on the island of Philae. The Frenchman Sylvestre de Sacy worked on the Demotic text and was able to decipher several names including that of Ptolemy, but he thought the script's complete decipherment impossible. The Swedish diplomat, J. D. Akerblad, succeeded in deciphering in the Demotic inscription all the proper names, and a few other words by careful comparison with the Greek text.

40 Napoleon in Egypt meeting the Savants, the scientific and artistic commission charged with the task of studying the Egyptian antiquities.

41 Frontispiece to Jomard's *Description de L'Egypte* (1809).

The next serious worker in this field was Dr Thomas Young (1773–1829), a Cambridge medical man and physicist, already famous for his discoveries in the field of optics and his wave theory of light. He worked on the Demotic inscription and his results were published in a Demotic vocabulary and an article in the *Encyclopaedia Britannica*. The main credit for the final decipherment, however, goes to the Frenchman Jean François Champollion (1790–1832). When a young child of eleven he was shown by the great mathematician Jean-Baptiste Fournier some hieroglyphic writing on papyri and tablets, and asked, 'Can anyone read them?' On being told no, he said, 'I will do it.'

And so he did. He was an infant prodigy, wrote a book when he was twelve, and at the age of thirteen was reading Arabic, Syriac and Coptic. From then on he devoted himself to Egyptology. He began work on the Rosetta Stone in 1808, but it took him fourteen years to complete his decipherment. In September 1822 he discovered a cartouche from Abu Simbel and was able to identify the name of the Pharaoh Ramesses and to appreciate that the hieroglyphs were used phonetically. He rushed to his brother and said, 'I've got it!' and fainted. Soon he was back at work and completed his famous *Lettre à M. Dacier, secretaire perpétuel de L'Académie royale des Inscriptions et Belles-Lettres, relative à l'alphabet des hiéroglyphes phonétiques*, which was published on 27 September 1822. In it he announced his decipherment. Two years later there appeared his *Précis du système*

42 The Great Sphinx at Giza as depicted, somewhat inaccurately, by Baron de Denon, who accompanied Napoleon to Egypt and published an account of his journeys there in 1802.

43

43 Jean François Champollion (1790–1832), who deciphered the Egyptian hieroglyphic writing.

hiéroglyphique, showing that the hieroglyphic script was a mixture of ideographic and phonetic signs.

He was appointed a curator in the Louvre and led an expedition to Egypt in 1828, assisted by his pupil Nicolo Rosellini. He returned to Paris in 1829, but died three years later: his *Grammaire Egyptienne* and *Dictionnaire Egyptienne* were published posthumously.

The Champollion-Rosellini survey extended as far south as Aswan. In 1840 Richard Lepsius made a survey of Nubian antiquities as far south as Khartoum. He dug at Memphis and elsewhere, discovered another 'Rosetta Stone' in the Decree of Canopus, and inscriptions of Egyptian copper miners in Sinai.

Less reputable people began to engage in what might charitably be called excavation but was really plain tomb-robbing. The most famous 44 of these was Giovanni Battista Belzoni (1778–1823), 'the Patagonian Sampson'. Born in Padua, he made a living in England by performing prodigious feats of strength at circuses, went to Egypt to sell hydraulic machinery for irrigation purposes, and, this failing, turned his strength and energy to collecting antiquities by tomb-robbing. He began his search for the pharaohs in 1817 at Thebes. He describes how he broke into one tomb, crashing his way through antiquities:

44 (*Opposite*) Giovanni Battista Belzoni (1778–1823), who robbed Egyptian tombs and provided valuable finds for the British Museum.

every step I took I crushed a mummy in some part or other . . . When my weight bore on the body of an Egyptian it crushed like a band-box. I sank altogether among the broken mummies with a crush of bones, rags and wooden cases . . . I could not avoid being covered with bones, legs, arms and heads rolling from above.

G. BELZONI.

C. Hullmandel's Lithography.

M. Gauci del.

45 Four lithographs from Belzoni's *Egypt and Nubia* (1823), illustrating some of his adventures in search of Egyptian antiquities.

It is not surprising that Belzoni fainted frequently during these outrageous escapades and that on one occasion he was so overcome that he 'wandered about in a trance'. Belzoni worked on behalf of the British Consul-General, as well as on his own account, and as a result much remarkable material found its way to the British Museum. Belzoni gave an account of his adventures in *Narrative of the Operations and Recent Discoveries within the Pyramids, Temples, Tombs and Excavations in Egypt and Nubia* (1823). It contains some marvellous entries such as 'Difficulties encountered from the natives . . . Shot at by soldier . . . Surprised by a hyena.' He was certainly one of the most bizarre, outrageous and colourful figures in the history of archaeology – which is saying a great deal.

45

Returning to England he displayed his collection in 1821 in the Egyptian Hall in Piccadilly – an exhibition building designed in 1812 with an Egyptian façade. It was a tremendous success and demonstrated the growing interest in antiquities: 1,900 people paid half a crown each to visit it on the opening day and Belzoni, just before the opening, invited a number of prominent doctors to assist him in unwrapping the mummy of a young man 'perfect in every part', as he subsequently described it.

Suddenly Belzoni tired of Egyptology and London and in 1822 went to West Africa to search for the source of the Niger. He had got as far as Benin when he was struck down by a severe attack of dysentery and died.

By the middle of the last century the major field antiquities of Egypt had been discovered and described from the *Description* through to Lepsius; and hieroglyphs and demotic had been deciphered. Popular books began to appear describing the antiquities of Egypt: such were John Kenrick's *Ancient Egypt under the Pharaohs* (1850) and Sir John Gardner Wilkinson's *Manners and Customs of the Ancient Egyptians* (1837, and 1841). And from that time there appeared writers claiming that Egypt was the earliest civilization and the progenitor of later civilizations. 'There is no difficulty in fixing on the country from which Ancient History must begin', wrote Kenrick. 'The monuments of Egypt, its records and its literature, surpass those of India and China in antiquity by many centuries.'

Auguste Mariette (1821–81) became interested in archaeology as a young man, growing up in Boulogne and then teaching there. In 1849 he obtained a minor post in the Louvre and next year was sent out to Egypt officially to collect Coptic manuscripts. He became more interested in field monuments than manuscripts and began excavating. He did not return to his post in the Louvre but stayed on working in Egypt: in 1858 he was appointed, by the Khedive, Conservator of Egyptian monuments, which made him Head of the newly created Egyptian Service of Antiquities, a post which he held until his death. He has very properly been described as the founding-father of Egyptian archaeology.

46 Bronze bust of Auguste Mariette (1821–81), French pioneer of Egyptology, in the Musée Municipal at Boulogne-sur-Mer.

During the thirty years of his reign he excavated over thirty sites of major importance, including the Serapeum at Memphis, the great temple of Osiris-Apis, with its cemetery of sacred bulls, the temple of the Sphinx at Giza, the cemeteries of Sakkara, the temples of Abydos, Medinet Habu, Deir-el-Bahri and Edfu. His technique of excavation has often been criticized. Petrie has described how Mariette made excavations near the Sphinx and blasted away with dynamite the fallen ruins of a temple. 'Nothing was done', wrote Petrie in 1883, 'with any uniform plan: work is begun and left unfinished: no regard is paid to future requirements of exploration and no civilized or labour-saving appliances are used. It is sickening to see the rate at which everything is being destroyed, and the little regard paid to preservation.'

It is true that Mariette was mainly concerned with finding precious objects and imposing monuments, that he never published his results adequately (some of his excavations were not published at all!), and that he was happy to amass a vast amount of material without recording the details of its provenance or studying its historical significance. But Mariette was introducing new methods into field archaeology, even if they did not measure up to the standards of Petrie, working at the end of the nineteenth century. He saw to it that no one but he dug in Egypt and prevented the kind of scramble for antiquities that was taking place at that time in Mesopotamia. He rid Egypt of tomb-robbers and art-collection touts masquerading as archaeologists. The Belzoni era was over, and for the first time Egypt was provided with a proper control of excavation and research.

Mariette devoted himself strenuously to preventing Egyptian antiquities leaving the country. It was his desire that the remains of ancient Egypt should remain in modern Egypt and portable antiquities be properly housed in Egypt: to this end he brought into being the National Museum of Egyptian Antiquities. The creation of the Egyptian Service of Antiquities, Mariette's appointment as Director, and the birth of the Museum did not come about as a result of the enlightened interest of the Khedive, Said Pasha; on the contrary, Said did not consider that Egyptian antiquities mattered at all. They were due to the secret machinations and intrigues of Fernand de Lesseps, then cutting the Suez Canal, and of Napoleon III. Maspero (see p. 116 below) said that Said Pasha reluctantly 'came to the conclusion that he would be more acceptable to the Emperor if he made some show of taking pity on the Pharaohs'. Mariette had a difficult task turning this diplomatic pity into real interest and finance. He could never secure regular and permanent grants from the government. He always had to apply for *ad hoc* grants and these were sanctioned or refused according to the Khedive's temper: some of his excavations had to be halted because of the sudden cutting off of funds.

To house his collection of Egyptian antiquities Mariette was first allocated a deserted and ruinous mosque, some filthy sheds and a house alive with vermin, in which he lived. Courageously he turned this into the first Egyptian Museum. It was Queen Aahotep's jewellery that eventually moved the Khedive. In 1859 Mariette's workmen found near Thebes the gilded sarcophagus of Queen Aahotep. Before Mariette could get it to Cairo, the Mudir of Keneh, a local potentate, stole it, opened it in his harem, and set off by boat with the jewellery to present it to the Khedive as a present from himself! Mariette gave chase in a steamboat, caught up with him, boarded the Mudir's boat and forced him by physical violence to surrender the jewellery. The Khedive thought all this very funny, kept a gold chain for one of his wives and a scarab for himself, and ordained that the rest of the jewellery should go to a specially built museum. In 1859 such a special museum was constructed at Boulak. Even so Mariette had to guard his museum as year after year it was filled with new treasures from fresh excavations. The Khedive often expressed the desire to give away some of the exhibits as presents to his friends, and on one occasion put forward the idea that the whole collection should be pawned as security for a loan he was negotiating!

But the museum prospered in a quiet way, eventually moving from Boulak to a disused palace at Giza in 1889, and in 1902 to its present position in the Qsar-el-Nil in Cairo. Whatever criticisms posterity may level at Mariette, when he died he could look back on three great personal achievements – the creation of the first National Service of Antiquities in the Near East, the creation of the first National Museum in the Near East, and the birth of a conscience about the export of antiquities from Near Eastern lands.

The beginnings of archaeology in Mesopotamia date from about the same time as the beginnings of archaeology in Egypt. Field archaeology began with Claudius James Rich (1786–1821), a brilliant linguist who joined the East India Company and at the early age of twenty-one was posted as British Resident in Turkish Arabia and took up his residency in Baghdad in 1808. He spent his free time visiting the sites of old Mesopotamian cities and collecting antiques and manuscripts. His first

47 Paul Emile Botta (1802–70), French consul in Mosul who excavated in the 1840s at Nineveh and Khorsabad.

visit to Babylon was in 1811 and he made a thorough survey and examination of the site, later publishing his *Memoir on the Ruins of Babylon* in 1812 followed by his *Second Memoir on Babylon* (1818). Lord Byron immortalized these memoirs in *Don Juan*:

> Claudius Rich, Esquire, some bricks has got
> And written lately two memoirs upon't.

Alas, Rich died of cholera in 1821: an account of his later travels appeared posthumously in 1836 in his *Narrative of a Residence in Koordistan and on the site of Ancient Nineveh, with Journal of a Voyage down the Tigris to Baghdad and an account of a Visit to Shiraz and Persepolis.*

Paul Emile Botta was French Consul at Mosul in 1842 and had been appointed to this post because of a growing interest among French scholars in Mesopotamia and its antiquities fostered by Rich's *Memoirs* and his *Narrative.* He excavated at Nineveh, which lies across the Tigris from Mosul, in 1842 and Khorsabad in 1843: they were the first excavations in Mesopotamia. While excavating in Nineveh he heard of sculptured stones found at Khorsabad fourteen miles to the north and so transferred his attentions there. Within a week he had discovered the remains of a huge Assyrian palace with large sculptured slabs and

47

cuneiform inscriptions. It was Rich who had, correctly as it turned out, identified the mounds across the river from Mosul as Nineveh. Botta thought he was wrong, and that Khorsabad was Nineveh, and he sent a cable to Paris from his Khorsabad excavations saying 'Ninive est retrouvé'. We now know that Khorsabad is in reality Dur Sharrukin, the city of the great Assyrian king, Sargon II (721–705 BC), and it was his palace that Botta had discovered. The French became excited by Botta's work, the government provided funds – he had hitherto financed his excavations himself – and sent out a skilled artist, M. E. Flandin, to record the finds and sculptures. On their return to France Botta and Flandin published the Khorsabad discoveries in their *Monument du Ninive* (Paris, 1849–50), a large work of five volumes, the first of text and the other four of Flandin's drawings. In 1846 many of the Khorsabad sculptures were sent to Paris, where they still are in the Louvre.

Meanwhile Austen Henry Layard (1817–94) had begun excavations at Nimrud. His excavations from 1845 to 1847 were at first financed by himself and Sir Stratford Canning, the British Ambassador to the Sublime Porte, but later by the British Museum. He dug not only at Nimrud but also for a short while at Kuyunjik and Ashur. At Nimrud he discovered the palaces of the Assyrian kings Ashur-nasirpal, Esarhaddon and Shalmaneser III. Many of his finds were sent to the British Museum, which they reached after many adventures, in 1848; they rested for a while on the quays at Bombay where they were displayed and lectures given on the remains. These treasures included the huge winged bulls, the Black Obelisk of Shalmaneser III and the sculptures of Ashur-nasirpal – some of the most valued possessions of the British Museum.

Much publicity was given to Layard's work: in 1847 the *Morning Post* published despatches from a correspondent who visited the excavations at Nimrud. Layard thought Nimrud was Nineveh: just as Botta thought that Khorsabad was. The British Museum proposed to spend £4,000 in publishing Layard's material in a form comparable with the five volumes of Botta and Flandin, but the British Treasury would not sanction this. A volume of drawings, *The Monuments of Nineveh*, was published privately in 1849 and a popular account, *Nineveh and its Remains*, in 1848–49. This latter book immediately became one of the earliest and most successful bestsellers – eight thousand copies were sold in one year, 'which', wrote Layard with pardonable pride, 'will place it side by side with Mrs Rundell's *Cookery*.' A year or two later John Murray, who had published the other books, started a series for reading in the train: they were for sale on the new railway station bookstalls which W. H. Smith had been opening. Among the first half-dozen titles published was *A Popular Account of Discoveries at Nineveh*.

Layard found he was famous: he was given an honorary doctorate by the University of Oxford in 1848 at the early age of thirty-one. He made a second expedition to Mesopotamia in 1849–51 financed by the British Museum. He dug at the actual site of Nineveh this time as well as at Nimrud, Ashur and Babylon. His main discovery was the palace of Sennacherib at Kuyunjik with its great library of cuneiform tablets. It

48

49

48 (*Opposite*) Austen Henry Layard (1817–94), excavator of Nimrud, Kuyunjik and Ashur, as a young man in Bakhtiyari costume.

must be confessed that Layard's criteria of the success of his excavations was the finding of works of art and portable antiquities. He was disappointed by his poor finds at Ashur and Babylon and concentrated on the Assyrian palaces. On his return to England he found himself more famous than ever: he was made a freeman of the City of London and was knighted. In 1853 he published *A Second Series of Monuments of Nineveh*, and a new popular work, *Discoveries in the Ruins of Nineveh and Babylon*.
50

Recently, in his *Quest for the Past* (1978), Brian Fagan has been fiercely critical of Layard's methods, describing how at Kuyunjik in a short time he dug two miles of bas-reliefs and cleared seventy rooms in the palace at Sennacherib. Fagan says of Layard that 'he shovelled his way into the past . . . tore Nimrud and Nineveh apart, and in the process wiped out priceless archaeological information.'

Rouet, who had replaced Botta as French Consul at Mosul, sent agents all round the countryside, opening mounds at random to stake a French claim and prevent the British under Layard from digging in them. As a result Layard was compelled to do the same thing. There was a moment, bizarre even in the strange story of nineteenth-century digging, when the French, disbelieving Layard's claims to have permission to dig, were themselves digging little pits while Layard was excavating in the same mound!

Although he had only worked in Mesopotamia for just over five years Layard gave up archaeological excavation in 1851: his work was continued by Hormuzd Rassam, an English national though a Moslawi, who had been his assistant. Rassam engaged unashamedly in what Seton Lloyd has described as 'an undignified scramble for archaeological loot'. Using Mosul as his base Rassam 'examined' mounds over an area of two hundred miles and left behind groups of his workmen

49 (*Opposite*) Layard sketching Assyrian relief slabs at Kuyunjik.

50 (*Above*) Layard's reconstruction of an Assyrian hall, from *Monuments of Nineveh* (1853).

51 The earliest known
picture of the ziggurat at
Ur-of-the-Chaldees, as
seen by William Kennett
Loftus in 1849 while
exploring the mounds of
southern Mesopotamia.

digging away in an attempt to snatch treasures before rivals claimed the
right to excavate. And Rassam had no compunction in digging into
mounds already assigned to other nations. His discovery of the library
of Ashur-banipal in the Kuyunjik mound at Nineveh was an act of
unashamed piracy. Kuyunjik had, with the approval of the British,
been divided into a northern or French area and a southern or British
area. Victor Place succeeded Botta in 1851 in charge of the French
excavations: he had resumed work at Khorsabad and recovered the
plan of Sargon's palace. In 1853 Place's men were digging in the
northern part of Kuyunjik and Rassam in the southern. Rassam was
mortified to find Place's team, working in their own allotted sector,
approaching what he thought might be the most exciting part of the
mound. At the risk, he said, 'of getting into hot water with M. Place',
Rassam excavated in the French concession at night and discovered
Ashur-banipal's palace and its library and the famous lion-hunt gallery.
Rassam described this extraordinary episode as 'using strategy':
maintaining – can we believe him? – that Place accepted his behaviour
without protest and congratulated him on his 'good fortune'.

　　Rassam's work at Nineveh was carried on by William Kennett
51　Loftus, who had already worked in southern Mesopotamia visiting
mounds which, he said, 'from our childhood we have been led to regard
as the cradle of the human-race'. In the early 1850s he excavated
Warka, the site of the biblical Erech and the home of the mythical
Sumerian hero, Gilgamesh, where he discovered coloured mosaics of
terracotta cones, and some cuneiform tablets.

　　J. E. Taylor, the British Vice-Consul at Basra, excavated in 1854–55
Tell Mukayyar, a mound containing the fine ziggurat of Ur-of-the-
Chaldees, and Tell Abu-Shahrein (ancient Eridu). The excavations of

Loftus and Taylor, important as they were to become for their discovery of early Sumerian buildings, attracted little interest at the time: they did not produce spectacular sculptures like those being found in excavations in Assyria.

The French, in addition to sending out Place to succeed Botta, provided money for 'a scientific and artistic expedition to Mesopotamia and Media': it consisted of Fresnes, Oppert and Félix Thomas who dug in various sites such as Kish and Babylon in southern Mesopotamia. In 1855 the boats and rafts which were carrying downstream the finds of the French expedition and also two hundred and forty cases of material from Khorsabad and from Ashur-banipal's palace at Nineveh were deliberately, and with malicious intent, capsized by Arab brigands at Kurnah, at the head of the Shatt al-Arab.

The Kurnah disaster was a very great loss to archaeology and especially to the European museums waiting for the Assyrian material to display in their galleries. Yet Mesopotamian archaeology was already well represented in European collections. When Place's successor asked the French authorities for more money to carry out further excavations he was told: 'Non . . . les fouilles sont finies, on a trop dépensé'. The British Museum became so full of material from Mesopotamia that a special Assyrian Room was organized in the Crystal Palace. In 1855 the outbreak of the Crimean War put a stop to excavation in Mesopotamia: there was a lull of nearly twenty years.

Meanwhile cuneiform writing had been deciphered. At the turn of the century a German scholar, G. F. Grotefend, was working on the copies that Niebuhr had made of the trilingual inscriptions from Persepolis. In 1802 he had deciphered three royal names in Old Persian, the simplest of the three scripts; later he was able to decipher correctly a third of the letters in this language. But Grotefend was not an Oriental scholar and could not take his researches further. He submitted a dissertation embodying his discoveries to the Göttingen Academy: it was not accepted for publication. In fact it was not published until 1893, when it was purely of historical interest. Henry Creswicke Rawlinson (1810–95) is always described as the man 53 responsible for the decipherment of cuneiform. He had no knowledge whatsoever of Grotefend's work, but he had a very considerable knowledge of Oriental languages which Grotefend had not.

Rawlinson worked first on two short trilingual inscriptions near Hamadan and then on the famous trilingual inscriptions engraved in 516 BC on the orders of Darius Hystaspes (521–485 BC), on the great rock of Behistun or Besitun, near Kermanshah. These inscriptions are 52 400 feet (122 metres) from the ground on the face of a rock-mass rising 1,700 feet (518 metres) from the plain. Rawlinson began copying the Old Persian and Elamite inscriptions in 1835. He returned to the task in 1844: the inscriptions were, of course, very difficult to get close to. Eventually, in 1847, with the assistance of one of the most attractive and anonymous figures in the history of archaeology, 'a wild Kurdish boy who had come from a distance' and who performed the most remarkable feats, hanging on to a cleft in the rock face with his fingers and toes, swinging on ropes across gaps and taking paper squeezes from a swinging painter's cradle, the Babylonian inscription was recorded.

52, 53 Henry Creswicke Rawlinson (1810–95) (*opposite*), British Consul-General in Baghdad, who deciphered cuneiform using the trilingual inscription (*above*) carved in 516 BC on the great rock of Behistun, near Kermanshah.

By the end of 1837 Rawlinson had translated the first two paragraphs of the cuneiform inscription in Old Persian; in 1846 he published, in two volumes, *The Persian Cuneiform Inscription of Behistun*, which was a complete translation. Dr Edward Hincks published an independent translation in the same year. Rawlinson, Hincks, Oppert, Fox Talbot and others then began work on the Babylonian inscription and soon that, too, was translated, and the key obtained to Babylonian and Assyrian. In 1857 Rawlinson translated for the British Museum an inscription on a cylinder of Tiglath Pileser I. Before publication, Hincks, Fox Talbot and Oppert were asked to make their own independent translations: these, sent in sealed envelopes to the President of the Royal Asiatic Society, were examined by a committee, which pronounced that the translations were so much alike that there could no longer be any doubt that cuneiform had been deciphered.

It was this decipherment that enabled the mounds across the river from Mosul to be identified by Rawlinson as Nineveh, Sinkara to be the ancient city of Larsa, Tell Mukayyar to be Ur-of-the-Chaldees and Tell-Abu-Shahrein the biblical Eridu. Rawlinson found himself as famous as Layard: he, too, was given an honorary doctorate by the University of Oxford, and was knighted in 1856.

54 Lord Elgin, British ambassador to Turkey from 1799 to 1803, obtained permission to remove some of the marble friezes from the Parthenon in Athens (*above*). In 1816 they were bought from him for £35,000 and exhibited in the British Museum, where they have remained ever since. Whatever the propriety of transporting the marbles to Britain and keeping them there, they would undoubtedly have suffered great damage if left in their original home.

Greece and Rome: the Beginnings of Classical Archaeology

Travellers from France, Germany and Britain in the eighteenth and early nineteenth centuries had no scruples about carrying away to museums in north-western Europe the portable antiquities of Italy, Greece and the Near East. Their justification was that the local inhabitants were unworthy to possess, and unable to look after, works of ancient art. 'Inscriptions we copied as they fell in our way', said Robert Wood in his *Ruins of Palmyra* (1753), 'and carried off the marbles wherever it was possible, for the avarice and superstition of the inhabitants made the task difficult and sometimes impracticable.'

Lord Elgin (1766–1841), a Scottish lord and diplomat, was, at the early age of thirty-three, sent in 1799 to be British Ambassador at Constantinople. His friend, Thomas Harrison, an architect, asked him to make plaster casts of some Greek sculpture. Elgin conceived the idea of doing drawings and casts of as much as possible. When he visited the Acropolis in Athens he realized that the statuary was constantly being exposed to wilful destruction and to general neglect. Eventually he received permission to remove some of the metopes of the Parthenon. Three hundred to four hundred workmen were kept busy for a year carrying off the decorative sculpture of the Parthenon. Much damage was done to the original monuments: as was said 'Quod non fecerunt Gothi, fecerunt Scoti'. Lord Elgin was recalled in 1803: his collection in two hundred cases, filling several ships, was sent off to England. The brig *Mentor* was wrecked off Cape Malea: skilled divers took three years to recover the treasures, but they were not eventually despatched until 1812. After many vicissitudes the Elgin 'marbles' were bought from him for the nation in 1816 for the sum of £35,000 and exhibited in the British Museum. There has been, and still is, endless controversy about the propriety of transporting the 'marbles' to Britain and discussion as to whether they should now be returned to Greece. What is beyond dispute is that they have survived admirably in the British Museum, where they are now beautifully displayed: they would have suffered great damage if left in their original home.

The Cambridge don, Edward Daniel Clarke (1769–1822), who became the first Professor of Mineralogy and later University Librarian, had travelled extensively in Greece. He discovered the tomb of Euclid in Athens – not the mathematician, but Clarke thought he was, and wrote, 'How interesting . . . such an Antiquity must be for the University of Cambridge, where the name of Euclid is so particularly revered.' And his account of the removal of the colossal Cistophoros of Eleusis, now in the Fitzwilliam Museum, is a very fascinating revelation of the methods of the time:

> I found the goddess in a dunghill; buried to her ears. The Eleusinian peasants, at the very mention of moving it, regarded me as one who would bring the moon from her orbit. What would become of their corn, they said, if the old lady with the basket were removed? I went to Athens and made an application to the Pasha, aiding my request by letting an English telescope glide between his fingers. The business was done.

John Disney was a gentleman of Essex and a lawyer. He was called to the bar in 1803, the same year in which Lord Elgin, passing through Paris, was arrested under a decree of Napoleon. Disney was a dilettante and a collector and a friend of E. D. Clarke. He, like Clarke, presented his collections to the University of Cambridge but went one better than Clarke and founded a Professorship of Archaeology in 1851. The declaration and agreement between the donor and the University was quite clear: 'It shall be the duty of the professor to deliver in the course of each academic year . . . six lectures at least on the subject of Classical, Medieval and other Antiquities, the Fine Arts and all matters and things connected therewith.' Although the Disney Professorship of Archaeology was the first such chair in the British Isles it was by no means the first in Europe. We have already referred to the creation of a Chair of Antiquities in the University of Uppsala in 1662 with Olof Verelius as the first holder. Then in 1818 Caspar Jacob Christiaan Reuvens was appointed to the newly created Chair of Archaeology at Leiden: his field was specified as 'Egyptology, numismatics, architectural history, classical and non-classical archaeology'.

The French consul at Athens, Fauvel, was active in collecting antiquities and it was due to him that the Louvre possesses an extremely fine plaque from the Parthenon frieze. A group of men consisting of the Englishmen C. R. Cockerell and J. Foster, two Danes, Bröndstedt and Koes, the Livonian Baron Otto Magnus Von Stackelborg and the Nuremberg architect Baron Haller von Hallerstein excavated the supposed temple of Zeus at Aegina and the temple of Apollo at Bassae in 1811. Sculptures from these sites, restored by the sculptor Thorwaldsen, were bought by King Louis I of Bavaria and the British Museum. In 1829 a French archaeological mission worked in the Peloponnese, publishing their results in *Expédition scientifique de Morée*.

In 1821 the Vicomte de Marellus, Secretary to the French diplomatic mission in Athens, working on the instructions of his superior, the Marquis de Rivière, ambassador at Constantinople, bought the famous statue of the Venus de Milo, now in the Louvre. He wrote of it: 'O Vénus, charme de mes yeux et de mon souvenir, après avoir sommeillé plus de mille ans sous des moissons stériles et des herbes sauvages, elle s'est réveillée à ma voix . . .'

55

Greece was liberated from Turkish rule in 1829 and as a new nation began to take an interest in its own past, assisted by many foreign archaeologists. The French Ecole française d'archéologie was set up in 1846 – the first of such foreign schools in Greece, to be followed, in due course, by similar institutions by Germany, Britain, America and Italy. The day of consular officials and ambassadors indulging in archaeology on the side was coming to an end, but the career of the Englishman, Charles Thomas Newton, was characteristic of the interpenetration of archaeology and diplomacy. Newton was an official of the British Museum who arranged to be sent by the Foreign Office for seven years of diplomatic service in the Levant and to combine his duties with collecting material for the British Museum. He succeeded in identifying the site of the Mausoleum of Halicarnassus, one of the wonders of the Ancient World, and assembled in the British Museum all that was left of it, including fragments that had been taken to Geneva, Constantinople and Rhodes. He discovered the plan of the Greek city of Cnidos in 1858–59: the first time that an old city plan had been carefully and accurately recovered. He made very extensive use of photography in all his archaeological work.

In Italy the eighteenth-century excavations at Herculaneum and Pompeii were carried out over many years by small groups of four, eight or at most thirty workmen. They were treasure hunts and not serious excavations. Houses were exposed and looted, paintings were sawn off and the robbed houses allowed to fall into decay. Complete excavation of houses was rarely, if ever, done: the usual practice was to dig the upper storey and let it collapse into the trenches, burying the lower levels. Right at the end of the eighteenth century and at the beginning of the nineteenth, owing to the generosity and enthusiasm of the Napoleonic kings of Naples, carefully planned excavations at Pompeii were mounted. They were directed by a scholar from Naples, Michele Arditi: this was the first large planned excavation in history and sufficient money was forthcoming to implement it – at times six hundred men were being employed.

Giuseppe Fiorelli took over the excavations in Pompeii in 1860. He uncovered whole *insulae*, digging them very carefully, layer by layer, preserving features of interest *in situ*. He set up a *Scuola di Pompeii* where foreign archaeologists, as well as Italians, could learn these new archaeological techniques. He himself made a special study of the materials and technique of building at Pompeii. He developed the technique of making casts of bodies by pouring plaster into the hollows formed in the volcanic ash when the bodies had disintegrated: and he developed this technique to make casts of doors, furniture and even roofs.

56, 57

55 (*Opposite*) The Venus de Milo bought in 1821 by the French in the Greek island of Melos and now in the Louvre, Paris.

Fiorelli was a thoroughly scientific man and a pioneer of stratigraphical analysis. In describing Fiorelli's methods, as initiated at Pompeii, Gaston Bossier said:

He declared and repeated in his reports that the centre of interest in the Pompeian excavations was Pompeii itself: that the discovery of works of art was a matter of secondary importance: that efforts were directed, above all, to reviving a Roman city that would depict for us the life of bygone ages: that it was necessary to see the city in its entirety and in its minutest details in order that the lesson it taught might be complete, that knowledge was sought, not only of the houses of the wealthy, but also of the dwellings of the poor, with their common household utensils and crude wall decoration. With that end in view, everything became important, and nothing could legitimately be overlooked.

A very remarkable and modern statement.

56, 57 The inhabitants of Pompeii, human (*above*) and animal (*left*), were given little warning in AD 79 as Vesuvius erupted, burying them in hot ashes and suffocating them with sulphur fumes. Giuseppe Fiorelli, who took over the Pompeii excavations in 1860, developed the technique of making casts of the bodies by pouring plaster into the hollows formed in the volcanic ash.

Barbarian Europe

The Etruscans were studied in the early nineteenth century by Micali, Inghirami and Gerhard. The richly coloured mural paintings of Corneto were discovered in 1827; other decorated sites and tombs were later opened at Veii, Chiusi, Cerveteri and Orvieto. The discovery in 1836 of the Regolini-Galassi tomb at Caere, with its fabulously rich contents, did much to excite interest in the Etruscans, but also to attract treasure hunters. The Etruscans were made known to English readers by George Dennis's *Cities and Cemeteries of Etruria* (1848), a widely read and delightful book. Dennis had no doubt of the great role played by the Etruscans in spreading Mediterranean civilization to northern and north-western Europe. 'Antiquarians are now generally agreed', he wrote, 'that all the ancient bronzes found in various finds north of the Alps from Switzerland to Denmark, and from Ireland to Hungary and Wallachia, are of Etruscan origin.'

The Scythians had been described by Herodotus. The earliest discoveries of the Scyths by modern archaeologists were those of Paul VII, VIII Dubrux at Kul Oba near Kerch in 1830. Later work was described in *Les Antiquités de la Scythie d'Hérodote* (1866–73), published by the Imperial Archaeological Commission of St Petersburg. The Imperial Odessa Society of History and Antiquities was created in 1839: ten years later it became the Imperial Archaeological Society. An Archaeological and Numismatic Society had been founded in Russia in 1846.

58 The archaeology of the Celts, and of the pre-Roman Iron Age in Europe in general, came into its own in the fifties and sixties of the nineteenth century. Of course archaeological material belonging to the pre-Roman Iron Age in Europe was recognized as such even before Thomsen and his successors had defined the Iron Age; but this material was variously labelled British, Teutonic or Gaulish and there was uncertainty between pre-Roman, Roman and post-Roman ascription. Colt Hoare had described the bridle-bits, iron tires and axle mounts from Hampden Hill as pre-Roman and British. The Baron de Bonstetten described the heap of iron weapons, horse-harness, parts of chariots, Celtic coins and pottery found at Tiefenau near Berne as Alemannic of the third or fourth century AD. Colonel Schwab first excavated the site of La Tène on Lake Neuchâtel in 1858: these excavations were continued for many years and brought to light, among other things, a splendid series of iron swords which Ferdinand Keller studied and declared to belong neither to the Roman period nor the Bronze Age but to be Celtic, part of the Helvetic phase of Swiss prehistory and of the Iron Age.

In 1846 excavations, by Ramsauer, began at Hallstatt in Austria on behalf of the Vienna Museum and continued for nearly twenty years. In 1866 an international party of highly reputable archaeologists dug at Hallstatt: they included John Evans, Lubbock, Franks, Lartet and Morlot. Evans wrote of this dig: 'we arranged with the Bergmeister to set some men at work digging and are going up there early tomorrow morning to see the result: it may be that we shall stop there all day.' And, next day, he wrote:

58 Celtic head on the handle of an early La Tène bronze flagon, from Waldalgesheim, Germany, early fourth century BC. Ht of head *c*. 4 cm.

We found our diggings too pleasant for us to be able to tear ourselves away from them. Lubbock and I breakfasted soon after 6 and about half past seven were up at the cemetery . . . and found the men had already discovered a bronze bracelet and a broken fibula. I subsequently found in one of our trenches and dug out with my own hands one of the iron socketed celts with a part of the handle remaining in it and having on one part the impression of a fine twilled cloth against which it had lain.

The result of nearly twenty years' digging was summarized in Baron von Sacken's *Das Grabfeld von Hallstatt* (1868): some 993 burials were uncovered. The cemetery seemed to demonstrate the transition from the Bronze to the Iron Age in Europe. In 1872 Hildebrand proposed that the European Iron Age should be divided into an earlier or Hallstatt phase and a later or La Tène phase.

John Kemble drew attention to a group of objects ornamented in the style of La Tène which were being studied in the British Museum by Franks. Franks, in arranging and describing the plates which Kemble had intended to illustrate his *Horae Ferales* (published after Kemble's death in 1863), ventured to term them 'Late Celtic'. He deliberately used the label Celtic because their distribution appeared to coincide with that of Celtic occupation, and because the ornamental patterns seemed linked with those of Early Christian art in Ireland, and were entirely different from the art of the Roman, Saxon and Danish antiquities found in England.

The first definite evidence for the date of La Tène art was provided by the excavations at Mont Auxois (Alesia) and Mont Réa at Alise Ste-Reine in Burgundy, carried on from 1861 to 1865 by order of Napoleon III. In the ditches of a Roman camp were found swords and spears associated with Roman and Gaulish coins, none of the former being later than 54 BC, which seemed to date the La Tène objects to the pre-Roman period, and at least to the middle of the first century BC. This was the first reliable date for La Tène art and enabled archaeologists in France or Spain to assign finds and graves to the pre-Roman Iron Age. At the same time the extent of the Celtic La Tène civilization began to be appreciated. In 1870 de Mortillet saw that objects from graves at Marzabotto, near Bologna, were identical with objects from La Tène graves in the Marne and so identified archaeologically the La Tène Celtic invaders of Italy.

We have already referred to the Reverend Bryan Faussett as one of the first excavators in England. Thrown on the fire as a child by the family pet monkey, he survived to excavate burial mounds in the eighteenth century which he thought were Roman in date but were actually Anglo-Saxon. Faussett's diary of his work was not published until Charles Roach Smith did so in his *Inventorium Sepulchrale* (1856), the year before J. Yonge Akerman published his *Remains of Pagan Saxendom*. Inspired by Akerman, Kemble found resemblances between Anglo-Saxon pottery in England and urns from Hanover, publishing his discovery in 1856. The following year an Anglo-Saxon hut was excavated in Oxfordshire: Anglo-Saxon archaeology was born in the 1850s.

Joseph Dubrovsky (1753–1829) began studying in 1781 the burial rites of the Old Slavs and tried to put these finds into their historical setting; he was one of the first archaeologists in the world who insisted on applying the method and principles of prehistoric archaeology to written sources: he called his archaeological finds 'speaking proof'. He also wrote an account of the 1803 excavations of Iron Age barrows near Lochovice in Bohemia – the first professionally conducted and documented dig in what is now Czechoslovakia.

America

We have already referred in Chapter 1 to the interest in archaeology of the American Philosophical Society and the circular sent out by Thomas Jefferson as President in 1799. In 1812 Isaiah Thomas, a publisher, founded the American Antiquarian Society in Mass-achusetts, the first of its kind in the New World: its purpose was 'The collection and presentation of the antiquities of our country and of curious and valuable productions in art and nature [which] have a tendency to enlarge the sphere of human knowledge . . . and to improve and instruct posterity.' The Society held its first meeting in Boston, a

library was established, material for a museum collected, research planned and encouraged and the first volume of the Society's *Transactions* published in 1820. It contained a paper by Caleb Atwater (1778–1867) entitled 'Description of the Antiquities Discovered in the State of Ohio and other Western States', in which the author described and planned many mounds near his home town of Circleville, Ohio and the surrounding region. His classification of and speculation about the mounds was not so useful as his survey work: he divided them into three periods, the most recent that of the modern European, then preceding that those mounds of the modern American Indian, while the earliest mounds, he claimed, were built by the original mound-builders who were Hindus from India on their way to Mexico.

Dr James H. McCulloh Jr, a man who did no fieldwork, published his *Researches in America* in 1817 and *Researches Philosophical and Antiquarian Concerning the Aboriginal History of America* in 1829: he denied Atwater's claim of a separate mound-builder people and said that the mounds were built by the American Indians, as indeed they were.

In 1848 there was published *Ancient Monuments of the Mississippi Valley* by E. G. Squier, an Ohio newspaperman, and E. H. Davis, a doctor from Chillicothe, Ohio. They surveyed a large number of mounds, excavated some, and published a section through the Grave Creek Mound, dug by its owner Abelard B. Tomlinson in 1838. Their book was a synthesis of their own work and that of others: they did little

59 An artist's conception of the Grave Creek Mound in West Virginia, from Squier and Davis's *Ancient Monuments of the Mississippi Valley* (1848).

59

in the way of speculation but did believe in the great mound-builders race theory, and were sure that the American Indians and their ancestors could not have had the skill to build the mounds.

Tomlinson claimed to have found in the Grave Creek Mound an inscribed sandstone tablet with writing in an unknown alphabet. Henry Rowe Schoolcraft, a geologist and ethnographer, studied these and other finds and declared, 'there is little to sustain a belief that these ancient works are due to the tribes of more fixed and exalted traits of civilisation . . . of either an Asiatic or European origin.' They were, he said, 'the antiquities of barbarism, not of civilisation'. His views gained little attention, hidden as they were in his six-volume work *Historical and Statistical Information Respecting the History, Condition and Prospects of the Indian Tribes of the United States* (1851–57).

In 1837 Samuel Haven (1806–81) was appointed Librarian of the American Antiquarian Society, a post which he held until his death. In 1856 he published *The Archaeology of the United States, or Sketches Historical and Bibliographical of the Progress of Information and Opinion Respecting Vestiges of Antiquity in the United States*, which has been described as 'a model of reasoned description and discussion' by Willey and Sabloff (*A History of American Archaeology*, 1974, 47). 'We desire to stop where evidence ceases,' he wrote, 'and offer no speculations as to the direction from which the authors of the vestiges of antiquity in the United States entered the country, or from whence their arts are derived.' He declared, however, that the native Americans were of great antiquity and that 'all their characteristic affinities are found in the early conditions of Asiatic races and a channel of communication is pointed out through which they might have poured into the country.'

Haven's book, a foundation stone of modern American archaeology, was published by the Smithsonian Institution. James Smithson, an eccentric and very wealthy Englishman, who had never visited the United States or shown the slightest interest in it, left, subject to the life interest of a nephew, over five hundred thousand dollars to found an institution in Washington 'for the increase and diffusion of knowledge among men'. The Smithsonian Institution, today one of the world's great research institutions, opened its doors in 1846.

George Peabody, a wealthy American businessman and philanthropist living in London, founded the Peabody Museum of Archaeology and Ethnology at Harvard in 1866. Peabody's nephew, Othniel Marsh of Yale, became interested in American archaeology through reading Sir Charles Lyell's *The Antiquity of Man* and Lyell, whom he met, urged him to take up archaeology in America. This he did and it was while excavating a mound near Newark, Ohio, that the idea came to him of persuading his uncle to found an archaeological and ethnological museum. George Peabody required little persuasion. The Smithsonian Institution in Washington and the Peabody Museum at Harvard have had, and still have, a tremendous influence on the development of archaeological research in America.

Little had happened in the study of Meso-American archaeology while the mound-builders were being disputed in North America. Then, in 1804, Charles IV of Spain sent a Frenchman, Guillermo Dupaix, to examine the pre-Conquest ruins of Mexico. This he did, but

his reports were left unstudied in Mexico City. Other archaeological travellers and explorers, like John Galindo, an Irishman by birth and Guatemalan by naturalization, and Jean Frédéric Waldeck, tried to interest the world in Palenque and other sites. Waldeck's *Voyage pittoresque et archéologique dans la Province d'Yucatan pendant les années 1834 et 1836* was published in 1838 in Paris.

These early travellers aroused interest in learned circles and two scientific expeditions were undertaken. The first, locally organized in Honduras by a soldier, Lieutenant John Caddy, and a civil servant, Patrick Walker, produced the earliest scientific account of Palenque, which was forgotten about until its rediscovery a few years ago; it was in any case overshadowed by the expedition of Catherwood and Stephens which was organized with the backing of the United States Government. John Lloyd Stephens (1805–52) was an American lawyer who had travelled in the Old World in Egypt and Palestine and published in 1837 his *Incidents of Travel in Arabia Petraea*. Frederick Catherwood was an English artist and architect. They set out from Belize in 1839 and published their travels in *Incidents of Travel in Central America, Chiapas and Yucatan* (1841) and *Incidents of Travel in Yucatan* (1843). These books, with Catherwood's beautiful drawings, stimulated fresh interest in Middle American archaeology.

The work of Stephens and Catherwood was mainly descriptive, but they became certain that the remains they were studying were inspired and made by the native Indians. Stephens wrote:

60 View of the Castillo at Tulum, northern Yucatan, published by Frederick Catherwood in 1844.

61

60, 62

61, 62 John Lloyd Stephens (1805–52) (*below*) was one of the founding fathers of modern Mesoamerican archaeology. Together with the artist, Frederick Catherwood, he explored and recorded the ruins of the ancient Maya, and his two books, *Incidents of Travel in Central America* ... (1841) and *Incidents of Travel in Yucatan* (1843) became bestsellers. Catherwood's lithograph (*right*) shows a broken stele from the Maya site of Copán.

We are not warranted in going back to any ancient nation of the Old World for the builders of these cities: that they are not the work of people who have passed away and whose history is lost, but that there are strong reasons to believe them the creations of the same races who inhabited the country at the time of the Spanish conquest, or of some not very distant progenitors.

We have already mentioned Daniel Wilson (1816–92), whose *The Archaeology and Prehistoric Annals of Scotland* (1851) was the first major attempt to apply the Scandinavian three-age system to Britain. A product of the Scottish enlightenment, he migrated to Canada and became the first Principal and Vice-Chancellor of the University of Toronto. His influence on the development of archaeological and anthropological studies in Canada and North America as a whole was considerable. In 1862 he published *Prehistoric Man: Researches into the origin of civilization in the Old and New Worlds*. He argued for independent parallel evolution resulting from the psychic unity of man: a position much like that later set out by Lewis H. Morgan.

India and Asia

Some European travellers in India wrote in the seventeenth century about Indian monuments, but the beginnings of Indian archaeology came with the establishment of the Asiatic Society of Bengal in Calcutta in 1784. The founder was Sir William Jones (1746–94), a friend of Samuel Johnson, who came to Calcutta as Supreme Court judge in 1783. The purpose of the Society was 'to inquire into the history and antiquities, the arts, sciences and literature of Asia'. Its museum was founded in 1814 and its *Archaeological Researches* first published in 1788.

In 1790 Roman coins were found near Nellore north of Madras. In a letter to the Asiatic Society, Alexander Davidson, Governor of Madras, wrote that a peasant's plough was 'obstructed by some brick-work; he dug and discovered the remains of a small Hindu temple under which a little pot was found with Roman coins and medals of the second century.'

James Prinsep (1799–1840), Assay Master of the Mint in Calcutta, took a very keen interest in Indian antiquities and was for several years

Secretary of the Asiatic Society. He was a close associate of General Alexander Cunningham, who founded the Archaeological Survey of India in 1861.

In 1823 Babington discovered iron implements in some megaliths in Malabar. In 1845 James Fergusson, an indigo-planter, published his *Rock-Cut Temples of India*: this was the beginning of his archaeological and architectural interests which led to his *History of Architecture* (1865–67) and his *Rude Stone Monuments in all Countries: their Age and Uses* (1872), the first general survey of megalithic architecture.

In 1863 Robert Bruce Foote reported for the first time the discovery of Palaeolithic implements in Madras, and world prehistory had begun.

Archaeology in 1867

1867 is a convenient date at which to end this chapter, which has chronicled some of the developments in archaeology since the last few years of the eighteenth century when John Frere sent his Acheulian hand-axes from Hoxne to London claiming that they were to be referred 'to a very remote period, indeed, even beyond that of the present world', and Napoleon's savants had begun work on the antiquities of Egypt. The seventy years between 1797 and 1867 had seen the establishment of the new fluvialist geology, the acceptance of the great antiquity of man, and the adoption of the Danish three-age model of the past as modified by Lubbock into the four-age system.

1859, that *annus mirabilis* as it was often called, saw not only the acceptance of the antiquity of man but the publication of Charles Darwin's *The Origin of Species by Means of Natural Selection or the Preservation of Favoured Races in the Struggle for Life*. It was, incidentally, the reading of Lyell's *Principles of Geology* that suggested to Darwin the general theory of evolution, just as it was the reading of Malthus's *Essay on Population* that suggested to him the ideas of the struggle for existence and the survival of the fittest.

It has often been said that *The Origin of Species* had a profound effect on the development of archaeology. At first Darwin expressed no opinion of the effect of his theory on man's ancestry, nor did he in that book comment on the anatomical likenesses between man and the apes, except to say that the acceptance of his theory suggested that 'much light will be thrown on the origin of man and his history'. The scholar who extended Darwinism to man was T. H. Huxley (1825–95), 'Darwin's bulldog' as he styled himself: his *Man's Place in Nature* was published in 1863. Darwin expounded the extension to man of the theory of evolution in *The Descent of Man* (1871) and his *Expression of the Emotions in Man and the Animals* (1872). When the dust of the battle between the evolutionists and anti-evolutionists had settled and Darwinism was widely accepted, it was obvious that the theory of organic evolution made people more ready to accept the antiquity of man. It made the roughly chipped stone axes from the Somme and Suffolk not only credible but essential, and a belief in Neanderthal man credible and essential.

The Great Exhibition of 1851 in London had no archaeology and indeed why should it? Its purpose was to summarize the material

63

advances made during the first half of the nineteenth century and reveal the prospects of further progress. But the planners of the Paris Exposition of 1867 wanted to look back as well as forward and there were displayed collections of prehistoric and protohistoric material. The French collections of prehistory included artifacts from Aurignac and Les Eyzies, a case of rockshelter art, material from the Breton megaliths and from the lake villages on the Lac du Bourget. Gabriel de Mortillet wrote a guide called *Promenades préhistoriques à l'Exposition Universelle* (1867), and at the end of the guide claimed that three main facts had already emerged from the scholarship of prehistoric archaeology and he printed them in capitals:

LOI DU PROGRES DE L'HUMANITE
LOI DU DEVELOPPEMENT SIMILAIRE
HAUTE ANTIQUITE DE L'HOMME

Mariette arranged the Egyptian collections at the Paris Exposition. The Empress Eugénie was so delighted by the Egyptian jewellery that she informed the Khedive Ismail that she would be pleased to receive the whole collection as a present. The Khedive, surprised by the request, but anxious to please France, and, as ever, short of money, made the giving of this present conditional on the consent of Mariette. He told the Empress's agent, 'There is someone at Boulak more powerful than I and you must address yourself to him.' The much surprised agent did so and met with a firm refusal by Mariette: the collection of Egyptian antiquities returned safely from Paris to Boulak.

It was a great moment for archaeology as was the presence of archaeology in the Paris Exposition. Four years later, in his *Primitive Culture* (1871), E. B. Tylor wrote: 'The history and prehistory of man take their proper places in the general scheme of knowledge.' He was over-optimistic: some would say a century and more later that archaeology and prehistory have still not taken their proper place in the general scheme of knowledge. But at least in 1867 it could be said that archaeology had come of age.

63 Charles Darwin portrayed in *Punch* magazine's tongue-in-cheek musing on the implications of evolutionary theory, 1881.

3

Excavators and Explorers (1867–1914)

The Palaeolithic and Palaeolithic Art

The acceptance of the authenticity of Upper Palaeolithic art after the Lartet/Christy paper, 'Les cavernes du Périgord', of 1864 was not universal or immediate. In 1869 Worsaae, in the Copenhagen Congress of Archaeology, publicly accepted the authenticity of Chaffaud and Upper Palaeolithic art was now a fact of man's prehistory and a very surprising one.

Six years later a Spaniard, Marcellino de Sautuola, began excavating in the cave of Altamira, near Santander, and found paintings in black on the back wall of the cave; these he claimed to be of the same age as the Palaeolithic deposits in the cave. Four years later his small daughter, aged five, bored by her father's excavations, wandered into the back depths of the cave, which was very low and which her father had not visited because of its relative inaccessibility. There, by the flickering light of her lantern, she saw on the roof of the inner cave the now very famous vigorous, bold and striking polychrome paintings of I, II   bulls, bison and charging boars. She tottered out to tell her father what she had seen, saying 'Toros!, Toros!, father come and see the bulls.' He crawled inside, saw the wonderful paintings and immediately told the world of his discovery. Meanwhile in 1878 Chiron had found drawings on the walls of Chabot in the Ardèche, which he claimed were Upper Palaeolithic.

These discoveries and claims brought on a great dispute among prehistorians, some insisting they were forgeries or, at earliest, Gallo-Roman in date, others believing them authentic. In 1877 Gabriel de Mortillet accepted the authenticity of cave art, declaring: 'C'est l'enfance de l'art, ce n'est pas l'art de l'enfant'; and ten years later Edouard Piette claimed the paintings were Magdalenian in date, accepting their authenticity in *Equidés de la Période quaternaire d'après les Gravures de ce Temps*. But Emile Cartailhac in *La France Préhistorique* and Salomon Reinach in *Alluvions et Cavernes* – both books were published in 1889 – are full of doubts and reservations, and rejected the authenticity of Palaeolithic cave art.

In 1895 E. and G. Bertoumeyrou discovered some drawings on the walls of the rock shelter of La Mouthe near Les Eyzies, and the next year Emile Rivière excavated La Mouthe fully: deposits of Palaeolithic and Neolithic date completely blocked the entrance before excavations began, and in the cave were found paintings and engravings including the famous one of a Palaeolithic hut. That is why La Mouthe is so important in the history of archaeology, as Rivière himself realized. The engravings and paintings were discovered only after the deposits of human occupation had been cleared away, so that they were as old as, or older than, the Palaeolithic occupation of the cave shelter. This is what Rivière maintained in his publication to the French Académie des Sciences in 1896. A number of archaeologists and geologists who went to visit La Mouthe were convinced of the authenticity of the paintings and engravings and of the existence of Upper Palaeolithic cave art.

Meanwhile François Daleau had, since 1874, been excavating the rockshelter of Pair-non-Pair in the Gironde, some sixty-two miles west of Les Eyzies. In 1883 he saw some engraved lines on the wall of the cave but did not think much of them until, having heard of the discoveries at La Mouthe, he washed down the walls with a strong spray and was able to distinguish the engravings of twelve animals, which had been buried by Upper Palaeolithic occupation levels.

The Abbé Breuil, to become the doyen of Palaeolithic scholars and the greatest authority on Palaeolithic art, but then a young man of twenty-three, visited La Mouthe in 1900, and realized that the Pair-non-Pair engravings were stylistically identical with La Mouthe and that the La Mouthe evidence precluded any view other than that the engravings were Upper Palaeolithic. His tracings were published in the *Revue Scientifique* for 1901.

The tide was turning. In that same year, 1901, a man who had worked for Rivière at La Mouthe said he had seen similar engravings in a cave nearby and on 8 September, Capitan, Peyrony and Breuil were led to the now celebrated cave of Les Combarelles and saw the engravings. On 15 September of the same year Peyrony discovered the paintings in the cave of Font-de-Gaume, less than a mile from Les Combarelles.

At the congress of the Association Française pour l'avancement des sciences held in Montauban in 1902, the discoveries at Les Combarelles and Font-de-Gaume were discussed but mainly disbelieved in as still were Altamira, La Mouthe and Pair-non-Pair by most archaeologists. But a field excursion was organized to Les Eyzies and the savants were at last convinced.

In his *Four Hundred Centuries of Cave Art* (1952) the Abbé Breuil published a photograph of the A.F.A.S. excursion to La Mouthe on 12 August 1902 which we reproduce here. It shows Rivière, Peyrony, 62 Cartailhac, Adrien de Mortillet, Daleau and the Abbé Breuil. It is, Breuil rightly claimed, 'a really historical document for it dates the day when the scientific world officially recognized the wall art of the caves of the Reindeer Age.'

Cartailhac, Professor at Toulouse and the doyen of French prehistoric archaeology, had disbelieved in Altamira and thought the paintings so obviously a modern forgery that he had not been to see them since their discovery was announced. After La Mouthe, Pair-non-Pair, Font-de-Gaume and Les Combarelles he realized he was almost certainly mistaken: he also recognized the stylistic identity of Font-de-Gaume and Altamira. He took the young Breuil with him to see Altamira. They were excited. Breuil brought back stacks of copies he had made of the polychrome paintings. Cartailhac wrote his famous

64 The meeting of savants at the entrance to La Mouthe in 1902, including the young Henri Breuil.

paper published in *L'Anthropologie* in 1902, entitled 'Les Cavernes ornées de dessins: La grotte d'Altamira. *Mea culpa* d'un sceptique', in which he recounted his conversion to the authenticity of cave art. From now on Palaeolithic art, both from rockshelters and caves, was treated as the first – or at least the first surviving – artistic manifestation of man.

Niaux was discovered in 1906 and in the following year Piette wrote his *L'Art Pendant l'Age du Renne*. The Prince of Monaco interested himself in these new and remarkable discoveries: he founded the Institut de Paléontologie Humaine in Paris, and sponsored and financed a magnificent series of volumes describing the Palaeolithic art in the caves. The first of these, published in 1910, was *La Caverne de Font-de-Gaume*, written and illustrated by Breuil, Capitan and Peyrony.

The content of rockshelter art was also changing. In 1892 the broken ivory statuette of a woman was found at Brassempouy in south-west France and more 'Venus-figures' were found, notably that of Willendorf in Austria. So well established was Palaeolithic art that in 1913 Reinach produced his *Répertoire de l'Art Quaternaire*.

In 1912 the Bégouen brothers discovered the cave of Le Tuc d'Audoubert in the Pyrenees. Two stalagmite pillars had to be broken in order to reach the two modelled clay bison.

During this period, however, Palaeolithic man was found not only to have been an artist but to have had ideas about death and the afterlife. In 1868 workmen digging the hillside at Les Eyzies to construct the

66 (*Opposite*) Two bison modelled in clay, found in the cave at Le Tuc d'Audoubert in the Pyrenees in 1912.

railway from Perigueux to Agen, discovered in the rockshelter of Cro-Magnon (it is said now to be the garage of the Cro-Magnon hotel) chipped flints, animal bones and human remains. Edouard Lartet's son, Louis, excavated the rockshelter and, at the back, found five human skeletons together with ornaments including pierced sea-shells. These were now to be added to the Aurignac finds as deliberate Upper Palaeolithic burials. Buckland's early discovery of an Upper Palaeolithic burial at Paviland was then still regarded as Romano-British. Other discoveries of Upper Palaeolithic burials soon followed. In 1872 Rivière began excavating the nine caves of Grimaldi, or Baoussé-Roussé near Mentone. In the fourth, the Grotte du Cavillon, Rivière found a skeleton covered with powdered haematite. The skull was decorated with over 200 perforated sea-shells and 22 perforated red-deer canine teeth. In 1874/75 Rivière found in the cave, subsequently called Grotte des Enfants, the skeletons of two children associated with flint implements and the remains of what must have been two belts extending from navel to hips and made of more than a thousand perforated sea-shells.

Very soon the doubters had to accept that Upper Palaeolithic man was not only an artist, but also had what perhaps can be called religious beliefs.

The classification of the Stone Age went through various changes and developments in the period under review, culminating in Breuil's 1912 paper on 'Les Subdivisions du Paléolithique supérieur et leur Signification'. The problem of Tertiary man (that is, of man's existence in the geological period preceding the Quaternary) first came up in 1863, when J. Desnoyers found incised fossil bones from Saint-Prest

65 The so-called 'Venus of Brassempouy', found in the Grotte du Pape in the Landes in 1892, and now in the Musée des Antiquités Nationales at Saint-Germain-en-Laye. Ht 3.7 cm.

near Chartres, in Pliocene contexts. In 1867 the Abbé Bourgeois was finding what he claimed to be roughly chipped implements from these Pliocene beds at Saint-Prest and also from Miocene beds at Thenay (Loir-et-Cher). These and other finds allegedly proving the existence of Tertiary man were described as *eoliths* or 'dawn-stones', and there was considerable controversy for a very long time about the authenticity of these stones. The great antiquity of man, following discoveries in the last two decades in Tanzania, Kenya and Ethiopia, leaves no doubt as to the existence of Tertiary man, but the human artifactual nature of the so-called eoliths remains in considerable doubt. De Mortillet had an Eolithic or Thenaisian period at the beginning of his scheme of stone-age periods.

There was considerable discussion about the finds which dated to the end of the Palaeolithic or the beginning of the Neolithic. The Danish three-age system, as modified by Lubbock to a four-age system, described a very sharp break between the Old and the New Stone Ages: and this became an article of faith in European systematics. The Magdalenian hunters of the Upper Palaeolithic were supposed to have followed the retreating reindeer northwards and the Neolithic 'civilization', with its polished axes, domestic animals, crops and pottery, was brought from Asia to a depopulated Europe. The gap or *ancien hiatus* between the Palaeolithic and Neolithic was thought to be complete. French prehistorians pointed to sterile layers that in some sites lay between Magdalenian and Neolithic as geological and incontrovertible proof of this hiatus.

In the last quarter of the nineteenth century finds in various sites in France produced artifacts that were post-Magdalenian but pre-Neolithic. How could they (sites such as Mas d'Azil and Fère-en-Tardenois) be fitted in the Lartet-de Mortillet sequence? What was the position of the Azilian and the Tardenoisian?

Eventually a Mesolithic period was suggested between Palaeolithic and Neolithic. In addressing the Royal Anthropological Institute in 1866 – a year after the publication of Lubbock's *Prehistoric Times* – Hodder Westropp had proposed that the period of man's past when he used stone artifacts should be divided into Palaeolithic, Mesolithic and Kainolithic; and he elaborated this idea in his *Prehistoric Phases, or Introductory Essays in Prehistoric Archaeology*, published in 1872. His Mesolithic or 'hunting stage' included the Lartet and Christy Upper Palaeolithic finds from Dordogne, as well as the material from the Danish kitchen middens; and he compared the economy of the prehistoric people of this stage with that of American Indians.

Hodder Westropp's Kainolithic was soon forgotten, even by him, and his Mesolithic was not used. The *Oxford English Dictionary* attributes the first use of the word Mesolithic to J. Allen Brown, who read a paper to the Anthropological Institute in 1892 describing some flint artifacts and saying that 'it is to these forms which appear to be of transitional age, that I would apply the term Mesolithic.' It is curious that in 1892 archaeologists had forgotten Westropp's work of only two decades before, and that they did not know that Otto Torell, a professor of geology at Lund, had used the term Mesolithic at the International Congress of Archaeology and Anthropology at Stockholm in 1874.

TEMPS	AGES	PÉRIODES	ÉPOQUES
Quaternaires actuels. — Historiques.	du Fer.	Mérovingienne.	Wabenienne. (*Waben, Pas-de-Calais.*)
		Romaine.	Champdolienne. (*Champdolent, Seine-et-Oise.*)
			Lugdunienne. (*Lyon, Rhône.*)
		Galatienne.	Beuvraysienne. (*Mont-Beuvray, Nièvre.*)
			Marnienne. (*Département de la Marne.*)
			Hallstattienne. (*Hallstatt, haute Autriche.*)
Protohistoriques.	du Bronze.	Tsiganienne.	Larnaudienne. (*Larnaud, Jura.*)
			Morgienne. (*Morges, canton de Vaud, Suisse.*)
		Néolithique.	Robenhausienne. (*Robenhausen, Zurich.*)
			Campignyenne. (*Campigny, Seine-Inférieure.*)
			Tardenoisienne (*Fère-en-Tardenois, Aisne.*)
Quaternaires anciens. — Préhistoriques.	de la Pierre.	Paléolithique.	Tourassienne. (*La Tourasse, Haute-Garonne.*) Ancien Hiatus.
			Magdalénienne. (*La Madeleine, Dordogne.*)
			Solutréenne. (*Solutré, Saône-et-Loire.*)
			Moustérienne. (*Le Moustier, Dordogne.*)
			Acheuléenne. (*Saint-Acheul, Somme.*)
			Chelléenne. (*Chelles, Seine-et-Marne.*)
Tertiaires.		Éolithique.	Puycournienne. (*Puy-Courny, Cantal.*)
			Thenaysienne. (*Thenay, Loir-et-Cher.*)

67 The 'epochs' of prehistory according to G. de Mortillet, as set out in his *Formation de la Nation Française* (1897).

Anyhow, by the end of the century, the term Mesolithic was firmly established: in 1895 Piette's excavations at Mas d'Azil provided the famous section which showed that the *ancien hiatus* did not exist. But the proper description and assessment of the Mesolithic had to wait until the thirties of the twentieth century, when Grahame Clark published *The Mesolithic Age in Britain* (1932) and *The Mesolithic Settlement of Northern Europe* (1936).

De Mortillet continued to subdivide the various ages into periods, although he did not recognize the Mesolithic Age. A good example of

his period subdivisions is provided by the table published in 1897 in his
67 *Formation de la Nation Française* reproduced here: in that table the
Mesolithic is represented by the Tourassienne which is sub-titled
ancien hiatus. De Mortillet and his colleagues were taking an essentially
geological outlook towards the problem of the description of artifacts;
they were dividing man's prehistoric past into epochs or periods
characterized by assemblages of type or zone fossils.

Various classifications of the Neolithic, Bronze and Iron Ages were
68 devised. The Swedish archaeologist Oscar Montelius (1843–1921), in
Les Temps Préhistoriques en Suede (1895), devised a fourfold classification of the Neolithic in northern Europe and distinguished, in post-
kitchen-midden times, first a period characterized by pointed polished
axes and no megalithic tombs, secondly a period characterized by thin-
butted axes and 'dolmens' (single megalithic burial chambers in round
or long barrows), a third period characterized by thick-butted polished
axes and passage graves – megalithic tombs with chambers approached
by a passage – and the fourth and final period characterized by long

68 The Swedish
archaeologist Oscar
Montelius (1843–1921)
(right) being shown the
Oseberg ship excavation
by Gabriel Gustafson in
1904.

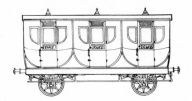

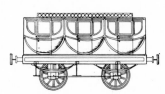

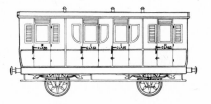

69 Montelius used the
evolution of the railway
carriage as an example of
typology: *top left*, England
1825; *bottom left*, Austria
1840; *right*, Sweden/
Germany *c.* 1850.

stone cists. Montelius did not give names to these four periods in the
way that Lartet and de Mortillet had named their periods. He was
content to number them, and his division of the Neolithic was into
Periods I, II, III and IV, a comparatively objective device not tied to
type-sites in particular countries.

Italian archaeologists like Pigorini, Colini and Orsi, in the last
quarter of the nineteenth century, proposed an Eneolithic period
between the Neolithic and the Bronze Age. Von Pulszky in Hungary
proposed the recognition of a Copper Age. Sir William Wilde in his
Catalogue of the Antiquities in the Museum of the Royal Irish Academy
(Dublin, 1863) had distinguished between a copper industry and a
bronze industry. Much, a German, and many French archaeologists
were of the same view. Chantre, who had in the early seventies been
publishing papers proposing a threefold division of the Bronze Age,
wrote his *L'Age du Bronze* in 1875–76, in which he regarded the Bronze
Age as a unitary phase of human culture, preceded by a Copper Age.

It began to look as though the Danish three-age system might now be
further modified by a Copper Age or Eneolithic. That this did not
happen was largely due to the writings of Montelius, to whose
classification of the Neolithic we have already referred. At the age of
twenty Montelius joined the Swedish Archaeological Service and
worked in the Swedish National Museum for fifty years. He believed
very firmly in the exact description and classification of prehistoric
artifacts: he may be considered the founder of prehistoric taxonomy.
He meticulously classified prehistoric artifacts according to form,
design and ornament. He further taught the importance of studying the
associations between these properly described and classified artifacts,
and began to arrange them in sequences based on changes in form,
design and ornament. The notion of typology, the arrangement of
artifacts in typological sequences, had been initiated by Worsaae.
Montelius's development and refinement of typology allowed him to
establish a relative time sequence for Scandinavian artifacts.

After extensive travels and comparative archaeological studies all over Europe and the East Mediterranean, Montelius proposed a detailed subdivision of the Bronze Age into numbered periods, the first of which, Bronze I, was in reality the Copper Age of Pulszky and Wilde and the Eneolithic of the Italians. His schemes were published in papers and books between 1885 and 1904. He recognized five phases in the Bronze Age of northern Europe from I to V. In adapting his scheme to Italy he distinguished four periods, splitting Period I into I.1, the Copper Age, and I.2, the Early Bronze Age proper. His use of numbers to describe his periods based on artifactual assemblages was an attempt to get away from the French idea of 'epochs': his aim was to provide in the Neolithic and Bronze Ages an objective scheme of classification which was essentially techno-typological.

Schemes to classify and subdivide the Iron Age were also proposed in the last quarter of the nineteenth century. In 1872 Hildebrand had already divided the pre-Roman Iron Age into an earlier, or Hallstatt, phase and a later phase which he named after La Tène. In 1875 de Mortillet adopted the same dual division of the Early Iron Age, but called the second the Gaulish or Marnian Iron Age. In 1885 Otto Tischler, following a detailed examination of the La Tène material in France, divided it into three phases, which were Early, Middle and Late.

A remarkable and brilliant attempt to synthesize what was known about European prehistory was made after the turn of the century by a French businessman from Roanne, Joseph Déchelette, in his great *Manuel d'Archéologie Préhistorique, Celtique et Gallo-Romaine*. The first volume, *Préhistorique*, was published in 1908; volume II, *Celtique ou Protohistorique*, came out in several volumes, the Bronze Age in 1910, Hallstatt in 1913 and La Tène in 1915, with appendices in 1910 and 1913. Déchelette was killed early in the First World War in 1914 and his work completed by Albert Grenier.

Though invaluable, Déchelette's work, in many respects, was an extension of the de Mortillet-Montelius vision of European prehistory. It was still the tradition of minutely subdividing the three-age system into epochs and periods – the construction of a chest of drawers or series of pigeon holes into which the artifacts of the past could be placed. But, gradually, archaeologists began to realize that this epochal subdivision of the three-age system was a means to a classificatory end in prehistory and not really the full story of prehistory. One great problem was the geographical one: it was seen that it was not possible to make a classification which was applicable to Europe as a whole. As early as 1858 Worsaae suggested that Europe in the Bronze Age would have to be studied on the basis of different geographical groups: he set out this idea again clearly in 1873–74. And in his *L'Age du Bronze* Chantre distinguished three 'provinces' in the European Bronze Age, which he called the Uralian (comprising Siberia, Russia and Finland), the Danubian (Hungary, Scandinavia and the British Isles) and the Mediterranean (the Graeco-Italian and Franco-Swiss groups). Then Déchelette found it impossible to apply the Montelian sequence of periods to the Neolithic of the West Mediterranean and Western Europe. Capitan, in studying the Neolithic of France, distinguished five groups, which he called the old European Neolithic, the Nordic, the Campignian, the megalithic and the lake-dwelling.

In 1909, at the Grotte de Valle near Gibaja (Santander) in northern Spain, Breuil and Obermaier discovered a classic Azilian deposit together with typical artifacts of the Tardenoisian: after this it was clear that the Azilian and Tardenoisian were not epochs of the Mesolithic but contemporary assemblages of artifacts. What was demonstrated here as true for the Mesolithic, namely the contemporaneity of some of the supposed 'epochs', appeared also to be true of the other great technological stages of prehistory.

The problem of prehistoric classification in Europe was illuminated by the discoveries in Greece and the Aegean. The classification of the remains at Hissarlik (Troy) by Schliemann (see below) was an objective one based on the stratigraphy there and eschewed the use of divisions of the Bronze and Iron Age; and in the Aegean the tendency was to refer finds to the Mycenaean, the pre-Mycenaean and other named periods. When Arthur Evans studied the great Bronze Age civilization of Crete he called it Minoan, after the legendary King Minos, and divided it into three main sections – Early, Middle and Late, each with three sub-periods. And when in 1890 he had published his finds of the 'Late Celtic' urnfield at Aylesford in Kent, he recognized the people buried there as a separate group within the La Tène period.

Was the three-age system, which was the basis of all archaeological work, now being undermined? Was it no longer a suitable model of the past? Had it served its usefulness?

There were some who thought that from the beginning it was an unsuitable model of man's past, or at least only suitable for museum classification. The nineteenth century produced many classifications of man's past based not on technology but on the supposed sequence of economics. Even Coleridge declared roundly that 'the progress from savagery to civilization is evidently first from the hunting to the pastoral stage'. Sven Nilsson had distinguished four stages in the human past: these four stages of the evolution of society became widely known in Western Europe when Lubbock published a translation of Nilsson as *The Primitive Inhabitants of Scandinavia* in 1867. Sir Edward Tylor recognized the Danish system and agreed that the Stone Age was the beginning of man's prehistoric development, but he proposed to distinguish in man's past three stages which he labelled Savagery, Barbarism and Civilization. In *Anthropology: An Introduction to the study of Man* (1881) Tylor defines barbarism as beginning with agriculture, and civilization with writing. These terms were defined by Lewis H. Morgan, the American anthropologist, in his *Ancient Society: or Researches in the Lines of Human Progress from Savagery through Barbarism to Civilization* (1877). Morgan admitted that the three-age technological system was useful for certain purposes, such as the classification of artifacts, but thought that man's economy provided a better basis: he devised seven 'ethnic periods' concerned with the gradual enlargement of the sources of man's subsistence, as follows:

1 *Lower Savagery*, from the emergence of man to the discovery of fire.

VI   Grave goods from the Sutton Hoo Ship Burial of a seventh-century Saxon king, discovered in 1939 in Suffolk. (*Above*) Gold purse-lid inlaid with coloured glass. (*Below*) Two heavy gold clasps, each secured by a link-pin on a chain.

Overleaf:
VII   Gold mask of a third-century Scythian queen, buried in a marble sarcophagus near Kerch in the Ukraine.

VIII   A Scythian stag in gold, from Kul Oba in the Crimea, fifth century BC.

IX   Procession of Maya musicians in the murals of Room 1 at Bonampak, Mexico, *c.* AD 800. Celebrating a battle and its aftermath, these are the finest Maya wall paintings known. From a copy by Felipe Dávalos G.

2   *Middle Savagery*, from the discovery of fire to the discovery of the bow and arrow.

3   *Upper Savagery*, from the discovery of the bow and arrow to the discovery of pottery.

4   *Lower Barbarism*, from the discovery of pottery to the domestication of animals.

5   *Middle Barbarism*, from the domestication of animals to the smelting of iron ore.

6   *Upper Barbarism*, from the discovery of iron to the invention of a phonetic alphabet.

7   *Civilization*, from writing and the alphabet onwards.

Morgan's classification was mainly based on the postulated sequence in the Old World: he had slightly different criteria for his ethnic periods in America where there was no iron nor any domestic animals. He distinguished between, on the one hand, the ancient civilizations of Egypt, south-west Asia and classical lands, and, on the other, the modern civilization of which he was a part.

Morgan, as Daniel Wilson before him, thought of these periods as universal and as showing a sequence developed naturally in different regions: but he realized that they were homotaxial and not contemporary all over the world. 'The condition', he wrote, 'is the material fact, the *time* being immaterial.' His scheme was as rigid as the subdivisions of the three-age system: it was not concerned in detail with artifacts and surface antiquities, but it fitted not unreasonably with the archaeological record. It achieved fame and popularity because it was adopted and much approved of by Engels, who wrote of it in his *Origin of the Family* (1884) as follows: 'Morgan is the first man who, with expert knowledge, has attempted to introduce a definite order into human prehistory.' This was not true: the value of the Danish technological model was that it *had* introduced a definite order into human prehistory. The value and interest and attractiveness to many of the Morgan scheme was, that by using a model of hypothetical periods based on subsistence, he would appear to have surmounted the apparent and real limitations of prehistoric archaeology: that it was confined to a description of the material culture of man's past.

What was necessary, whether you accepted the ages of stone, bronze and iron or the Morgan ethnic periods, was some way of dating the technological and economic development of man. Worsaae had attempted to give very generalized dates for the Neolithic and Bronze Ages in Europe on the basis of apparent synchronisms with the archaeology of the East Mediterranean and Egypt. Petrie and others had gone far in establishing an absolute chronology for Aegean and Mycenaean contexts by cross-dating them with Egypt. Montelius attempted to extend this cross-dating across Europe to Italy, France, Britain and Scandinavia. An example of his method is provided by his paper in *Archaeologia* for 1909, when he says that the British Bronze Age covered 1,700 years from 2500 to 800 BC, and dated his division of it into five periods as follows: I, the Copper Age, 2500–2000 BC; II, 2000–1650 BC; III, 1650–1400 BC; IV, 1400–1150 BC; and V, 1150–800 BC. It surprised people then, and is even more surprising now, how

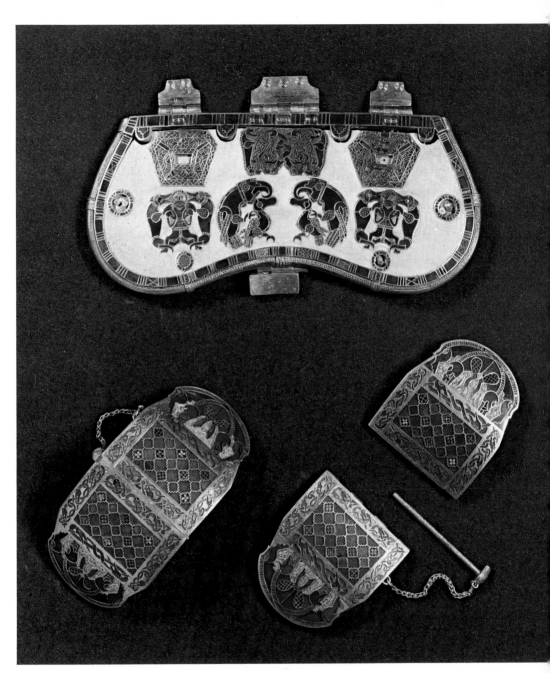

VI

VII

VIII

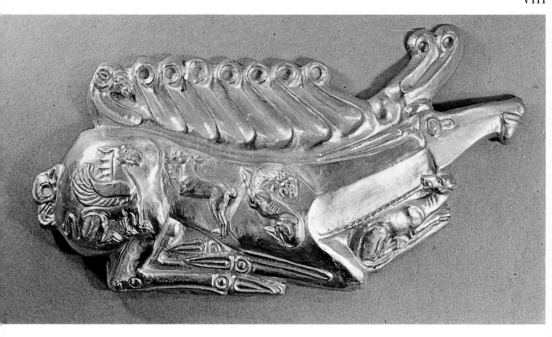

IX

confidently Montelius proposed these dates and his refinement of dates to half-centuries, such as 1650 and 1150 BC. Yet this technique of cross-dating was used until the advent of radiocarbon (C14) dates after the Second World War and is still used by those who continue to remain suspicious of the validity of C14 and thermoluminescence (TL) dating. Admittedly most of these dates were guesswork, but guesswork by those apparently best equipped to make the guesses. Even so, it was a hazardous and shaky affair: thirty years after Montelius, Gordon Childe, who was a fervent disciple of Montelian thinking in many ways, admitted ruefully that no date in the prehistory of barbarian Europe was certain before 1700 BC.

Absolute chronology was one problem that exercised the nineteenth-century archaeologists. The other was the explanation of culture change. From the very first writings of Thomsen and Worsaae the problem was there: namely, did the succession stone to bronze to iron occur naturally in Scandinavia or was it the result of invasion or trade? The early Danish archaeologists did not regard the three ages as forming a natural sequence in Scandinavia. Worsaae was always ready to argue that the Bronze Age in Denmark did not develop step by step out of the Stone Age: 'the transition is so abrupt', he wrote, 'that the bronze period must have commenced with the irruption of a new race of people, possessing a higher degree of civilization than the earlier inhabitants.' Worsaae also thought that the Iron Age was the result of another invasion. He fully appreciated that the spread of the workers in bronze and iron from south-east Europe to Scandinavia must have been slow and gradual, and that therefore the terms Bronze Age and Stone Age had no exact and universal chronological value. He declared, 'The universal diffusion of metals could only take place by degrees.' Here then, in the first half of the nineteenth century, were the ideas of diffusion, invasion and homotaxy which formed for many people the explanation of European prehistory right through to the middle of the twentieth century.

Sven Nilsson, on the other hand, while prepared to accept the view that several waves of invaders had brought changes in the material culture of Scandinavia, believed firmly that prehistoric archaeology as a whole showed the gradual evolution of material culture everywhere. Geology showed the long development of the organic world: prehistoric archaeology showed the long development of man. Independent invention and progress were the keynotes of his thesis; in *The Primitive Inhabitants of Scandinavia* (1867) he declared, 'Nations spring into existence and in their turn, decline and fall: but civilization and humanity are steadily progressing, spreading themselves more and more, and will one day be disseminated over every spot inhabited by man.' One of the three things that de Mortillet thought, in his *Promenades*, had emerged from prehistory so far was parallel development – the *loi du développement similaire*. The Darwinian doctrine of organic evolution was bound to suggest forcibly to people that organic evolution should and did continue into cultural evolution. On the other hand, a study of European and Near Eastern history showed that it was filled with invasions and migrations. The post-Roman period in Europe was the period of the *Völkerwanderung* – the

X View of the excavations near Mount Li, China, where a vast army of terracotta figures has recently been found, buried to protect the emperor Huang Ti (221–209 BC) in the afterlife.

time of the barbarian invasions of the Dark Ages. Was it not reasonable to interpret the marked changes observed in the pre-Roman record as due to similar invasions and migrations?

The German anthropologist Adolf Bastian (1826–1905) was an out-and-out evolutionist: he refused to acknowledge the possibility of any form of diffusion. He declared that there was a general law, namely, that the psychic unity of man everywhere produced similar ideas. He admitted that different geographical environments might produce different responses and there could be, as there manifestly were, cultural contacts in later historical times, but the basic teaching of Bastian was the psychic unity of man and therefore the independent and parallel evolution of culture. He preached very clearly a form of supra-organic or cultural or social evolution.

And this was basic to Morgan's ideas. 'Mankind', he declared, 'commenced their career at the bottom of the scale and worked their way up from savagery to civilization through the slow accumulation of experimental knowledge.' Everything he studied showed, he thought, 'the unity of the origin of mankind, the similarity of human wants in the same stage of advancement, and the uniformity of the operations of the human mind in similar conditions of society.' And these views were carried on through Engels into Marxism and became an essential part of the official thought of Marxist-dominated archaeologists such as the Russians of today.

Montelius was a forthright anti-evolutionist and argued very forcibly for the derivation of all European culture in pre-Roman times from the Near East. In *Der Orient und Europa* (1899) he said, 'At a time when the peoples of Europe were, so to speak, without any civilization whatsoever, the Orient and particularly the Euphrates and the Nile valley, were already in enjoyment of a flourishing culture. The civilization which gradually dawned on our continent was for long only a pale reflection of Oriental culture.'

Salomon Reinach denounced this doctrine of *ex oriente lux* in *Le Mirage Oriental* (1893), declaring the European prehistorians had for too long looked for simple explanations of culture change in terms of invasion and diffusion from the East Mediterranean and the Near East, and had underrated the native European contribution to cultural development – here he may well be right. The Minoan, Mycenaean, Etruscan and Celtic civilizations were, to his mind, native and European.

Many, like Arthur Evans and John Myres, refused to see a complete dichotomy in theories of cultural origins: Myres said, 'To recognize adequately the eastern background of European origins is no *Mirage Oriental*. The "independent European element" is not extinguished by its own capacity for assimilation.' Many others held the same view: the early Scandinavian archaeologists believed in the possible truth of both evolution and diffusion; so did Pitt-Rivers; and E. B. Tylor recognized several agencies of cultural change – the like working of men's minds, blood relationship and intercourse. Robert Lowie, in his *History of Ethnological Theory* (1937), says that in the Anthropological Institute of London in the late nineteenth century 'evolution ... lay down amicably beside diffusion'.

This was so for moderate and sensible thinking prehistorians, but for many others then, and right through to the present day, the great issue was polarized as Evolution *v.* Diffusion and the issue, and the difference between the two points of view, was exacerbated by the extravagant position taken up by some of the militant diffusionists.

The most influential and extremist school of militant diffusionists was the so-called Manchester School. Grafton Elliot Smith (1871–1937) was an Australian who came to England as a medical student, became the first occupant of the Chair of Anatomy at the Government Medical School at Cairo, and was subsequently Professor of Anatomy at Manchester and later University College, London. He was fascinated by Egypt and began a study of the ancient human remains from excavations. He was the first person to make a detailed study of the Egyptian technique of mummification. He believed this technique was so complicated that it was highly unlikely it could have been developed independently elsewhere, and when therefore he heard of similar practices of embalming and mummification in other parts of the world he was forced to the conclusion that they were diffused from Egypt. He put forward the theory, and held it very strongly, that civilization had been invented once and once only, and that was in the valley of the Nile. All civilization, he said, and indeed all advances from the savagery of the Old Stone Age, were due to settlers from ancient Egypt. He first set out this doctrine of Egyptocentric hyperdiffusionism in 1911 in his book *The Ancient Egyptians*, which caught the imagination of many people then and in the next quarter of a century.

Another problem which much concerned archaeologists was the extent to which national and linguistic labels could be applied to the periods and peoples of prehistory. The early Danish archaeologists spent a great deal of time arguing whether the Stone Age was the work of the Lapps, the Bronze Age that of the Finns or Phoenicians, and the Iron Age the work of Celts or Goths. Various archaeological groups in the Mediterranean were labelled Phoenician, Graeco-Phoenician, Trojan, Phrygian, Dorian, Achaean, Siculan, Ligurian, Iberian and so on. There was a general acceptance of the view that the La Tène and probably late Hallstatt epochs or cultures were the work of Celts. Sir John Rhŷs, in his various statements on early British archaeology such as his *Early Britain: Celtic Britain* (1882), set out the view that the Neolithic in Britain was the work of the Iberians, the Bronze Age of the Q-Celts or Goidels, and the Iron Age of the P-Celts or Brythons. And the problem of the Aryans began to loom over prehistory.

The comparative study of languages as a key to the study of the past goes back to the now famous Presidential Address and the ten discourses by Sir William Jones to the Asiatic Society in Calcutta in 1788. The suggestion by Jones that Sanskrit, Greek, Latin, Celtic and the Germanic languages were all derived from a common mother tongue was confirmed by Franz Bopp in his *Vergleichende Grammatik* (1833–35) when he used the term Indo-Germanic, a term first suggested by Klaproth in 1823. Max Müller proposed the term Aryan as an alternative and this superseded Indo-Germanic and was in turn eventually superseded by Indo-European. The prehistory of Europe was seen in terms of the movements of Finno-Ugrians and subsequently the Aryans. If languages from Ireland to Central Asia and India all came from one parent source, who were these people and with what archaeological material could they be identified? What was the homeland of the Aryans (or the Indo-Europeans)? Two typical summaries of the linguistic prehistories of the late nineteenth century are Isaac Taylor's *The Origin of the Aryans: An Account of the Prehistoric Ethnology and Civilization of Europe* and T. H. Huxley's *The Aryan Question and Prehistoric Man*, both published in 1890.

Egypt and Mesopotamia

When Mariette died in 1880 he was succeeded by Gaston Maspero (1840–1910), a Frenchman of Italian origin and a person of enormous energy and great ability. His Directorship of Archaeology in Egypt began with the excavation of the pyramid of Unas at Sakkara and the discovery of the famous 'Pyramid' Texts. He reorganized and rearranged the collections in the Museum and also found time to write many popular books about ancient Egypt and its antiquities: these works of *haute vulgarisation* did much to encourage interest in Egyptology and create a vogue for Egyptian travel among ordinary non-archaeological people.

Miss Amelia Edwards (1831–92) was one of these. A prolific novelist and writer of popular books and papers on art and history, she visited Egypt and Syria in 1873–74, and published a delightful account of her travels in *A Thousand Miles up the Nile* (1877). Egyptology now became her chief interest: she argued that scientific excavation was necessary and the only cure for the widespread destruction of monuments and pillaging of tombs that was going on. She got together interested people and founded in 1882 the Egyptian Exploration Fund, acting as its secretary and giving up all her other work. She gave lectures on Egyptology and these were published in her book *Pharaohs, Fellahs and Explorers* (1891). When she died she founded at University College, London, a Chair of Egyptology: the first holder of the Edwards Chair, by her wish, was Flinders Petrie.

The Cairo authorities still maintained Mariette's traditions and reserved the right to retain any objects excavated in Egypt, but permission was now granted for excavations to be carried out by representatives of other countries. The French Mission Archéologique was founded in Cairo at about the same time as the Egypt Exploration Fund, and later organizations and institutions were set up by the Swiss, the Germans and the Americans. The first man to dig for the Egypt Exploration Fund was Henri Naville, a Swiss archaeologist who had been trained by Lepsius and went on working for the fund until 1913. From 1883 onwards, and off and on, Flinders Petrie worked for the Fund until he founded his own Egyptian Research Account in 1894, renamed in 1906 the British School of Archaeology in Egypt.

70 (Sir) William Matthew Flinders Petrie (1853–1942) – his grandfather was Captain Matthew Flinders, the explorer of Australia – was a keen archaeologist from his early childhood. In his autobiography, *Seventy Years in Archaeology* (1931), he says that at the age of eight he was horrified at the way a Roman villa had been unearthed on the Isle of

70 William Matthew
Flinders Petrie
(1853–1942), the great
archaeologist who
introduced scientific
methods of study and
recording into
Egyptology.

Wight: 'I protested', he said, 'that the earth ought to be pared away
inch by inch to see all that was in it, and how it lay.'

Petrie and his father were fascinated by reading a book published in
1864 entitled *Our Inheritance in the Great Pyramid*, written by Charles
Piazzi Smyth, Astronomer Royal of Scotland and Professor of
Astronomy in the University of Edinburgh. Piazzi Smyth was one of the
first of the pyramidiots who are unfortunately still with us. He
invented the 'Pyramid inch' corresponding to 0.999 of a British inch:
he thought the Great Pyramid stood at the centre of the world and
declared of his pyramid measurements that 'employing a suitable unit
of measure and a considerable degree of patience, I can easily shew that
the dimensions yield the distance of Timbuctoo or the average weight
of an adult goldfish.'

Fortunately Flinders Petrie was not for long carried away by these
pyramidiocies and eventually made the first accurate survey of the
pyramids. But he began his work as an archaeological surveyor in
Britain: some of his results are published in *Stonehenge* (1880).

71 Jar decorated with horned animals, from the prehistoric cemetery at Naqada dug by Petrie in the 1890s. Ht 25.5 cm.

When he was financed by the Egypt Exploration Fund, he wrote to Miss Edwards: 'the prospect of excavating in Egypt is a most fascinating one to me, and I hope the results may justify my undertaking such a work.' They most certainly did. He began work at Tanis in 1885 and excavated year after year, each season followed by publications and by public exhibitions in London, many in the Egyptian Hall in Piccadilly which Belzoni had used. Among his famous finds were the remains of Tell el-Amarna and the Tell el-Amarna correspondence, the discovery of Mycenaean and pre-Mycenaean pottery at Gurob and Kahun, and the discovery of the predynastic Egyptian civilization.

In 1891 Petrie visited Mycenae to test there the dating of the Gurob and Kahun sites. Here he was helped by his former pupil, Ernest Gardner, then Head of the British School in Athens. He recognized Egyptian influences and actual Egyptian objects at Mycenae, all of the eighteenth dynasty: at Kahun he found what he called Aegean or proto-Greek pottery mixed with that of the twelfth dynasty. He had now established two synchronisms: between the 'proto-Greek' ware and the twelfth dynasty on the one hand, and Mycenae and the eighteenth dynasty on the other. He now declared that the Aegean civilization had come into being about 2500 BC and that the dates of the late Mycenaean civilization were between 1500 and 1000 BC. It was a most remarkably fine piece of cross-dating and the first of its kind in the field of comparative archaeology. Gardner said that Petrie had 'done more in a week than the Germans had done in ten years to clear up the matter from an Egyptian basis', and Petrie, looking back in 1931 on his work on the absolute chronology of Greece, said, 'there seems little to alter in the outline reached then, though forty years have since elapsed.' What is sometimes not realized is that Petrie confidently and correctly called the foreign pottery at Kahun Aegean or proto-Greek, whereas no such pottery had as yet been found and described in the Aegean itself!

Our knowledge of predynastic Egypt comes from Petrie's work at Naqada and Ballas in 1894–95 and at Diospolis Parva (Hu) in 1898–99. Naqada turned out to be a prehistoric cemetery of over 2,000 graves and has given its name to the Naqada period of Egyptian prehistory. The British Museum, to its shame, declined Petrie's offer of the type series from Naqada on the grounds that they were advised the material was 'unhistoric rather than prehistoric': the material went to the Ashmolean instead. In his publication *Diospolis Parva* (1901) Petrie arranged the predynastic Egyptian material by means of the technique of what he called sequence-dating. He did not approve of any system based on subdivisions of the three-age system: his sequence dates were based on the typological sequence of prehistoric pottery. He started his sequence with S.D. 30, assuming, correctly, that he had not yet discovered the earliest prehistoric material, and carried on to dynastic times at S.D. 80. 'This system', he wrote, 'enables us to deal with material which is entirely undated otherwise . . . There is no reason now why prehistoric ages, from which there are groups of remains, should not be dealt with as surely and clearly as the historic ages with recorded dates.' His optimism was not justified, and his system of sequence dates was not generally adopted; but it was a remarkable and interesting innovation and worked well for his own Egyptian material.

In 1892 Petrie published *Ten Years' Digging* and in 1904 his *Methods and Aims in Archaeology*, where he set out not only his schemes of cross-dating and sequence-dating but his principles and practice of survey and excavation. He complained that the Egypt Exploration Fund had given him no training or advice, that he had had to work out methods and techniques for himself: he said his work was 'a case of breaking new ground in archaeology'.

He declared that his method was based on the following four principles: 1. care for the monuments being excavated and respect for future visitors and excavators; 2. meticulous care in the actual excavation and the collecting and description of everything found; 3. the detailed and accurate survey and planning of all monuments and excavations; and 4. the complete publication of results as soon as possible. He also began the scientific study of the materials used by prehistoric and protohistoric man. He declared that the archaeologist must study 'all details of material, colour, fabric and mechanical questions of tools'.

Furtwängler had developed the study of painted and decorated pottery as an archaeological chronometer. Petrie did the same for unpainted pottery. He began to appreciate this when, in the 1880s, he was digging at Naucratis, but it was his excavation of a Palestinian tell, Tell el-Hesi, in 1890, that showed him the way to deal with this difficult problem. In this tell he was dealing with sixty feet (about eighteen metres) of occupational debris clearly divided into levels characterized by pottery types although, as he also realized, the pottery types and levels did not coincide exactly. He was also able to synchronize some of the Tell el-Hesi levels with Egyptian dynasties and so built up an absolute chronology of the whole sixty feet of occupation – as important a piece of cross-dating as his work at Mycenae. His work at Tell el-Hesi was a pioneer achievement in the study of a stratified surface occupation site: one far in advance of the work of Schliemann and Dörpfeld at Troy.

Petrie was one of the giants among archaeologists. His techniques and methods, as well as his actual discoveries, certainly justified calling the last quarter of the nineteenth century the Heroic Age of Egyptian archaeology.

After a period of no activity following the outbreak of the Crimean War, western interest in Mesopotamian archaeology revived in the 1870s. George Smith, who was a minor official in the Assyrian Department of the British Museum, published *The History of Ashur-bani-pal translated from the Cuneiform Inscriptions* in 1871. The following year, while translating clay tablets from the Nineveh libraries, he discovered a fragmentary inscription which contained the statement that 'the ship rested on the mountains of Nizur', followed by an account of the sending forth of a dove and its finding no resting place and returning. 'I saw at once', said Smith, 'that I had discovered a portion at least of the Chaldean account of the Deluge.' He discovered 73 more fragments and was able to translate an account of the Babylonian flood story which he read to the Society for Biblical Archaeology in 1872. The interest caused by this discovery was enormous. A piece of

the Deluge tablet was still missing: *The Daily Telegraph* offered £1,000 to equip an expedition led by Smith to look for the missing fragment. Smith was not a trained excavator and had never been to Mesopotamia before, but he began work at Kuyunjik in 1873 and by an amazing stroke of beginner's luck found the missing fragment on the fifth day. He did more work in the field for the British Museum but died at Aleppo in 1877 on his way home from his third season of excavations. He published popular accounts of his work in *Assyrian Discoveries* and *The Chaldean Account of Genesis*, and joined Layard as an archaeological bestseller.

Smith was succeeded as Director of the British Museum excavations in Mesopotamia by Hormuzd Rassam, who returned after an absence of many years. His last campaigns were from 1878 to 1882 and he ranged very widely over the country, digging into mounds everywhere looking for treasures and inscriptions for his sponsors in London. In 1878 he discovered at Tell Balawat the famous bronze gates of Shalmaneser II. In 1880 he began excavations which went on for eighteen months at Abu Habbah, in southern Mesopotamia, and was able to identify it as Sippar and as a temple dedicated to the Sun-god Shamash. Here Rassam found a very large number of inscribed tablets and cylinders: one inscription recording how Nabonidus (whom we have already mentioned), the last king of Babylon, had himself dug in the foundations of the temple to discover who first built it and found, eighteen cubits beneath the pavement, a foundation stone laid by Naram-Sin, son of Sargon of Akkad 'which for 3,200 years no previous king had seen'. This invaluable chronological document also recorded perhaps the first archaeological activities of modern man (see p. 14).

72 Diorite statue of Gudea from Lagash (Telloh), now in the Louvre. Ht 105 cm.

73 One of the tablet fragments from Ashurbanipal's palace at Nineveh which George Smith recognized contained part of the Chaldaean account of the Deluge.

74 Hormuzd Rassam (1826–1910) as an old man, proudly displaying photographs of the bronze gate reliefs from Balawat, whose provenance was at one time doubted by the British Museum.

Gradually scholars were becoming aware of a civilization in Mesopotamia that lay before and behind the Babylonian and Assyrian civilizations and which we now call the Sumerian – traces of which had been already found by Loftus, Taylor and Rawlinson. In 1869 Oppert had postulated on linguistic grounds the existence of a pre-Babylonian, non-Semitic people in Mesopotamia.

The Sumerians became a reality thanks to the excavations at Telloh by Ernest de Sarzec, French Consul at Basra. In 1874 Arabs informed de Sarzec that stone statuettes were being found at Telloh and he began digging there in 1877, continuing his work intermittently until 1900. He thought the site was the Sumerian city of Lagash, and discovered many archaic sculptures of the late third millennium BC, including the portrait statues of Gudea, seventh governor of Lagash. The Louvre Catalogue of 1901 described Lagash as 'the Pompeii of early Babylonian antiquities', and Oppert declared that 'since the discovery of Nineveh . . . no discovery had been made which compares with the

72

recent excavations in Chaldea'. It is due to de Sarzec's work that we owe our first familiarity with the art, history and language of the ancient Sumerians. He was however wrong in his identification of Lagash. It was now known to be not at Telloh but at the neighbouring site of Tell al-Hiba. Telloh was the ancient Girsu, in the state of Lagash (see Seton Lloyd, *The Archaeology of Mesopotamia*, 1978, 106).

In 1884 the first American expedition to Mesopotamia took place: it was a reconnaissance, but three years later Peters and Hilprecht began digging at Nippur. The first season ended in disaster: tribesmen sacked their camp. The excavations were started again in 1890 and continued until 1900. Over 50,000 inscribed tablets were found, mostly in the Sumerian language, and extending over a thousand years.

Ten years after de Sarzec had started work at Telloh a German expedition under the auspices of the Deutsche Orient Gesellschaft made a reconnaissance of many important Sumerian sites, but did not excavate any of them completely. This was the beginning of serious German involvement in Mesopotamia. From 1899 until the outbreak of war in 1914 the Germans, led by Robert Koldewey and Walter Andrae,

75, 76

75, 76 Robert Koldewey's work at Babylon from 1899 to 1914 was the first thorough excavation of a Mesopotamian site. The best-preserved structure he unearthed was the Ishtar Gate (general view, *opposite*, close up, *left*), erected by Nebuchadrezzar in the sixth century BC and ornamented with bulls and dragons in brick relief.

excavated thoroughly two sites: Babylon and Ashur. Koldewey's work at Babylon was summarized in his book *The Excavations at Babylon* (1914): he brought to Mesopotamia the techniques of excavation already developed by the Germans in classical lands, and his work was the first complete and scientifically conducted excavation of a large site in Mesopotamia. Walter Andrae dug at Ashur from 1903 to 1914. Here he not only excavated with great skill and care the first capital of the Assyrian nation, but adopted for the first time in Mesopotamian excavation the sondage method. The Germans cut through the Temple of Ishtar and the remains of other temples beneath it to an original archaic Sumerian temple. Seton Lloyd has described the work at Ashur as 'a brilliant feat of excavating and the prototype of all stratigraphical investigations in later times' (*Foundations in the Dust*, 1947, 202). The buildings which archaeologists excavated in Greece and Egypt were of stone: the architecture of Mesopotamia is largely of sun-dried bricks, and the technique of tracing these was quite unknown to earlier excavators. Koldewey and Andrae were the first successfully to trace walls of sun-dried brick.

77 Alexander Conze at work at Samothrace in the 1870s.

Classical Archaeology

The development of archaeology in Greece and Italy in at least the first half of the period under review is dominated by the work of Germans and Austrians – professional and amateur. Alexander Conze dug in Samothrace in 1873 and 1875: he had two architects working with him and a photographer as well as a man-of-war placed at his disposal by the Austrian Government. He published a complete and lengthy account of his excavations which has been described as the first 'modern' excavation report in existence; it was accompanied by beautifully drawn plans and photographs – the first time photographs had been used in an archaeological publication.

A branch of the German Archaeological Institute was set up in Athens in the 1870s and excavations begun at Olympia under the Director, Ernst Curtius, assisted by his architect, Friedrich Adler. This great work occupied the six winters of 1875–80: the State paid £30,000 and the expenses of the last winter were personally borne by the Emperor William. The Greek Government allowed only duplicates of artifacts to be exported: the German Government therefore had to renounce all claims to the material they found. A small museum was built at Olympia to house the finds. Like Mariette's policy in Egypt, here was the birth of an archaeological conscience. The stratigraphy of Olympia was studied in detail and very carefully recorded. A moving spirit in developing new methods of preservation and excavation was Dörpfeld.

The work of Conze and Curtius initiated a period of thirty years and more of great classical excavations in which not only the Germans but French, British, Americans and the Greeks themselves carried on the traditions established at Samothrace and Olympia.

However, the name that most people associate with the development of classical archaeology in the late nineteenth century is not that of a professional scholar but of an amateur who spent most of his early and middle years as a businessman: Heinrich Schliemann (1822–90). It is to this remarkable man that we owe our first and enduring knowledge of prehistoric Greece and the Aegean. He was, as Walter Leaf said, 'the creator of prehistoric Greek archaeology'. There had been isolated discoveries of prehistoric material between 1826 and the first excavations at Troy but they amounted to little, and had not captured the enthusiasm of scholars or the imagination of the public.

Schliemann was the son of a German pastor who gave him as a Christmas present a copy of Jarrer's *Universal History*. In this book was a picture of Troy in flames and Schliemann, excited by the Homeric sagas, kept this picture in his mind through a long business career in Holland, Russia and America. He firmly believed in the truth of the events related by Homer, and when at the age of forty-six he had amassed a great fortune he retired from business to devote himself to archaeology and particularly to finding Troy. He travelled extensively, dug in Ithaka in 1869 and published his *Ithaka, the Peloponnese and Troy* in which he argued that the graves of Agamemnon and Clytemnestra were not the so-called Treasuries outside the citadel at Mycenae, but were in the citadel itself, and that the city of Troy was not a myth but situated at Hissarlik, on the site of the historic Ilion.

Two years later he began excavating at Hissarlik and had four periods of excavation there, 1871–73, 1879, 1882–83, and from 1889 until his death. In his first campaign he worked alone with his beautiful young Greek wife Sophia. In the last two seasons he had the expert assistance of Dörpfeld, who continued work at Troy, after Schliemann's death, until 1894.

Between the first and second campaigns at Hissarlik Schliemann excavated at Mycenae and Ithaka, in 1880 the Treasury of Minyas at Orchomenos and in 1884–85, Tiryns. He published his work rapidly and fully: *Trojan Antiquities* in 1874, *Mycenae* in 1876, *Ilios* in 1880, *Troja* in 1884 and *Orchomenos* in 1887. These books first appeared in German and were quickly translated into French and English. W. E. Gladstone, then Prime Minister, wrote a preface to the English translation of *Mycenae* in 1877, and attended the meeting of the Society of Antiquaries of London in March 1877 when Schliemann lectured on Mycenae: the lecturer had arrived only on the morning of the lecture after what was described as 'eight days and nights of incessant travelling'.

Even among people who disbelieved in his findings, his excavations aroused tremendous interest and excitement: indeed they were the first

78 Heinrich Schliemann (1822–90) was a highly successful businessman with a burning ambition – to confirm the truth of Homer and dig up Troy. At the age of forty-six he retired from commerce (the photograph shows him shortly before this time) and in four campaigns confounded his critics by laying bare the walls of Troy.

79 Schliemann's excavations at Troy, from his *Ilios: City and Country of the Trojans* (1880).

great excavations whose progress was followed avidly by the informed public all over the world.

Schliemann proved that Hissarlik was a heavily fortified prehistoric settlement of great antiquity: he distinguished seven cities, identifying the second as Homeric Troy, 'the citadel of Priam'. On the day before the end of the 1873 excavations Schliemann discovered a magnificent collection of gold treasures dating from the second city which he claimed to be Priam's treasure. Although he made the wrong identification of Homeric Troy (three years after his death Dörpfeld identified the sixth city as that of Homer), he had achieved his object: to prove by archaeology the truth of Homer. But he achieved much more: he discovered centuries of pre-Homeric and prehistoric occupation at Hissarlik and a non-Greek 'barbaric' civilization.

At Mycenae he hoped to find, and believed he did find, the tombs of Agamemnon and Clytemnestra. He dug in the circle of stones inside the Lion Gate and found the graves he was looking for – the now famous shaft-graves. The contents of these shaft-graves were

80, 81

82, 83

spectacularly rich: vases of gold and silver, inlaid swords of gold, silver, copper and bronze, finger rings and bracelets, thin gold ornaments for the clothing of the dead and gold face-masks. He believed that what he had found was the Mycenaean Heroic age of Homer. Scholars were divided over his claims: some, like Mr Gladstone, accepted them, others said the finds were Byzantine in date or the work of Celts, Goths, Avars, Huns or just, vaguely, 'orientals'. Curtius, who was understandably jealous of the fantastic successes of his non-professional countryman, declared that one of the gold masks was a portrait of Christ of Byzantine date! Many scholars argued that the finds, while authentic and Greek, were not Homeric but pre-Homeric and they were right: Schliemann had discovered at Mycenae, as he had at Hissarlik, a prehistoric civilization.

III

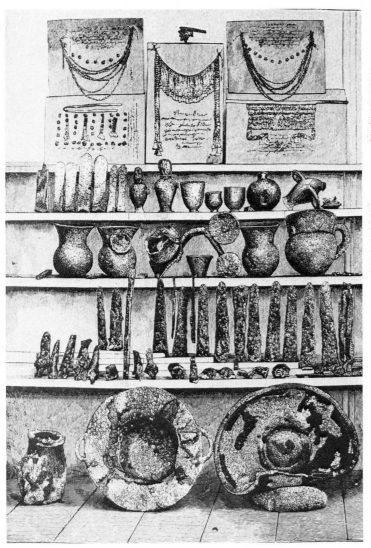

80, 81 The rich haul of objects found by Schliemann at Troy astonished the world. Imagining them to be 'Priam's treasure', he adorned his wife Sophia with the excavated jewels as Helen of Troy (*above*). A less colourful picture of the hoard appeared in his official account of the excavations (*left*).

82, 83 A modern air photograph of the citadel of Mycenae (*right*) and a view of the Grave Circle (*below*; visible also just inside the walls in the photograph) from Schliemann's *Mycenae* (1878), the introduction for which was written by Gladstone.

There has been much dispute about Schliemann's archaeological techniques and methods. To some he was a complete stranger to any archaeological skill, a man whose reputation was built entirely on the wealth and splendour of his finds. To others he was the first modern archaeologist: Stanley Casson, rather extravagantly, called him the founder of modern scientific archaeological method and said that his work 'constituted an innovation of the first order of importance in the study of the antiquity of man by archaeological methods' (*The Discovery of Man*, 1939, 221). His work at Troy was the first excavation of a tell, as Sir John Myres has put it, 'the first large-scale dissection of a dryland settlement unguided by the remains of great monuments such as simplified the task in Babylon and Nineveh.' Schliemann demonstrated the applicability of stratigraphy to a mound consisting of superimposed occupation levels. From 1882 onwards he was assisted very considerably by Dörpfeld, who brought with him the system and efficiency of the German classical archaeologists as demonstrated at Olympia.

Schliemann's discovery of two hitherto unknown prehistoric civilizations immediately posed the questions of their dates, origins and inter-relations. While he was working at Troy and Mycenae traces of a pre-Mycenaean civilization were being unearthed in Cyprus and the Greek islands. In 1894–95 the British School at Athens, under Sir Cecil

Smith of the British Museum, excavated at Phylakopi on the eastern coast of Melos. It was the first stratified site to be excavated in the East Mediterranean after Hissarlik, and it provided a relative sequence for the development of the pre-Mycenaean, or, as it began to be called, the Cycladic or Aegean civilization. The first occupation of Phylakopi was that of an open village comparable archaeologically with finds from cist graves in other Cycladic islands; then a second occupation revealed a fortified site with copper and bronze in use, obsidian and local marble traded to the Greek mainland, with pottery resembling that of Troy II and the earliest shaft graves; and thirdly a settlement of mainland Greek type with a small Mycenaean palace.

There were sporadic excavations in Cyprus from the mid-1860s onwards, undertaken by men like General Louis Palma di Cesnola and Alexander di Cesnola and Max Ohnefalsch-Richter. These were unscientific treasure hunts, but their results to discerning observers like Salomon Reinach and Dümmler in the 1880s revealed that Cyprus had an Early Bronze Age civilization comparable with that of Troy II but developing differently, and a colonial equivalent of Mycenae intruding into the Late Bronze Age development of the native Cyprus Bronze Age. Sir John Myres excavated in Cyprus in 1894, and in 1899 published with Ohnefalsch-Richter *The Cyprus Museum Catalogue*. British Museum excavations in Cyprus, published by Murray, Smith and Walters in *Excavations in Cyprus* (1900), revealed tombs rich in goldwork which, though not as rich as the Mycenaean shaft-graves, were richer than the shaft-graves in imports from Egypt and Syria.

The finds from Phylakopi were not published until 1904, by which time Arthur Evans's discoveries in Crete had thrown a new light on the pre-Mycenaean background of Greece and the Aegean, stressing the Cretan rather than the Cycladic component. Schliemann himself came within an ace of excavating in Crete and discovering the great Cretan Bronze Age civilization. Pursuing the study of the legends that had taken him to Troy, he noted that Knossos in Crete was the home of the Minotaur, of King Minos and the Labyrinth. In 1883, in his *Anfänge der Kunst in Griechenland*, the German scholar Milchhöfer observed that there were being found in Crete peculiar types of carved seal-stones bearing symbols resembling a kind of primitive writing, and affirmed that Crete would prove to be one of the oldest homes of Greek civilization and art.

In that same year, 1883, Schliemann obtained permission to dig at Kephala, the site of Knossos. He could not at first find time to take up his permit; later, a very rich man getting miserly in his old age, he was not prepared to pay the quite large sums demanded by the owner of the site and was still negotiating for permission to dig at the time of his death in 1890.

84   Meanwhile, Arthur Evans (1851–1941), who had been appointed Keeper of the Ashmolean Museum, acquired the site in 1894 and in that year elaborated Milchhöfer's ideas in his *Cretan Pictographs*. In 1898 Crete declared herself independent of Turkey and next year Evans, with D. G. Hogarth, began excavations at Kephala.

Their work was crowned with immediate success: in nine weeks digging more than two acres of a very large prehistoric building were

84 Sir Arthur Evans (1851–1941), who excavated Knossos in Crete and discovered the Minoan civilization. A portrait by Sir William Richmond now in the Ashmolean Museum, Oxford.

uncovered which Evans identified as the palace of Minos. He carried on digging at Knossos for over twenty-five years but the outlines of the great story were early established. He had discovered a completely unknown civilization, which preceded the Mycenaean, and which he labelled the Minoan. Behind and before this Bronze Age civilization of Crete he found an earlier Neolithic period which at Knossos itself formed a tell twenty-one feet (six-and-a-half metres) thick. First published in 1901, and much publicized in many books in the next fifteen years, Evans's own definitive report appeared in four volumes between 1921 and 1935 entitled *The Palace of Minos at Knossos*. He divided this Minoan civilization into three – Early, Middle, and Late – each with three sub-periods; and, turning to study the Phylakopi material, he similarly divided that into Early, Middle and Late Cycladic, equated with the Minoan periods. He dated the beginning of the Early Minoan period to 3400 BC and the end of the Late Minoan to

86

1100 BC. By calculating from the thickness of deposits he suggested that the Cretan Neolithic began between 12,000 and 10,000 BC, but nowadays this date would be set nearer to 6000 BC at the earliest.

Evans had been initially attracted by the Cretan writing and in 1909 published the first volume of his *Scripta Minoa*, containing the hieroglyphic writing such as that on the Phaestos disc and the two linear scripts A and B that had resulted from a simplification of the Cretan pictorial writing. Since his time Linear B has been deciphered (see p. 204 below) but the pictorial writing and Linear A have so far defied decipherment.

Schliemann's discoveries at Troy and Mycenae had been received with scepticism. Evans's work had few doubters. He was in any case a professional scholar digging after many years of research and archaeological experience. His discoveries soon captured the imagination of the world as the discoveries in Assyria had done and Schliemann's finds had done, and the discovery of Tutankhamun's tomb and the Royal Tombs at Ur were to do in the 1920s. The 'cup-bearer' fresco, the bull-leaping frescoes of boys and girls, the walls covered with double-axe symbols, and the faience snake-goddesses brought the vanished Minoan civilization and archaeology gloriously alive.

85, 86 Knossos proved a rich source of Minoan artifacts and architecture. The faience statuette of a Snake Goddess (*opposite*), made in about 1600 BC, was found in a stone-lined pit in the Palace of Minos. A photograph of the restored palace itself (*above*) first appeared in Sir Arthur Evans's *The Palace of Minos at Knossos* (1921–35).

133

Iran and Anatolia

In 1891 Jacques de Morgan had visited the ruins of Susa in Khuzistan province, and persuaded the French Government to interest themselves. In 1897 the French purchased from the Shah the exclusive rights of excavation in Persia; and in that year the *Délégation Française en Perse* went out with de Morgan to dig for Persian antiquities. The *Délégation* has been described as 'probably the most important archaeological expedition that has ever left Europe' (Carleton, *Buried Empires*, 34). It worked through until the First World War.

87 While the excavations at Susa were in progress the American R. Pumpelly and the German archaeologist, Hubert Schmidt, dug, in 1902, two occupation mounds, the North and South Kurgans, each 30–40 feet (9–12 metres) high, at Anau, near Ashkabad in Russian Turkestan or Transcaspia. Four cultural levels were distinguished at Anau and were described as cultures, not as epochs or periods, in the full publication by Pumpelly, Schmidt and others in their *Explorations in Turkestan: Expedition of 1904: Prehistoric Civilisations of Anau: Origins Growth and Influence of Environment*. The excavations at Anau occupy an important place in the development of archaeological field techniques and methods. The actual digging, preservation and recording was done by Hubert Schmidt, of the Berlin Museum für Völkerkunde, who had been trained by Dörpfeld at Troy. Schmidt sank large pits at Anau which were deepened two feet a day: the position of everything found was most carefully recorded. The Anau reports contain phrases such as this: 'Much of the earth was sifted to save small objects', and 'the importance of considering even apparently insignificant objects as documents containing a story, and of recording their vertical and horizontal position in the column of culture strata became evident at every stage of the analysis of results.' The human bones from Anau were studied by Sergi and Mollison, the animal bones by Duerst of Zürich, the remains of cultivated grains by Schellenberg, while F. A. Gooch made chemical analyses of the metal objects. It was a thoroughly modern excavation. Schellenberg was able to identify wheat and two-rowed barley from casts and from siliceous skeletons of the chaff of these cereals. Duerst, complaining that the animal bones weighed half a ton and that their analysis occupied his whole time for three years, declared that he could show the transition of *Bos nomadicus*, pig and sheep from a wild to a tame state.

The period under review is important for the archaeological discovery of the Hittites. Our modern knowledge of the ancient Hittites dates from 1736, when Jean Otter discovered the famous Neo-Hittite relief at Ivriz in southern Cappadocia. In 1812 Burckhardt found one of the Hamath inscriptions. Other similar finds, and finds of seals and seal impressions, were made during the early nineteenth century, but there was no quickening interest in the Hittite problem until the 1860s and 1870s. In 1861 Georges Perrot, the art historian, was sent to investigate the monuments of Augustus at Ankara and went on from there to the Cappadocian hills farther east where, at a Turkish village called Boghazköy, within the bend of the River Halys, he found the remains of a vast fortified city with sculptures quite unlike the art of the

87 (*Opposite*) Air view of Susa, Iran.

134

ancient world then known from Egypt, Mesopotamia or the classical world of Greece and Rome. Perrot had discovered the archaeology of another unknown civilization.

The Hamath inscription was rediscovered in 1870 and then several new ones were found. Richard Burton in his *Unexplored Syria* (1872) published a transcription of the Hamath inscription, and Dr W. Wright, an Irish missionary at Damascus, had the Hamath stones sent to the museum in Constantinople; at the same time sets of plaster casts of them were sent to the British Museum, which also obtained a number of inscriptions from Jerablus, the ancient Carchemish.

Burton demonstrated that the writing on the Hamath stones was in a hitherto unknown script. Perrot had argued that the Boghazköy sculptures belonged to an unknown people. Wright now suggested that the writing and the art were the work of the people known to the Bible as the Hittites, and in 1884 published his *Empire of the Hittites*, bringing together all the then available archaeological information and an attempt at the decipherment of the cuneiform script by A. H. Sayce, Professor of Assyriology at Oxford. Four years later, in *The Hittites*, Sayce brilliantly re-created the forgotten empire of the Hittites.

In 1906–8 German and Turkish scholars under Professor Hugo Winckler excavated the fortified city found by Perrot and revealed Boghazköy as the capital of the Hittites, the city of Hattusas. These 88 excavations, though limited in time and incomplete in scope, brought to light thousands of tablets forming the official archives of the Hittite foreign office during the period 1350 to 1300 BC, in which are mentioned ancient peoples such as the Egyptians, the Babylonians, the Cypriots and the Ahhiyawa, a people described as settled on the southern coasts of Asia Minor and Cyprus and now identified with the Achaeans.

In 1907 in the *Mitteilungen der Deutschen Orient Gesellschaft* (vol. 35) the Czech scholar, Friedrich Hrozny, published the key to the translation of the Hittite documents which he set out in detail in *Die Sprache der Hethiter* (1917).

Carchemish, a southern outpost of Hittite civilization in northern Syria, was excavated before the 1914–18 war by a British Museum expedition under Hogarth, Campbell-Thompson, T. E. Lawrence and Leonard Woolley.

Barbarian Europe

The period under review – it might be called from Napoleon III to Pitt-Rivers – was one of great activity in the archaeology of post-Palaeolithic Europe and we have already referred to it in general terms in discussing, above, the various attempts at classifying the Neolithic, Bronze and Early Iron Ages. Napoleon III himself took a keen interest in the archaeology of France, was much concerned with looking behind the Roman occupation of Gaul and indeed in getting portrayed, favourably if possible, the role of the pre-Roman Gauls in the evolution of France.

Of the many major figures who worked in European archaeology in this period none is more colourful, and affected British and eventually

88 (*Opposite*) A tunnel under the ramparts at Boghazköy, the city identified in the 1900s as Hattusas, the capital of the Hittites.

89, 90 General Pitt-Rivers's excavations in 1893–94 at Wor Barrow, Dorset (*above*), from which he derived the schematic but accurate drawing of the ditch (*opposite*), published in his *Excavations in Cranborne Chase*, vol. IV (1898).

European archaeology more profoundly, than Pitt-Rivers. The man who is generally referred to in archaeological literature as General Pitt-Rivers was born Lane Fox and changed his name in 1880 when he inherited the very large Rivers estates comprising over 29,000 acres of land, including much of Cranborne Chase in southern England. As Colonel Lane Fox, and before, he had been professionally concerned with the use and evolutionary history of the musket; he studied the development of firearms and found himself arranging collections of types in developing or evolutionary sequences. He decided that all material culture could be seen as objects to be arranged in typological sequences that developed in an evolutionary way. Here he was following in the footsteps of the earlier Danish and Swedish archaeologists and working in a parallel way to John Evans in England and Montelius in Sweden.

To prove this thesis of the typological development of all artifacts he began collecting everything he could lay his hands on: soon his own house was an inadequate repository. In 1851 his collections were lent to the museum at Bethnal Green: they moved later to South Kensington and then to Oxford, where a special annexe of the University Museum was designed for them. The objects in the new Pitt-Rivers Museum were set out on a taxonomic and typological basis. By his arrangements, and advocacy in lectures and writing, he demonstrated the value of ethnography to prehistoric archaeology. He, like Flinders Petrie, insisted that archaeology was not a study of art objects but of all objects.

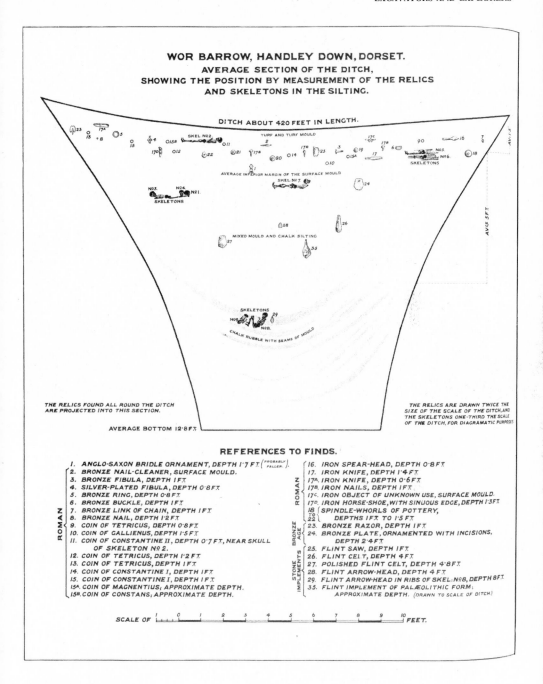

WOR BARROW, HANDLEY DOWN, DORSET.
AVERAGE SECTION OF THE DITCH,
SHOWING THE POSITION BY MEASUREMENT OF THE RELICS
AND SKELETONS IN THE SILTING.

DITCH ABOUT 420 FEET IN LENGTH.

TURF AND TURF MOULD

AVERAGE INFERIOR MARGIN OF THE SURFACE MOULD

SKEL. Nº 7

SKELETONS

MIXED MOULD AND CHALK SILTING

SKELETONS

CHALK RUBBLE WITH SEAMS OF MOULD

THE RELICS FOUND ALL ROUND THE DITCH
ARE PROJECTED INTO THIS SECTION.

THE RELICS ARE DRAWN TWICE THE
SIZE OF THE SCALE OF THE DITCH, AND
THE SKELETONS ONE-THIRD THE SCALE
OF THE DITCH, FOR DIAGRAMATIC PURPOSES.

AVERAGE BOTTOM 12·8 FT.

REFERENCES TO FINDS.

ROMAN

1. ANGLO-SAXON BRIDLE ORNAMENT, DEPTH 1·7 FT. (PROBABLY FALLEN.)
2. BRONZE NAIL-CLEANER, SURFACE MOULD.
3. BRONZE FIBULA, DEPTH 1 FT.
4. SILVER-PLATED FIBULA, DEPTH 0·8 FT.
5. BRONZE RING, DEPTH 0·8 FT.
6. BRONZE BUCKLE, DEPTH 1 FT.
7. BRONZE LINK OF CHAIN, DEPTH 1 FT.
8. BRONZE NAIL, DEPTH 1·2 FT.
9. COIN OF TETRICUS, DEPTH 0·8 FT.
10. COIN OF GALLIENUS, DEPTH 1·5 FT.
11. COIN OF CONSTANTINE II, DEPTH 0·7 FT., NEAR SKULL OF SKELETON Nº 2.
12. COIN OF TETRICUS, DEPTH 1·2 FT.
13. COIN OF TETRICUS, DEPTH 1 FT.
14. COIN OF CONSTANTINE I, DEPTH 1 FT.
15. COIN OF CONSTANTINE I, DEPTH 1 FT.
15A. COIN OF MAGNENTIUS; APPROXIMATE DEPTH.
15B. COIN OF CONSTANS; APPROXIMATE DEPTH.

ROMAN

16. IRON SPEAR-HEAD, DEPTH 0·8 FT.
17. IRON KNIFE, DEPTH 1·4 FT.
17A. IRON KNIFE, DEPTH 0·6 FT.
17B. IRON NAILS, DEPTH 1 FT.
17C. IRON OBJECT OF UNKNOWN USE, SURFACE MOULD.
17D. IRON HORSE-SHOE, WITH SINUOUS EDGE, DEPTH 1·3 FT.
18 TO 22. SPINDLE-WHORLS OF POTTERY, DEPTHS 1 FT. TO 1·5 FT.

BRONZE AGE

23. BRONZE RAZOR, DEPTH 1 FT.
24. BRONZE PLATE, ORNAMENTED WITH INCISIONS, DEPTH 2·4 FT.

STONE IMPLEMENTS

25. FLINT SAW, DEPTH 1 FT.
26. FLINT CELT, DEPTH 4 FT.
27. POLISHED FLINT CELT, DEPTH 4·8 FT.
28. FLINT ARROW-HEAD, DEPTH 4 FT.
29. FLINT ARROW-HEAD IN RIBS OF SKEL. Nº 8, DEPTH 8 FT.
35. FLINT IMPLEMENT OF PALÆOLITHIC FORM; APPROXIMATE DEPTH. (DRAWN TO SCALE OF DITCH)

SCALE OF 1 0 1 2 3 4 5 6 7 8 9 10 FEET.

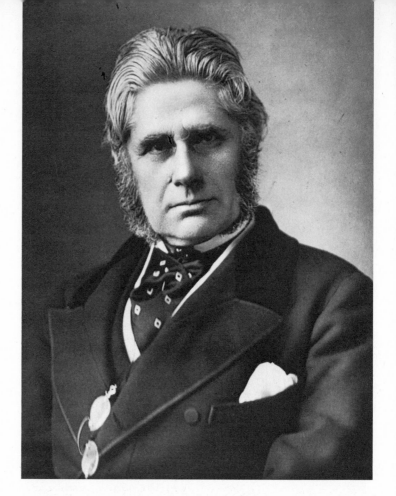

91 General Pitt-Rivers
(1827–1900), who
transformed excavation
from a pleasant hobby to
an arduous scientific
pursuit.

He stressed that his collection was 'not for the purpose of surprising anyone, either by the beauty or value of the objects exhibited, but solely with a view to instruction. For this purpose ordinary and typical specimens rather than rare objects have been selected and arranged in sequence.'

Even before he had inherited the Cranborne estates he had carried out many excavations in England and Wales, and even at Haithabu in Schleswig. Between 1880 and 1900, and not limited by considerations of finance, time or labour, Pitt-Rivers excavated camps, villages, cemeteries, barrows and ditches, including Wor Barrow, Bokerly Dyke, Woodyates and Rotherly. He initiated and practised the total excavation of sites, stressing the importance of stratigraphy and the necessity of recording the position of everything found. He caused 90 accurate plans and sections, detailed drawings and descriptions to be made of all his excavations and made models of the main sites. The result of his excavations were quickly published in four privately printed volumes between 1887 and 1898 under the title *Excavations in Cranborne Chase*. In every way his work was of the highest standard: in fifteen years he had transformed excavation from a pleasant hobby to an arduous scientific pursuit. He was far in advance of his contemporary diggers: R. G. Collingwood has suggested that in many ways he was in advance of modern archaeological techniques: many present-day practitioners of archaeological excavation envy his resources and the way in which he conducted his digs with the efficiency, thoroughness and discipline of a military operation. His influence was considerable on another para-military figure, Mortimer Wheeler, as we shall see below. Recently Michael Thompson has published a full and fair portrait of this remarkable figure in his *General Pitt-Rivers* (1977).

There is no space to record in detail some of the archaeological discoveries made during these years, but special mention must be made of the finding of the Gokstad and Oseberg ships.

In 1880 the son of a farmer owning a barrow at Gokstad on the west side of Oslo fjord began to dig into the mound. He was looking for treasure but found instead a Viking ship eighty feet (twenty-four metres) long dating from the second half of the ninth century AD. The human remains in the burial chamber were perhaps those of King Olaf Geirstadralf of the Ynglingar dynasty. A quarter of a century later, when he was celebrating his birthday in the National Museum at Oslo, Professor Gustafson was interrupted by a farmer who said he had found the remains of a comparable ship on his land. This land was at Oseberg, ten miles north of Gokstad and about thirty miles south of Oslo. Gustafson excavated the vessel – a sailing ship seventy feet (twenty-one metres) long. The Gokstad and Oseberg ships are now in a special museum built for them just outside Oslo.

92 The excavation of a Viking ship burial at Oseberg, Norway in 1904 (cf. ill. 68).

America

Haven's *Archaeology of the United States* and the illustrated travels of Stephens and Catherwood mark an important watershed in nineteenth-century American archaeology. They were followed by more travellers, such as Désiré Charnay, whose *The Ancient Cities of the New World* was published in 1887, the extraordinary and eccentric Augustus Le Plongeon, who made some excavations and whose *Queen Moo and the Egyptian Sphinx* came out in 1900, and the Englishman Alfred P. Maudslay, who published the results of his travels and surveys in the four volumes of *Biologia Centrali Americana* (1889–1902).

The first really large-scale and important excavations in Central America were those undertaken by the Peabody Museum of Harvard at Copan, the Maya centre in Honduras, work conducted by M. H. Saville, John Owens (who died during the excavations) and G. H. Gordon: published in part in Gordon's *Prehistoric Ruins of Copan, Honduras* (1896). The beginnings of stratigraphical observation in Middle American archaeology can be seen in the demonstration by Gamio and Boas of a three-period culture sequence in the valley of Mexico, based on pottery and figurines.

Peru was fortunate to benefit from the services of the German Max Uhle (1856–1944). Trained as a philologist, he switched to archaeology and ethnography, and, when on the staff of the Dresden Museum, he met Alphons Stübel who had, with Wilhelm Reiss, dug a cemetery on the coast of Peru. Uhle collaborated with Stübel in a book entitled *Die Ruinenstaette von Tiahuanaco* (1892), based on Stübel's field notes and photographs. Uhle then took to the field in South America and worked there off and on for thirty years, first in Peru and Bolivia and later in Chile and Ecuador. His major excavation in Peru was at Pachacamac, south of Lima. He was aware of the sequence produced by stratigraphy and was influenced by the work of Flinders Petrie in Egypt. His monograph *Pachacamac* (1903) has been described as 'one of the monuments of American archaeology' (Willey and Sabloff, *A History of American Archaeology*, 1974, 78). He realized the necessity of a time scale in American archaeology and wrote: 'In American studies, the first thing that had to be done was to introduce the idea of time, to get people to admit that the types could change.'

In this period of American archaeology we record not only travel, field survey and the beginnings of excavation but the study of hieroglyphic inscriptions and native literature. The Frenchman Abbé Brasseur de Bourbourg (1814–74) from the north of France was, from the age of seventeen, possessed of 'a lively interest in all geographical facts relating to America' and was most excited by reading an account in the *Gazette de France* that a Brazilian farmer had found a flat stone, Macedonian arms and armour, all bearing Greek inscriptions. He devoted his life to the study of Mexican Indian history, language and culture and translated native manuscripts. His work on Landa's *Relación de las Cosas de Yucatan* and on native Maya documents provided data by which the archaeologist could understand and interpret his finds. Ernst W. Förstemann, who has been called 'the father of Maya hieroglyphic research', deciphered parts of the original

93

Maya book known as the Dresden codex, concentrating on the numerical and calendrical data, so that it became possible for archaeologists to date Maya monuments from their inscriptions. His *Commentary on the Maya Manuscript in the Royal Public Library at Dresden* was published in 1906. Edward Seler's researches on codices and Maya iconography were published in his five volume *Gesammelte Abhandlungen zur Amerikanischen Sprach und Alterthumskunde* (1902–23). Charles P. Bowditch of the Peabody Museum at Harvard became an authority on Maya astronomy: his *The Numeration, Calendar Systems and Astronomical Knowledge of the Mayas* was published in Cambridge, Mass., in 1910. Bowditch launched from the Peabody a long campaign of fieldwork, excavation and library and museum study into Maya archaeology.

The new light being thrown on Middle American archaeology was synthesized by H. J. Spinden in his *A Study of Maya Art* (1913) and Thomas A. Joyce's *Mexican Archaeology* (1914). Both set up chronological systems based on excavation, dated monuments, the evolution of art styles and correlations with native traditions. Here was the beginning of a new age in Middle American archaeology.

In North American studies Cyrus Thomas, in papers such as 'Who were the Mound Builders?' (1884) and 'Report on the Mound Explorations of the Bureau of American Ethnology' (1894), was able to confirm what Haven and others had said earlier, namely that the Indian peoples of the present showed continuity with the mound-builders of the past. F. W. Putnam, a Director of the Peabody, taught his students the modern techniques of fieldwork and excavation: a good example of his doctrines is found in a paper entitled 'On Methods of Archaeological Research in America' published in the *Johns Hopkins University Calendar* (Vol. V. no. 49, 1886).

But if we can look at the last decade of the nineteenth century and the first of the twentieth century as full of hope for American archaeology, the period under review highlights dramatically the dangers inherent in archaeological explanation.

The nineteenth century, and alas, the twentieth century even more, was subject to the development of myth America, the creation of invented pasts for the pre-Columbian Indians. Edward King, Viscount Kingsborough (1795–1837), an eccentric Irish peer, while an undergraduate at Oxford, was fascinated by a Mexican codex in the Bodleian Library and immediately fell in love with Mexican antiquities. He published his *Antiquities of Mexico* (1831–48) in nine imperial folio volumes at his own expense – an expense which ran him into debts, for which he was imprisoned on three occasions and died during his third term, some say of typhus or typhoid fever, others of a broken heart. During his work Kingsborough became passionately convinced that the Indians of Mexico were descendants of the Lost Tribes of Israel. It was sad that he moved away to the wilder shores of archaeology and we should not forget the good part of his work. H. H. Bancroft wrote of him:

> There is a scholarly dignity about his work which has never been attained by those who have jeered and railed at him; and, though we may smile at his credulity and regret that such strong zeal was so strangely misplaced, yet we should speak and think with respect of one who spent his lifetime and his fortune, if not his reason, in an honest endeavour to cast light upon one of the most obscure spots in the history of man.

Waldeck (see above) eventually came to the conclusion that the New World civilizations were older than those of the Near East by which they were linked by Atlantis. The Abbé Brasseur de Bourbourg after years of detailed work on Maya documents took leave of his senses. He decided that the texts he had worked on for so long were allegories, had no historical basis, and that they, like the Egyptian records, were derived from Atlantis, where all civilization started. Augustus Le Plongeon linked the Maya not only with Atlantis and Egypt, but also with the Lost Tribes of Israel, the Indian Rig-Veda, and the Chinese books of the Chou King, and were involved in the birth of Christianity. He declared that the last words of the dying Christ, 'Eli, Eli lama sabachthani', spoken in Aramaic and translated into English as 'My God, my God, why hast thou forsaken me?', were really the Maya words 'Helo, helo lamah zabac ta ni', meaning 'Now, now, sinking, black ink over my nose'. He insisted on Maya colonies on the banks of the Nile, visited by Queen Moo, driven away from Chichén Itza, visiting Atlantis on the way.

There was only limited attention paid to the writings of Kingsborough, Waldeck, Brasseur de Bourbourg and Le Plongeon, but immense popularity was achieved for the idea of Atlantis by Ignatius Donnelly, who published *Atlantis: the Antediluvian World* in 1882. The people of Atlantis, he argued, represented a lost civilization that came to North and Middle America – the mounds were their relics – and that went south to Mexico when attacked by the native savages. Donnelly's *Atlantis* went through fifty printings – it is still being reprinted – and has done even more damage to good thinking than Elliot Smith's *The Ancient Egyptians*. Mr Gladstone, Prime Minister of England, who was so impressed by the work of Schliemann, was sure Donnelly was right: he asked Parliament for funds to organize the search for Atlantis, but his request was fortunately turned down.

Archaeology in 1914

The archaeologists and geologists who had in the middle of the nineteenth century gladly abandoned the short world view of man's origins in 4004 BC were still finding it difficult at the end of the nineteenth century, and in the early years of the twentieth, to find a relative or absolute chronology with which to date their archaeological epochs or cultures. James Geikie, in *The Great Ice Age and its relation to the Antiquity of Man* (1874) and *Prehistoric Europe* (1881), propounded a system of four large and a fifth smaller glaciation for the Pleistocene and argued that man had appeared for the first time in the second interglacial. Between 1910 and 1919 Penck and Bruckner produced their system of four Pleistocene glaciations which they termed Günz, Mindel, Riss and Wurm after Swiss sites, and argued that man first appeared in Europe during the Mindel-Riss glaciation.

In post-glacial times the place of glacial and inter-glacial phenomena was taken by raised beaches and by changes in climate. By a macroscopic study of plant remains Blytt and Sernander distinguished five divisions of post-glacial times, namely pre-Boreal, Boreal, Atlantic, sub-Boreal and sub-Atlantic. These phases were confirmed by pollen-analytical methods first developed by Lennart von Post.

The translation of these glacial and post-glacial sequences into absolute dates was attempted in two ways: first by dead reckoning based on the thickness of deposits, and, secondly, by geochronological techniques. Arthur Evans had estimated the beginnings of the Neolithic in Crete at 10,000 to 12,000 BC; and at Anau Pumpelly made calculations based on a visit to Egypt in 1906–7 where he estimated the rate of accumulation of occupational debris there as 1.6 feet per century. Armed with these figures he dated the beginning of Anau I at somewhere in the tenth millennium BC; and a similar inflated chronology was proposed by de Morgan for Susa I. Schmidt, incidentally, did not agree with Pumpelly's dates and dated Anau I to the third millennium BC. The excavation report of Anau is a curiosity in that it includes both the Pumpelly and the widely differing Schmidt dates. Many estimates were made for the duration of the Pleistocene Ice Age according to the thickness of deposits; Penck himself estimated 600,000 years.

The second, or geochronological, method involved tree-ring and clay-varve counting. The Reverend Manasseh Cutler had used tree-rings for dating the American mound-builders (p. 40) and Thomas Jefferson had stressed the value of dendrochronology (p. 42). In 1811 Dr Witt Clinton was dating earthworks near Canadaigua (N. Y. State) by tree-rings. These interesting pioneer efforts were developed as a scientific technique by A. E. Douglass in 1901. By these techniques the early Basket Maker cultures of America have been dated to the early years of the Christian era – fifteen centuries before Columbus discovered America.

Clay-varve analysis – the counting of the varves left behind by the retreating glaciers at the end of the Pleistocene ice age – was first discussed as a possibility by the Swede Baron Gerhard de Geer as long ago as 1878. He began his field work in 1905. In 1910 he published his

94 Charles Dawson (*left*) and Sir Arthur Smith Woodward searching for Piltdown Man. A postcard which appeared around the time of the discovery in 1912.

famous paper, 'A Geochronology of the last 12,000 years'. De Geer took his zero-point as 6839 BC to designate the end of the Late Glacial and the beginning of the post-Glacial. There has been some confusion and revision of these dates but they immediately enabled us, for example, to say that the Upper Palaeolithic parietal art of southern France and northern Spain flourished before 13,000 years ago.

Chemical analysis of materials was also beginning in this period. In 1844 the English geologist, J. Middleton (*Proc. Geol. Soc. Lond.* IV, 431–33), and in 1893 the French mineralogist, A. Carnot (*Annales de Mines, Mémoires*, 9ième Ser. 3, 155–95), reported that the amount of fluorine in fossil bones increases with their geological age: the fluorine present in the soil-water steadily accumulates in bones and teeth. The possibilities of this interesting fact were forgotten about until these papers were re-discovered by K. P. Oakley many years later. Fluorine dating could have been applied to the finds of bones made at Galley Hill in the Swanscombe gravels of Kent in 1888 and at Piltdown near Lewes in Sussex in 1912. The Galley Hill skeleton was that of a modern man with allegedly primitive features. When found in 1888 it was said to be eight feet (two-and-a-half metres) deep in the gravels and associated with Lower Palaeolithic hand-axes and remains of extinct animals. When fluorine analysis was applied in the 1940s it was shown that the Galley Hill skeleton was an intrusive burial much later than the Middle Pleistocene gravels in which it lay. The 'discovery' of a human skull and an ape-like jaw by Charles Dawson at Piltdown was heralded as that of the Earliest Englishman and was given the name *Eoanthropus dawsoni* – the dawn man found by Dawson! For long it bedevilled

94

scientific writing on human palaeontology until in the 1950s fluorine then revealed that it was a forgery.

Air photography as an indispensable aid to the archaeologist was a product of the First World War and immediately afterwards, but the beginnings were long before this. The Paris photographer, Gaspard Félix Tournachon, who went by the name of Nadar, took air photographs of Paris from a balloon in 1858. King and Black took air photographs of Boston, and Negretti of London in the 1860s. The first archaeological air photographs were taken from a military balloon in 1906 by Lieutenant P. H. Sharpe R.E.: these were oblique and vertical photographs of Stonehenge and showed up as dark marks the avenue   95 which was no longer visible on the ground as a surface feature. These photographs were published at the time in *Archaeologia* (1907, plates 69 and 70). In the years immediately preceding the 1914–1918 war, H. S. Wellcome used large box-kites wth special automatically controlled cameras for photographing his excavations in the Sudan.

By the outbreak of the war it was clear that archaeology as it developed was going to rely more and more on scientific techniques and was no longer the study of artifacts in the field and in museums in isolation. The archaeologist was becoming dependent on scientists who studied the flora, fauna and environment of his sites and who would date his material independent of archaeological methods. These trends become very clear in the next two chapters.

95 The two earliest archaeological air photographs ever taken were of Stonehenge, and appeared in *Archaeologia* for 1907. This oblique view shows the avenue, which was invisible from the ground.

4

Archaeology comes of Age (1914–1939)

The Three Age System and Diffusion

The epochal idea of prehistory was already open to severe adverse criticism before the 1914–18 war. After the discoveries in 1909 at the Grotte de Valle it was clear that the Azilian and Tardenoisian 'periods' were contemporary: they were cultures not epochs. Breuil's great paper of 1912, 'Les Subdivisions du Paléolithique supérieur et leur signification', already foreshadowed the break-up of the old epochal system.

In the first half of the twentieth century four things contributed to the general realization that the epochal idea was dead. The first, as we have said, was the demonstration of the contemporaneity of periods or epochs. The second was the extension of research from France, where the epochal system had been canonized by G. de Mortillet, to other regions of Europe, to Africa and then gradually all over the world and the ready realization that the French straitjacket could not be used universally.

The third was the absorption by prehistorians, working in barbarian Europe, of the new approach to archaeological theory and nomenclature which was being developed in the Aegean and the Near East. As we have seen, when Schliemann studied the archaeological remains at Tiryns and Mycenae he did not nominate them with some reference to epochs of the Stone Age and Bronze Age: he boldly designated them remains of the Mycenaean civilization, and Arthur Evans designated the remains from Knossos as Minoan. Similarly, words like Aegean, Cycladic and Helladic were being used for civilizations and peoples not periods. Nothing distinguished the nature of these civilizations in the East Mediterranean from the epochs of the archaeologists studying western and northern Europe, except their content and the degree of complexity of their remains. It began to dawn on archaeologists that their epochs, already often demonstrated to be contemporary, were really types of 'civilizations'. Should not prehistory then follow the examples of Schliemann and Evans and refer to the Mousterian civilization rather than the Mousterian epoch, the Hallstatt civilization instead of the Hallstatt period, and so on? Some archaeologists were chary of using the word 'civilization' for the material remains of societies which were savage and barbarian, and would have liked to reserve this word, with its special overtones, to literate societies. This difficulty was met and resolved, as we have seen, by Pumpelly, who described the contents of his levels at Anau not as representing periods but 'cultures'. In his *Explorations in Turkestan: Expedition of 1904* (1908) he wrote, 'To avoid misunderstanding it may be added that the word *culture* is used as a synonym for *civilization* and that the term culture-strata (*Kulturschichte* of the Germans) stands for the debris slowly accumulated during occupation of an inhabited site.'

The fourth factor was the absorption by archaeologists of ideas from human geography and anthropology in the early twentieth century. Anthropologists and anthropogeographers studying modern primitive peoples distinguished their material, moral and mental culture and grouped them into cultures. Ratzel in his *Völkerkunde* (1885–88) and his *Anthropo-Geographie* (1882–91) distinguished 'cultural complexes' and his pupil, Leo Frobenius, developed these ideas through what he called the 'geographical-statistical method', and worked out 'culture-circles' in West Africa and Melanesia in the last years of the nineteenth century. These ideas were developed in Germany in the early twentieth century into a complicated study of culture-areas and culture-strata. In America the culture-area idea was developed by Boas and Wissler.

But although the seeds of the destruction of the epochal chest of drawers model of the past were germinating by the 1920s the old system was still being set out in textbooks, such as M. C. Burkitt's *Prehistory* (1921), G. C. MacCurdy's *Human Origins: A Manual of Prehistory* (1924) and H. Osborn's *Men of the Old Stone Age* (1918).

And still the Manchester School was pouring out books advocating Egyptocentric-hyperdiffusionism as the answer to all problems of culture change. The first edition of *The Ancient Egyptians* had been published in 1911 – twelve years later when the second edition came out Elliot Smith wrote in the preface: 'Little did I realize when I was writing what was intended to be nothing more than a brief interim report . . . that this little book was destined to open up a new view – or rather to revise and extend an old and neglected method of interpretation of the history of civilization.'

Elliot Smith went on preaching, with the enthusiasm of a zealot and a blind disregard for facts and adverse appraisal of his theories, that all higher culture in Europe, Asia, Africa and America came from ancient Egypt: this archaic Egyptian culture, or Heliolithic Culture Complex as he called it, was spread by Egyptian trade – the Children of the Sun, in their search for the Givers of Life. He set out his theory in a series of books such as *The Migrations of Early Culture* (1915), *The Evolution of the Dragon* (1919), *Elephants and Ethnologists* (1924), *In the Beginning: the origin of civilisation* (1928), *Human History* (1930) and *The Diffusion of Culture* (1933). His most enthusiastic disciple and collaborator was W. J. Perry, who was first Reader in Comparative Religion in the University of Manchester when Elliot Smith was Professor of Anatomy there and then Reader in Cultural Anthropology in London when Elliot Smith moved to be Professor of Anatomy at University College, London.

Perry was even more dogmatic and made even more far reaching claims than Elliot Smith, and in a series of books such as *The Children of the Sun* (1923), *The Origin of Magic and Religion* (1923), *The Megalithic Culture of Indonesia* (1918) and *The Growth of Civilization* (1924) he elaborated and disseminated the doctrine of Egyptocentric hyperdiffusionism. The *Growth of Civilization* was re-issued in 1937 by Penguin Books, and as one of the first archaeological paperbacks had a very large circulation and much influence.

Perry was once asked what was taking place in the rest of the world when Egypt, and allegedly Egypt alone, was laying the foundations of civilization. He answered simply, 'Nothing'. He went on to say, looking back at the original *Ancient Egyptians* of 1911, 'The accumulation of fresh evidence during the twenty-odd years that have elapsed has tended to confirm the essential accuracy of what was then an astonishing generalization.'

Astonishing indeed: the whole Elliot Smith/Perry thesis was a classic example of inventing the past, of imposing a pattern on the archaeological evidence which could only be argued by false parallels, false chronology and even faked evidence. Lowie, in his *History of Ethnological Theory*, refers to Elliot Smith's 'unfathomable ignorance of elementary ethnography'. One day Dr A. M. Tozzer, of the Peabody Museum at Harvard, pointed out to his colleague Dr Roland B. Dixon that soon the Manchester School with their spate of books would have everyone in the world believing that the American Indians came from the Nile and urged Dixon to write a rebuttal, which he did in *The Building of Culture* (1928). It was a masterly demolishing of the Elliot Smith–Perry fantasy but had little effect on the believers. Why did intelligent academics invent and believe this farrago of rubbish? They were deluding the world: did they delude themselves? The answer is yes. Elliot Smith in his 1928 Huxley Memorial Lecture said, 'The set attitude of mind of a scholar may become almost indistinguishable from a delusion.' This is what had happened to him: he had developed a set attitude of mind regarding the Egyptian origin of all culture and it had become a great delusion.

Two years after Elliot Smith's death Lord Raglan published his *How Came Civilisation* (1939), in which he substituted Sumeria for Egypt and put forward his Sumerocentric hyperdiffusionist theory that all culture started in Mesopotamia. He wrote:

> No invention, discovery, custom, belief or even story is known for certain to have originated in two separate cultures . . . The natural state of man is a state of low savagery . . . savages never invent or discover anything . . . many of the principal discoveries and inventions upon which our civilization is based can be traced with considerable probability to an area with its focus near the head of the Persian Gulf.

The advantage to the unlearned in archaeology of the theories of the Manchester School and Lord Raglan was that they were all embracing, a complete and simplistic account of cultural origins. They were not dangerous – but other, all-embracing, interpretations of prehistoric archaeology did become dangerous.

One such was the doctrine preached by Gustav Kossinna in Germany. The Comte de Gobineau, a French nobleman, wrote his *Essay on the Inequality of Human Races* between 1853 and 1857, in which he declared that the hope of the world lay and had always lain with the fair-haired Teutons whom he called Aryans. In 1899 Houston

Stewart Chamberlain wrote *The Foundations of the Nineteenth Century*, in which physical anthropology, language and archaeology were all confused and the mystique of the Great German Race propagated. Small wonder that when the Nazis came to power they readily carried on this mystique, which is well seen in Hitler's *Mein Kampf*. Great wonder that there were archaeologists prepared to pervert archaeology for political ends.

Kossinna (1858–1931) began as a philologist and then turned to prehistory. In 1902 he was appointed Professor of German Prehistory in the University of Berlin and held that post until his death. He complained that hitherto German prehistory was thought to be of less importance in German scholarship than the archaeology of Egyptian, Greek, Roman and Oriental antiquity: and he set out to prove the greatness of the Germans through the evidence of prehistoric archaeology. He built up an inflated chronology in northern Europe so that everything started in Germany and spread from the superior Germans to their inferiors in western, southern and eastern Europe. All this seems strange and unreal to us today, but it was very real at the time. Kossinna believed in it and his archaeological perversions were readily accepted by German racialists: here was apparent proof provided by the apparently unimpeachable discipline of archaeology of the antiquity and superiority of the Germans. It was not to them a mystique but a fact and a fact that was delightful to Nazi doctrine. Himmler once said: 'Prehistory is the doctrine of the eminence of the Germans at the dawn of civilization.'

The examples cited in the last few pages show the dangers of what is politely called these days 'alternate' archaeology. We shall see later that these dangers in a different form are still with us.

Egypt, the Near and Middle East

Flinders Petrie carried on his work in Egypt for the first quarter of the twentieth century until in 1926, after forty years' excavation in that country, he transferred his attentions to Palestine where he died in 1942. The cessation of excavation during the First World War enabled him to carry on with the work of synthesis that he had begun with his *Arts and Crafts of Ancient Egypt* (1909). *Scarabs and Cylinders* was published in 1915, followed by *Tools and Weapons* (1916), the *Corpus of Prehistoric Pottery* (1918) and *Prehistoric Egypt illustrated by over 1,000 objects in University College London* (1920).

But the great discoveries in Egyptian archaeology in the twentieth century were not made by Petrie. At Tell-el-Amarna in 1887 a peasant woman digging for brick-dust manure found the now famous Amarna letters, tablets of baked clay written in cuneiform in the diplomatic Babylonian of the period. These tablets, at first neglected, then said to be forgeries, were eventually recognized as important, although by then half of them had been lost. The tablets were eventually fully published and the site excavated by many (including Petrie in 1891–92) and from 1907 onwards by the Deutsche Orient Gesellschaft. When the German concession lapsed the Egypt Exploration Society took over in 1921: work continued for many years, directed successively by names to

96 The Egyptian pharaoh Akhenaten and his queen Nefertiti, carved in relief on a piece of limestone from Amarna, *c*. 1355 BC. Ht 22 cm.

96

97 (*Opposite*) Tutankhamun's tomb proved to be the richest archaeological find ever made. On 17 February 1923, three months after the antechamber was officially opened, Lord Carnarvon and Howard Carter broke through sealed doors to reveal the inner burial chamber and the treasures lying therein.

become famous in Near Eastern archaeology – T. E. Peet, C. L. Woolley, F. G. Newton, Llewelyn Griffith, Henri Frankfort and J. D. S. Pendlebury. The results of the latest excavations (summarized briefly in Pendlebury's *Tell el-Amarna*) produced a lively and detailed picture of life in the fourteenth century BC in this remarkable, though short-lived, city under Akhenaten.

Akhenaten, Ikhnaten or Amenhotep IV was 'the heretic pharaoh of Egypt'. He reigned with his queen Nefertiti for seventeen years (*c*. 1369–52 BC) towards the end of the eighteenth dynasty. He removed the capital from Thebes to Tell el-Amarna, and here a very remarkable development of literature and art – the so-called Amarna style – took place. He attempted to replace the many and complicated religions of Egypt, more especially that of Amun-Re, by a monotheism, a worship of the sun represented by the Aten or Aton. His successor, son of Amenhotep III, was Tutankhaten who reigned for nine years. He began restoring the worship of Amun-Re and changed his name to Tutankhamun. His orthodox successors attempted to get rid of his name and memory and very little is known about him, yet because of the accidents of preservation and of archaeological discovery his is probably the name best known to the general public in all Egyptology. This is due to the discovery of his tomb with its sensational and rich furnishings in the autumn of 1922.

Schliemann's discoveries at Troy and Mycenae had made him a household name, and the money he spent personally on his excavations and the treasures he found, the envy of the world. Professor A. H. Sayce of Oxford wrote furiously:

Why is it that Dr Schliemann's example has not yet been followed by some of the rich men of whom England is so full? Why cannot they spare for science a little of the wealth that is now lavished upon the breeding of horses or the maintenance of a dog-kennel? England must contain one or two, at least, who would be willing to help in recovering the earlier history of our civilization.

Such a one arose in the person of Lord Carnarvon (1866–1923) who, in ill health after a car accident, was told to travel to Egypt. Like many another he became fascinated by Egypt and Egyptology. Percy Newberry, the Egyptologist and a close friend, revealed that Carnarvon once said to him that 'he would rather discover an unrifled tomb than win the Derby'. He left for Egypt in 1907 and spent a part of each of the next sixteen years working there.

He began to work with Howard Carter (1873–1939), who had himself worked under Newberry, Petrie and Naville and was appointed in 1899 by Maspero to be Inspector of Monuments in Upper Egypt. From 1902 onwards Carter collaborated with Theodore Davis (1837–1915), a wealthy New York businessman, in the Valley of the Kings and together they discovered the tomb of Thutmose IV. Then in 1912 Davis decided that the Royal Valley was exhausted; Maspero agreed that Carnarvon should take over Davis's concession. He and Carter worked in the Valley, apart from the war years, until 1921. The following year Carnarvon told Carter he could not afford to spend any more money on what seemed a fruitless task. He was persuaded to mount one last season and on 4 November 1922 Carter's workmen discovered 'a step-cut in the rock'. Sixteen steps led down through one doorway to a second containing the seal of Tutankhamun. Officially opened on 29 November 1922 and excavated by Carter off and on for the next ten years, the tomb yielded nearly five thousand works of art: it caused a sensation throughout the whole world. Tutankhamun became a household word, and the discovery of his tomb the richest archaeological find ever made. It has never been fully published, but there is a three-volume work by Carter and Mace, *The Tomb of Tutankhamen*, published between 1923 and 1933. Those who wish to pursue the story of the Tutankhamun excavations should read Thomas Hoving, *Tutankhamun, the Untold Story* (1979), Arnold C. Brackman, *The Search for the Gold of Tutankhamen* (1976), and the interesting memoirs of Carnarvon's son, namely, *Ermine Tales* (1980).

97
V

Petrie's pioneer work at Naqada and on the prehistoric origins of Egyptian civilization was carried on in the 1920s and 1930s by various workers. In Lower Egypt Junker, Menghin and Scharff excavated the Neolithic settlement of Merimde-Beni-Salame. The Neolithic cultures of the Fayum depression were studied by Miss Caton-Thompson and Miss E. W. Gardner in 1924–28. In Upper and Middle Egypt the British School of Archaeology in Egypt excavated at and near Badari between 1922 and 1925. Guy Brunton excavated cemeteries at Badari and Miss Caton-Thompson a settlement at Hemamieh, between Qau and Badari. They together published their results in *The Badarian Civilization and Predynastic Remains near Badari* (1928), which established the Badarian as the immediate ancestor of the predynastic period in Upper Egypt. In 1928 and 1929 Brunton excavated a cemetery and village at Deir Tasa, near Mostagedda, and in his *Mostagedda and the Tasian Culture* (1937) claimed the Tasian as the ancestor of the Badarian. Petrie had very wisely begun his series of sequence-dates at S.D.30 and the Tasian and Badarian cultures were now fitted in before this, so that there was a sequence leading from Tasian right through to the first dynasty at S.D.79.

Excavations were started again in Mesopotamia immediately after the end of the First World War: indeed R. Campbell-Thompson, on behalf of the British Museum, began digging at Ur and Eridu before the 1918 Armistice, and later H. R. Hall found at Al 'Ubaid, a new site four miles west of Ur, a small temple platform, prototype of the later Sumerian ziggurats. In 1922 a joint expedition of the British Museum and the University Museum of Pennsylvania carried on the work of Thompson and Hall, digging at Ur and Al 'Ubaid under the direction of Leonard Woolley. It was in 1926 that the great prehistoric cemetery at Ur with its Royal Tombs was excavated: the splendid treasures of gold and lapis lazuli and the remarkable evidence of funerary ritual caused a sensation comparable with that brought about by Schliemann's discoveries and that of Tutankhamun's tomb. The Ur excavations put the Sumerians on the map of general knowledge: the preliminary reports in *The Antiquaries Journal* from 1923 to 1934, and the full reports from 1927 to 1938, were made most accessible to the public by well-written, clear accounts by Woolley – one of the best practitioners of archaeological popularization – such as *Ur of the Chaldees* (1929), *The Sumerians* (1930), and *Abraham; Recent Discoveries and Hebrew Origins* (1930).

Parallel with the British/American excavations at Ur were the Oxford/Chicago excavations at Kish and Jemdet Nasr (later continued by the Frenchman Watelin), and the German excavations at Warka

98 The excavation of Ur from 1922 to 1934 by Sir Leonard Woolley must rank as one of the most spectacularly successful digs of the twentieth century. Not only did he excavate the city of Abraham's birth and recover its history, he also discovered in the deepest levels a Royal Cemetery containing some of the finest gold and other objects ever produced in antiquity. The photograph shows the excavation team at Ur in 1926: on Mrs Woolley's left stands Father Eric Burrows, the epigraphist, on her right Woolley himself, Hamoudi his foreman and M. E. L. Mallowan (later to dig at Nimrud).

99 An air view of the
ziggurat of Ur after
excavation.

(Uruk). In 1931 the Eighteenth Conference of Orientalists at Leiden
distinguished three predynastic periods in Mesopotamian prehistory,
first Al 'Ubaid, second, Uruk, and thirdly Jemdet Nasr. In the north of
Mesopotamia excavations took place at Tell Halaf, Arpachiyah, and
Tepe Gawra.

In 1933 a new Iraqi law prevented foreign archaeological expeditions
exporting the antiquities they had found. The French moved to Syria
where Parrot began work at Mari in 1934 and the British dug at Chagar
Bazar and Tell Brak in Syria, and at Atchana in the plain of Antioch.

Iran, Anatolia and Palestine

For some time the prehistoric archaeology of Iran and Transcaspia was
based on the work of Jacques de Morgan at Susa and Pumpelly at
Anau. In the period under review our knowledge of Middle Eastern
prehistory was enormously increased by excavations at sites such as
Tepe Hissar, Shah Tepe, Turang Tepe, Tepe Giyan and Tepe Sialk.
Of these excavations Tepe Sialk was the most important providing, as it
did, a fine stratigraphical sequence. Sialk is near Kashan and was

100 The 'Flood pit' at Ur, so-called because Woolley postulated a connection between the deepest water-laid deposit and the Biblical Flood.

excavated in 1933, 1934 and 1937 by Roman Ghirshman and was fully published in his *Fouilles de Sialk* (vol. I 1938; vol. II 1941). Of the four successive periods which he distinguished, Sialk I is the most interesting: characterized by *pisé* houses with contracted burials under the houses, their artifacts were sling stones, stone maces, stone axes and adzes, as well as pins and needles of hammered copper. The Sialk I peasants bred sheep and cattle and may have grown cereals: they were also hunters and collectors and perhaps to be seen as transitional between food-gathering Mesolithic folk and the food-producing chalcolithic cultures of the Near and Middle East. Ghirshman calculated the date of Sialk I on the basis of the accumulated debris. He allowed seventy-five years for each occupation level and gave a date of 4300 ± 200 BC for the first occupation of the site.

The remarkable work of Sir Aurel Stein (1862–1943) did much during this period to illuminate archaeology in India, Iran and Central Asia. A Hungarian who eventually became a naturalized British citizen, he worked first in the Indian educational service and then in the Archaeological Service of India. He was an indefatigable traveller and conducted four expeditions to Central Asia (1900–1, 1906–8, 1913–16, and 1930). The list of his published works indicates the breadth and extent of his researches: *Ancient Khotan* (1907), *Serindra* (1921), *The Thousand Buddhas* (1921), *Innermost Asia* (1928), *Archaeological Reconnaissances in N.W. India and S.E. Iran* (1937) and *Old Routes of Western Iran* (1940). Among his most famous discoveries was that of manuscripts in Turkestan, dating from the early centuries AD, written in the Tokharian language, a member of the Indo-European language family, which became extinct.

Hrozny's initial work on the translation of the Hittite documents was followed up by a team of workers, and soon the Boghazköy correspondence became a part of our general knowledge of the most ancient Near East. Other sites in Anatolia were excavated. An expedition of the Liverpool University Institute of Archaeology started work in Anatolia in 1907 under John Garstang, who continued there for over 40 years. Our knowledge of the Hittites from new excavations and from the reading of the Boghazköy tablets is summarized in A. E. Cowley's *The Hittites* (1920), G. Contenau's *Éléments de Bibliographie Hittite* (1922) and Garstang's *Hittites* (1929).

Forty years after Dörpfeld had brought to an end Schliemann's excavations at Troy, a new campaign of fieldwork was mounted there 101 by the University of Cincinnati under the general direction of Professor W. T. Semple. The field director was Carl W. Blegen, who conducted seven seasons between 1932 and 1938. The full results were published by Blegen and his associates in *Troy: Excavations Conducted by the University of Cincinnati 1932–38* (4 vols. 1950–58); a short summary by Blegen himself, *Troy and the Trojans*, came out in 1963. The object of this operation was to examine new areas, check the earlier stratigraphy, the chronology and Dörpfeld's identification of Troy VI (which he dated from 1500 to 1000 BC) as the Homeric city. Dörpfeld's chronology and the identification of Troy VI with the Troy of Homer had been criticized by Åberg in his *Bronzezeitliche und Früheisenzeitliche Chronologie* (1930–35).

Troy I was revealed by the Cincinnati excavations as a little township which Blegen dates to 3000 to 2500 BC. Troy II, which according to Blegen was to play a great part in the development of European metallurgy, is dated between 2500 and 2200 BC. Troy VI was a city destroyed by an earthquake. Troy VIIa is suggested as the Homeric city and dated by imports from Mycenae to the early twelfth and late thirteenth centuries BC. Blegen in 1963 gave his revised dates as 1300 to 1260 BC.

The evidence from Troy was supplemented by excavations at Kum Tepe, Yortan and at Thermi in Lesbos where Miss Winifred Lamb, as she described in her *Excavations at Thermi in Lesbos* (1928), found a succession of five superimposed townships, the first four contemporary with Troy I.

Excavations in central and eastern Anatolia began to reveal pre-Hittite civilizations and cultures comparable with those known from the early levels of Troy and Thermi. In 1926 de Genouillac published the Anatolian prehistoric painted pottery in the Louvre in his *Céramique Cappadocienne*. What was needed was some major excavation that would relate the painted wares to the Hittites and

provide a complete sequence of Central Anatolian prehistory. This was the aim of the Oriental Institute of the University of Chicago, when, in the 1920s, they planned a full investigation of the Hittite civilization and its precursors. In 1926, in one season of exploration, Von der Osten found over three hundred new sites in Anatolia of which the most promising was Alishar Hüyük, a mound over one hundred feet (thirty metres) high, which was excavated by him and E. F. Schmidt between 1927 and 1932.

This enterprise was a complete excavation carried out with great efficiency and it constitutes one of the most important contributions to archaeological scholarship in the twentieth century, as can be seen by studying E. F. Schmidt, *Anatolia through the Ages: Discoveries at the Alishar Mound 1927–29* and Von der Osten and Schmidt, *The Alishar Hüyük Excavations 1927–32* (1930–37).

Further detailed knowledge of the Anatolian sequence established at Alishar Hüyük was produced by the excavations of Dr Hamit Zubeyr Kosay, Director of Museums and Antiquities in Turkey at Ahlatlibel and Alaca Hüyük. A preliminary survey of remains in the Cilician plain by Gjerstad was followed in 1936–37 by the Neilson Expedition under Garstang, who then carried out many seasons' work in the Mersin tell. Here M. C. Burkitt studied the early Neolithic industry, claiming it as the earliest post-Palaeolithic culture in the Near East and dating it to 5500 BC.

101 Wilhelm Dörpfeld, Schliemann's successor at Troy, flanked by Professor W. T. Semple, who led a new campaign of fieldwork at the site from 1932 to 1938, and by Mrs Semple.

In Palestine, Megiddo, which had been first excavated by the Germans under Schumacher in 1903–5, was the site of large-scale excavations by the Oriental Institute of Chicago from 1925 onwards. The site of Ras Shamra (ancient Ugarit) was discovered almost by chance in 1929, and excavated for the next ten years until the war by Claude Schaeffer. The excavations revealed a long succession of cultures, from a Neolithic comparable with that of Mersin to a second-millennium city mentioned as Ugarit in the Tell el-Amarna letters, in Hittite correspondence and in Egyptian inscriptions. Ugarit was destroyed by an earthquake in the middle of the fourteenth century BC, was reconstructed and finally destroyed by people from the north and 'the peoples of the sea' at the end of the thirteenth and the beginning of the twelfth centuries BC. It was a kind of international port, and from the fifteenth to the twelfth centuries BC was variously under the influence of the Egyptians, the Hittites and the Mycenaeans.

In a library at Ras Shamra were found hundreds of clay tablets dating from the fifteenth and early fourteenth centuries BC. These bear texts in a cuneiform alphabet identified as Semitic and closely related to biblical Hebrew and Phoenician. The discovery of the Ras Shamra tablets, with the earliest known alphabet of which a full record survives, is one of the major archaeological discoveries. All alphabetic scripts, including Greek, have employed the device invented by the Phoenicians.

Jericho had been first excavated by the Deutsche Orient Gesellschaft in 1907–9: Garstang began work there in 1930, and dug until 1936, revealing a succession from a non-pottery Neolithic, which he dated 4500 to 4000 BC, through several cities, until its destruction by Joshua which he dated at 1400 BC.

Classical and Barbarian Europe

The brilliant discoveries of Arthur Evans at Knossos were followed by excavations in many other Cretan and Aegean sites. The Italians under Halbherr excavated the palace at Phaestos and the great chamber tomb of Hagia Triada which contained over 250 skeletons. The British dug at Gournia and the French at Mallia. The Cretans themselves took part in excavations: Hatzidakis dug a Minoan palace at Tylissos, and Xanthoudides the vaulted tombs of the Mesara. These developments of Cretan archaeology have been well summarized by D. Fimmen in his *Die Kretisch-Mykenische Kultur* (1921) and by J. D. S. Pendlebury in his *Archaeology of Crete* (1939), G. Glotz in his *Civilisation égeenne* (1923) and R. C. Hutchinson in his *Prehistoric Crete* (1962).

In 1914 Ernest Buscher brought the German excavations in Greece to an end for a while: they were resumed from 1925 to 1940. In 1925 there was published in Germany J. D. Beazley's great work on Attic red-figure vase painters based on a study of 10,000 examples: the English edition appeared in 1942, by which time Beazley had studied 5,000 more. In 1927 T. Wiegand resumed work at Pergamon and in 1938 K. Lehmann restarted excavations at Samothrace.

To turn to non-classical Europe, Breuil had already set out his views on the development of Palaeolithic cave art in 1902. His definitive

102 A stele of the god Baal, *c.* 1400 BC, from Ras Shamra, the ancient site of Ugarit excavated by Claude Shaeffer during the 1930s. Ht 1.44 m.

assessment was published in 1934 in his *L'Evolution de l'Art Pariétal dans les Cavernes et Abris Ornées de France*. This scheme was repeated, little changed, in his *Four Hundred Centuries of Cave art* (1934). Meanwhile discoveries of new sites continued: Peche Merle, for example, was found in 1920.

103   The turning point in the study of post-Palaeolithic European prehistory in this century occurred in 1925 when a young Australian, V. Gordon Childe, working as Assistant Librarian in the Royal Anthropological Institute in London, published *The Dawn of European Civilization*. No such book had appeared before in the English language, although Schuchhardt's *Alteuropa* (1921) was a remarkable synthesis along the lines Childe was moving and to which Childe may owe more than is often allowed. The *Dawn* was followed in 1929 by *The Danube in Prehistory*, by which time Childe had been appointed the first holder of the Abercromby Chair of Archaeology in Edinburgh. He held this chair from 1927 until his appointment as Director of the Archaeological Institute of the University of London in 1946, a post which he filled until his retirement in 1957. During thirty years of teaching and research Childe became one of the most important and outstanding archaeological scholars in the world. He was not himself particularly interested in or a good practitioner of excavation, but his knowledge of other people's excavations and the museum collections of Europe and the Near East was vast and encyclopaedic.

No longer, after Childe's writings, could any European country study its past parochially. His pan-European view of man's pre-Roman past set the style for students and scholars up to the Second World War and for twenty years afterwards. Not only did he produce the facts of prehistoric archaeology in ordered and intelligible form, but he interpreted them in two significant ways.

First, he eschewed the old epochal, chest-of-drawers outlook and replaced it by the notion of culture: this was most clearly set out in his preface to *The Danube in Prehistory*. In the second place, he explained the development of European prehistory in two ways, by the diffusion of people and ideas from the Near East and the East Mediterranean (after a brief flirtation with the Egyptocentric hyperdiffusionist doctrines of Elliot Smith he abandoned the Children of the Sun), and by their modification and development in Europe. He saw barbarian Europe irradiated by south-west Asia but itself creating something new and European out of its oriental ancestry.

During the years of his synthetic and interpretative teaching and writing fresh discoveries were continually being made, and Childe kept abreast of all these. He has often been described as a Marxist prehistorian, but far from it, as he strenuously pointed out himself (see *Antiquity*, 1979, 93–95). He did not belong to the Daniel Wilson-Lewis Morgan school of unilateral cultural evolutionists, although he tried this Marxist, psychic-unity-of-man approach to the past in *Scotland before the Scots* (1946). He remained firmly a diffusionist preaching a modified form of the excesses of the Manchester School. What always worried him was the balance in interpretative theory between diffusion and the independent products of diffusion: to what extent the achievement of the barbarians of Neolithic and Bronze Age Europe was

103 Vere Gordon Childe (1892–1957) photographed in Edinburgh in 1927, when he became the first holder of the Abercromby Chair of Archaeology.

the result of what they learned from south-east Europe and the Near East, or was their own inspired interpretation of what they had borrowed from outside. He never answered this question to his own satisfaction, which is understandable, for it is not a question that can be answered in simple historical terms.

Three remarkable Englishmen made outstanding contributions to archaeology in the quarter-century under review in this chapter: let us deal with them in alphabetical order – Crawford, Fox and Wheeler. Two of them wrote their autobiographies and Crawford's *Said and Done* (1955) and Wheeler's *Still Digging* (1955) are important documents, not only for our understanding of these men, but to the development of archaeology in and outside England in the twenties and thirties of this century. Fox did not write a full autobiography, but the essay which was printed at the beginning of the second edition of *The Archaeology of the Cambridge Region* tells us a great deal about him and the evolution of his ideas.

When we add to this brief list of three men the name of Childe who, though an Australian, spent all his working life in Britain, and remember Evans still working in Crete, the discoveries of Howard Carter and Carnarvon in Egypt, Woolley in Mesopotamia, Marshall in India, and Garstang in Anatolia and Palestine, it is only fair to say that this period was that of the domination of archaeology by the British as the second half of the nineteenth century had perhaps been by the Scandinavians and the French.

104 O. G. S. Crawford (1886–1957) setting out on one of his field trips.

104   O. G. S. Crawford (1886–1957) was trained in the Oxford School of Geography under Herbertson and after a brief career in the First World War as a navigator in the Flying Corps, and a longer one as a German prisoner of war, he was made the first archaeology officer of the Ordnance Survey. He saw that the Survey maps produced up-to-date, reliable and accurate archaeological information which made them the cynosure of the world, and he started a series of period maps (of which perhaps the *Map of Roman Britain* is justly the most famous) which put periods in our historical past graphically. His experience as an airman convinced him of the value of air observation and air photography to archaeology. He was not alone in this. The value of air photography to archaeology was appreciated during the First World War by other Englishmen as well as by German and French scholars working in military intelligence. The German Dr Wiegand traced the eastern end of the Roman *limes* to the Dobrudja from air photographs, and was later sent out specially with the German forces in southern Palestine and Sinai to photograph and describe archaeological sites. Léon Rey used air photographs for archaeological purposes in 1915 in Macedonia and Father Antoine Poidebard studied air photographs of the Near East

105 Air view of
Hambledon Hill, Dorset,
from Crawford and
Keiller's *Wessex from the
Air* (1928).

and in 1918 flew across Persia. The Royal Flying Corps took air
photographs of archaeological interest in the Near East and their value
was appreciated by men like Beazeley and Hamshaw Thomas. Colonel
Beazeley read a paper to the Royal Geographical Society in London
entitled 'Surveys in Mesopotamia during the War': it was published in
the *Geographical Journal* for 1920 and laid the foundations of
archaeological air photo interpretation.

O. G. S. Crawford had discussed with Dr Williams-Freeman before
the First World War the value of the air view of the ground: Williams-
Freeman had himself said that 'one ought to be a bird in order to be a
field archaeologist'. Crawford became a bird in the war: as we have
seen, he was a navigator and after the war developed the potentialities
of air photography. His pioneer work with Alexander Keiller was
published in 1928 under the title *Wessex from the Air*: a magnificent 105
work based on the hiring of an aircraft and the taking of three hundred
photographs of archaeological sites in two months.

Major Allen, a freelance flyer with his own aeroplane and using his
own hand-made cameras, inspired by turning over the pages of *Wessex
from the Air* took, in a few seasons' flying, many thousands of air 106

NORTH STOKE. 105.H8. 2.7.38 8.129

106 Cropmarks
photographed from the air
by Major Allen at
Crowmarsh (North
Stoke), Oxfordshire. The
rings represent the
remains of ploughed-out
Bronze Age barrows.

photographs in southern Britain. Père Poidebard worked in the Near East and his *La Trace de Rome dans le Désert de Syrie* (1934), *Un Grand Port Disparu, Tyr* (1939) and (with R. Mouterde) *Le Limes de Chalcis* (1945) are models of archaeological research based on aerial photography.

Crawford was sharply aware of the necessity of interesting the public in archaeology, and his *Man and his Past* (1921) was a pioneer effort to explain the importance of archaeology to the world. In 1927 he founded the journal *Antiquity* (and edited it for thirty years, until his death in 1957), to get the results of archaeology across to the world. Though given a short life by many professional critics, it succeeded beyond all reasonable expectation. The writer of this book is proud and happy to have succeeded Crawford as Editor of that journal which has done so much to make archaeology readable and relevant.

Cyril Fox began his career as a field archaeologist and museum man in the Cambridge region and his book, *The Archaeology of the Cambridge Region* (1923), was a pioneer work in the geographical approach to archaeology. The sub-title of that book is important: it was 'a topographical study of the Bronze, Early Iron, Roman and Anglo-Saxon Ages'. He was indebted in his ideas to the Aberystwyth School of anthropogeographers: the classic paper by Fleure and Whitehouse, 'The Early Valleyward Movement of Population in Southern Britain', was published in *Archaeologia Cambrensis* in 1916, and Crawford's *Man and his Past* developed the possibilities and techniques of the geographical approach to prehistory and early history. What Fox did was to apply the general notions of Crawford (and, before Crawford, the Herbertson School, the Fleure School and the work of Germans like Gradmann) to a small region – a region extending twenty to twenty-five miles around Cambridge. Here he studied prehistoric distributions against the background of natural vegetation: and of course in relation to the prehistoric and not the present vegetation cover.

Fox then applied his geographical interpretation of the past to the study of archaeology in general, and this was perhaps best seen in his book *The Personality of Britain* (1932), which had a tremendous effect on archaeologists everywhere. Professor E. G. R. Taylor described the effect of this publication as 'a minor earthquake corresponding to number 6 on the Rossi-Forel scale', which by definition means 'General awakening of those asleep. General ringing of bells . . . some startled persons leave their dwellings.'

Certainly some archaeologists comfortably installed in their dwellings were startled to learn through Fox and Crawford of a new environmental and ecological approach to their subject. A modern generation, which in England properly gives credit to men like Grahame Clark and Eric Higgs for stressing the importance of ecofacts – non-artifactual material remains with cultural relevance – will not forget that the environmental approach to prehistory of the 'thirties, 'forties and 'fifties is grounded in the work of Fox, Fleure and Crawford in the 'twenties.

The history of archaeology is difficult to write when one is trying to work out, for example, what actually happened in European thinking between Mercati, Goguet and the opening of the Copenhagen Museum in 1819. For example, in writing an account of the development of the three-age technical model hardly anyone gives any credit to the early eighteenth-century historian Johann von Eckart who set out the three-age system as a historical concept as clearly as did Vedel-Simonsen. This is perhaps because no one paid attention to what he said, as R. J. Sharer and Wendy Ashmore point out in their *Fundamentals of Archaeology* (1979, 52).

It seems even as difficult, if not more so, when one is writing about people one knows and with whom one has discussed the evolution of their ideas. It is obvious to any historian of archaeology and ideas that Cyril Fox's views were based on Halford Mackinder's *Britain and the British Seas* and the writings of Vidal de la Blache, the French human geographer who invented the idea of geographical personality. I knew Fox well and often discussed with him the origin and development of his geographical ideas. He had never heard of, let alone read any of the works of, either Mackinder or Vidal de la Blache! Here we may have in the realm of archaeological ideas, as we now seem to be insisting on in the realm of archaeological interpretation, independent evolution and parallel development.

The third Englishman was R. E. M. Wheeler (Sir Mortimer   108
Wheeler as he was known to the world after his knighthood in 1952). Born in 1890, he was anxious at one stage to become an artist but chose instead to pursue his academic interests and read classics in University

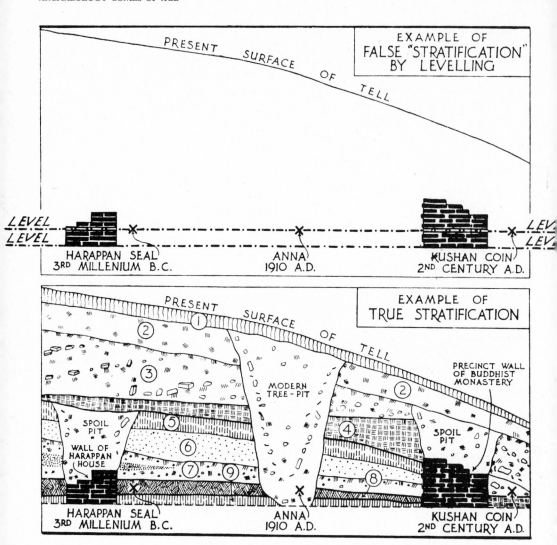

107 Modelling himself on Pitt-Rivers, Sir Mortimer Wheeler raised the science of excavation to a new standard of professionalism. His demonstration, illustrated here, of the difference between false and true stratification became a classic.

College London under, among others, A. E. Housman; he turned to archaeology with great success and to the lasting benefit of generations of archaeologists, particularly in Britain and India. He was in the main heroic tradition of field archaeologists and excavators – perhaps the last in a long line beginning with Layard and Mariette and continuing with Schliemann, Petrie, Pitt-Rivers, Arthur Evans and Woolley.

At an early age he found himself Director of the National Museum of Wales and his second book, *Prehistoric and Roman Wales* (1925), is a lively and forward-looking synthesis. His first excavations were in Roman sites such as Lydney, Caerleon, Caernarvon and Verulamium, but his most famous and most publicly known excavation was that of the Iron Age hillfort of Maiden Castle in Dorset. He followed this with extensive fieldwork and selected excavations in the hillforts of northern France. *Maiden Castle*, published in 1943, is one of the most clear demonstrations of the Wheeler method and will long be a classic of archaeological literature. Wheeler established a new system and technique of excavation, modelling himself, as he often said, on the then forgotten or ill-appreciated work of Pitt-Rivers. What the French call 'la méthode Wheeler' consists essentially of broad sectioning, excavation by squares or quadrants with key separating baulks, the rigorous recording of everything, accurate and detailed survey and full publication as soon as possible.

He moved from Cardiff to be Director of the London Museum and, with his wife Tessa Verney Wheeler, founded the Institute of Archaeology in the University of London. His own account of his life in *Still Digging* should be supplemented by the obituary notices by Stuart Piggott in the *Transactions of the Royal Society* (1977, 623–42) and by Jacquetta Hawkes in the *Proceedings of the British Academy* (1977, 483–507).

In 1943 Wheeler was appointed Director-General of Antiquities in India, and while his work in India and later properly belongs to the next chapter, it seems wrong to split up the career of a great archaeologist. He brought to the Indian subcontinent the scientific methods of archaeological survey and excavation which he had developed in Britain between the two world wars and a new inspiration to the study

109–11

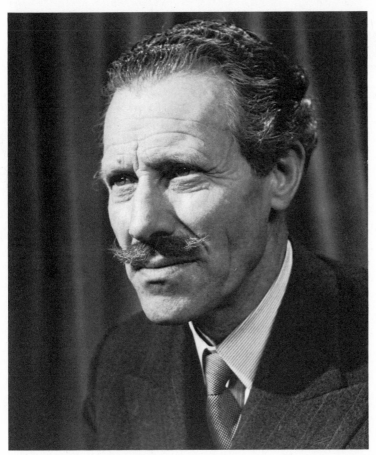

108 Sir Mortimer Wheeler (1890–1976). A photograph of him taken during one of his appearances in the BBC television programme *Animal, Vegetable, Mineral?* in 1954.

of ancient India, coupled with a genius for administration and a capacity for sustained and hard work which often, to the surprise of his Indian colleagues and students, paid scant attention to the rigours of the climate. He revitalized Indian archaeology, trained archaeologists and himself carried out a series of excavations of the greatest importance, first in the Indian cities of Mohenjo-daro and Harappa, where he was able to establish the true nature of these prehistoric cities, secondly at sites like Taxila and Chandragupta where the gap between Indian prehistory and its ancient history could be bridged and the relations established of these cities with the east and the west in Graeco-Roman times. Thirdly we remember his work at a site like the Indo-Roman trading station of Arikamedu, on the east coast near Pondicherry, which he discovered. By its excavation he was able to date some of the hitherto undated Indian prehistoric pottery and so date the Indian megalithic structures in the Deccan to the immediately pre-Christian centuries.

But although Wheeler's achievement in India was outstanding through excavation and direct research, his contribution to the archaeology of the subcontinent was also outstanding through his training of Indian archaeologists and the establishment in Asia of a school of highly efficient fieldworkers and museum men. He started the journal *Ancient India*, in itself a remarkable achievement in wartime in a country not noted for excellence in printing. There are few archaeologists over forty practising in India or Pakistan today who do not gladly recognize Wheeler as their *guru*. It is fascinating how the

109–111 Wheeler transformed Indian archaeology during his time as Director-General of Antiquities (1943–47). He introduced the disciplined grid-square method of excavation to the subcontinent (*opposite, above*, at Arikamedu, South India), and discovered massive ramparts at Harappa (*left*), twin capital city of the Indus civilization with Mohenjo-daro, where the bronze 'dancing girl' (*opposite, below*) was found.

charisma of one man could revolutionize the archaeology of a subcontinent: but, of course, as with the Wheelerian revolution in British field archaeology in the 'twenties and 'thirties, it was charisma masking and backed by rigorous methods, very hard work and inflexible purpose.

When Wheeler left India, and after partition, there survived two excellent archaeological departments: and excavation and research continue apace. One of the most interesting new sites was that dug in the late 'fifties and early 'sixties by Shri S. R. Rao at Lothal in Gujerat. This site was shown to be an Indus Valley town with the remains of a dock with an inlet channel and an eighty-foot (twenty-four-metre) long platform for loading and unloading merchandise; the port dated from the early to mature Harappan phase and yielded a contemporary Persian Gulf seal.

After his return to England Wheeler became Secretary of the British Academy and also resumed his British excavations by digging the hillfort of Stanwick in North Yorkshire. He regarded his work in India as his greatest achievement but it was only one, albeit a very important one, of many remarkable episodes in the career of a man who must without any doubt be hailed as one of the very great figures in the history of archaeology. His Indian achievements must be read in the context of what had gone on there in archaeology before he arrived, briefly discussed in the next section.

It has been said that Wheeler made no contribution to the theory of archaeology. To my mind the best theoretical position to adopt in archaeology is to use all possible means to make the fullest reconstruction of the past from the surviving material remains. He was always insistent on the purpose of archaeology. His words, oft-quoted, that 'the archaeologist is not digging up things, he is digging up people', is a statement of theory which not all archaeologists practise. Let us conclude this section with two other of his oft-quoted sentences: 'In a simple direct sense, archaeology is a science that must be lived, must be "seasoned with humanity".' 'Dead archaeology is the driest dust that blows.'

India and China

In 1913 Barrett began his book on *The Antiquities of India* with the Rigveda hymns and said, 'In India there is no twilight before the dark.' Writing the chapter on the ancient monuments of India in the first volume of *The Cambridge History of India*, published in 1922, Sir John Marshall said, 'It is the misfortune of Indian history that its earliest and most obscure pages derive little light from contemporary antiquities'; his account of the pre-Vedic antiquities of India contained no more than brief and fleeting references to the palaeoliths of the Deccan, the megaliths of southern India and various hoards of copper objects from the Ganges.

Just two years later, Marshall was announcing in *The Illustrated London News* the excavations of the prehistoric cities of Harappa and Mohenjo-daro in what is now Pakistan and comparing their discovery, aptly, with Schliemann's discovery of Tiryns and Mycenae. Harappa lies three hundred miles north-west of Delhi, close to the railway line from Lahore to Multan, which for about a hundred miles has its track built up by ballast consisting of bricks from the prehistoric city itself. In 1921 Daya Ram Sahni dug at Harappa and established the prehistoric nature of the site. These excavations were continued in 1923–25 by Sahni and in 1926–34 by M. S. Vats, whose full publication of the site appeared in 1940.

At the same time as Sahni was digging at Harappa, R. D. Banerji began work at Mohenjo-daro – 'the place of the dead', four hundred miles to the south and about one hundred and forty north-east of Karachi. His excavations in 1921–22 cut through buildings of the historic Indian period and then came to levels which contained seals like those found at Harappa. These excavations were continued by Vats, Dikshit, Marshall, Hargreaves, Sahni and Mackay. The results of ten years' excavations were published by Marshall in his three-volume work *Mohenjo-daro and the Indus Civilisation* (1931) and by Mackay in *Further Excavations at Mohenjo-daro* (1938).

While the major excavations at Harappa and Mohenjo-daro were being carried on, Majumdar in Sind and Hargreaves and Stein in Baluchistan were finding other sites of what was then being called the Indus or Harappan civilization. Some of these sites were small towns like Chanhu-daro, others villages. Other discoveries extended the geographical distribution of this ancient prehistoric civilization north-east to the Siwalik hills and south to the Gulf of Cambay, an area larger than that of the ancient civilizations of Egypt and Mesopotamia.

The discovery of the Indus civilization gave an entirely new perspective to the pattern of the past. Archaeology had in the previous fifty years revealed the prehistoric civilizations that lay behind the historic civilizations of Greece, Rome, Assyria and Egypt, and the Minoans, Mycenaeans, Hittites and Sumerians were now a commonplace of early historical thinking, but these were discoveries all made within the East Mediterranean and south-west Asia. The Indus civilization was two thousand miles away from Mesopotamia – with its grid-iron street plans, its skilled craftsmanship in metalworking, achievements in art like the dancer and the bearded priest: it added something very new, not only geographically but culturally, to the early history of civilization.

So did discoveries in China. The prehistoric past of China was for long regarded in the same way as that of India. In the early 1920s, although the antiquity and importance of early Chinese civilization was appreciated, it was not thought that China had been occupied by man in the prehistoric past. In his *Prehistoric Man* Jacques de Morgan said: 'Chinese civilization dates from the seventh or eighth centuries BC: we are completely ignorant of its prehistory.'

This ignorance was corrected first by the initiative and interest of J. Gunnar Andersson, a Swedish geologist who went to China in 1914 as an adviser on coal and oil resources. In 1921 he discovered a Neolithic dwelling cave at Yang Shao Tsun in Honan. He published a preliminary account in *An Early Chinese Culture* (1923), which defined what has since been known as the Yangshao culture. Pre-Yangshao Neolithic cultures were found in China in the next ten years.

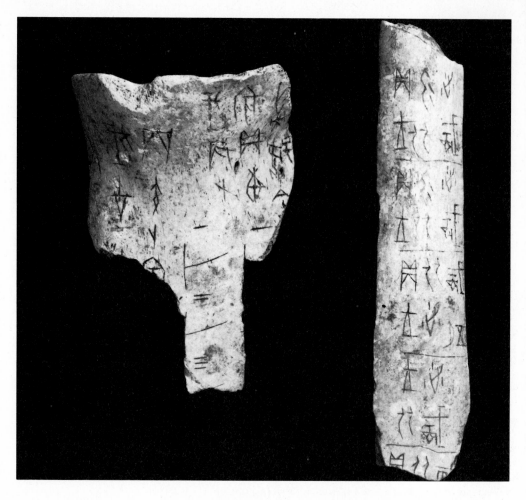

112 Two oracle bones of the Shang dynasty, China.

112

Towards the end of the nineteenth century farmers dug up near Anyang in the north of Honan province curious bits of bone, some of which were decorated with characters. In this century they were studied and correctly diagnosed as oracle bones. In 1928 the National Research Institute of History and Philology of Academia Sinica, together with the Smithsonian Institution, began excavating the site at Anyang. The excavations were directed by Drs Li Chi and Liang Ssu-yung and have been published in the four volumes of their *Preliminary Reports on Excavations at Anyang* (1929–33). They revealed the old city of Anyang as the capital of the Shang dynasty in the middle of the second millennium BC; the centre of an urban civilization making fine objects of bronze and carvings in bone, stone and ivory. Here were all the elements of an historic ancient Chinese civilization, but back in the second millennium.

China and India now were revealed by archaeology to have prehistoric civilizations. Their antiquity and their relationship to the ancient prehistoric civilizations of the ancient Near East were to exercise the minds of scholars for many years – and indeed still do.

While the results of the excavations of Marshall and his assistants and colleagues were exciting, their methods have aroused much critical comment. Mackay brought to the Indus excavations his training in Egypt and Mesopotamia, and as John Marshall himself admits, one of the main reasons why he was made Director-General of Archaeology in India was that he might introduce into that subcontinent the scientific methods of digging he had learnt in Greece. Yet the understanding of stratigraphy in archaeological sites as demonstrated by Dörpfeld at Troy, Schmidt at Anau, Petrie in Egypt and Palestine, and Pitt-Rivers in England had not yet penetrated to Marshall and Mackay. Their so-called stratigraphy of the Indus Valley sites depended, not on the recognition and detailed tracing of occupation levels, but on levelling every object found and tying it in at long range with the sea-level at Karachi, a system which Wheeler has described as 'incredible': and so it was for the twenties of the twentieth century. It is a good example of archaeologists not looking back at the history of their subject: had Marshall and Mackay never heard of Worsaae, Fiorelli and Pitt-Rivers, not to mention Thomas Jefferson? Apparently not.

American Archaeology

Willey and Sabloff in their *A History of American Archaeology* (1974, second edition 1980), and following up an original suggestion by D. W. Schwartz, proposed to distinguish four periods in the development of archaeology in America, as follows:

1. the *speculative* period from 1492 to 1840, and they use the phrase in the sense that speculation is forming conjectures regarding anything without experiment;
2. the *classificatory-descriptive* period from 1840 to 1914, and which saw the first professionalism in American archaeology;
3. the *classificatory-historical* period from 1914 to 1960; and
4. the *explanatory* period from 1960 onwards.

Our account of American archaeology in this chapter falls right in their classificatory-historical period, and its beginning coincides with the real stratigraphical revolution in American field methods. This revolution began with the work of Manuel Gamio, a student of Franz Boas, who, together with A. M. Tozzer of Harvard, encouraged him to conduct stratigraphical excavations in the valley of Mexico, with the express purpose of establishing objectively the sequence of Mexican pre-Columbian cultures. This Gamio did by sinking a seven-metre test pit into the refuse of the site of Atzcapotzalco. To quote Willey and Sabloff: 'With Gamio's single pit, Middle American archaeologists began to appreciate time, depth, and better yet, to realize that something could be done about it.' Gamio's work was followed by that of Nels C. Nelson in New Mexico in 1914 and onwards and then by the work of A. V. Kidder, a contemporary of Nelson's at Harvard. Kidder had been trained by Tozzer at Harvard and by the American Egyptologist G. A. Reisner. His work at Pecos in the Upper Pecos Valley of New Mexico was one of the largest investigations of its time in

North America and is of key importance in the development of American archaeological method.

Kidder's beginnings in archaeology in the field started when in 1907 Edgar L. Hewett – who must have been a kind of Mortimer Wheeler character – took him and two other Harvard students to the top of a mesa in the Four Corners area of south-west USA and showed them an area of several hundred square miles: to Kidder, as he said afterwards, 'it seemed about half the world'. Hewett pointed out features of archaeological interest in the landscape and said crisply: 'I want you boys to make an archaeological survey of this country. I'll be back in six weeks. You'd better get some horses.'

113 Kidder chose Pecos because it had still been occupied at the time of the Spanish colonization in the sixteenth century. His excavations, which lasted from 1915 to 1929, provided the basis for the first chronological statement of the pre-Spanish occupation of the American south-west. Kidder organized a conference in Pecos in 1927 of archaeologists from all over America: they pooled their experiences and researches and set out a cultural and chronological scheme which still serves as the basis for all modern work in this area. Kidder's *An Introduction to the Study of South-Western Archaeology* was first published in 1924 (new edition 1962, with an introductory essay, 'Southwestern archaeology today', by Irving Rouse): it is a classic in the history of American archaeology, and Kidder is clearly one of the very great figures in the development of modern American archaeology. In 1929 he became Director of Historical Research for the Carnegie Institution of Washington and in this position was able to plan and organize major archaeological research projects. He concentrated on the Maya, demanding both the study of the existing Maya as well as the excavation of sites to chronicle their ancient history. Sylvanus G. Morley had published in 1915 his fundamental *Introduction to the Study of Maya Hieroglyphs*. Three of the Carnegie major excavations were at Uaxactún in the rain forest of Guatemala, Chichén Itzá in arid Yucatan, and Kaminaljuyu (the Maya for 'hills of the dead') in the Guatemalan highlands.

113 Cross-section by A. V. Kidder of stratified walls and floors at Pecos, New Mexico, from his seminal work, *An Introduction to the Study of South-Western Archaeology* (1924). The terms 'Glaze 1, 2, 3' etc. refer to styles of pottery.

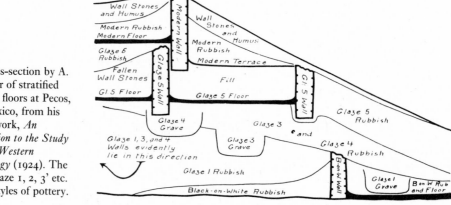

In his *The Pottery of Pecos* (1931, 6–7), Kidder sets out his considered scheme for research in a particular area; here, in his own words, is his plan:

1 Preliminary survey of remains under consideration;
2 Selection of criteria for ranking these remains in chronological order;
3 Comparative study of the manifestations of the criteria to arrive at a tentative chronological ranking of the sites containing them;
4 Search for and excavation of sites in which materials may be found in stratigraphic relationship in order to check up on the tentative ranking and also to obtain a large number of specimens for morphological and genetic studies;
5 A more thorough resurvey of the area in the light of the fuller knowledge now at hand in order definitely to rank all sites and, if necessary, to select for excavation new sites which may be expected to elucidate problems raised during the course of the research.

Here was a blueprint for archaeological research that seems to us, fifty years later, still impeccable and inspiring. Although what Kidder wanted was going on in certain parts of Europe (only in limited areas), no one to the best of my knowledge spelt it out so clearly as did Kidder. But of course Cyril Fox in the Cambridge Region of eastern Britain was doing precisely what Kidder demanded.

There was during this period a dispute among American archaeologists as to what was the nature of archaeological stratigraphy. Many people insisted that it was a matter of measurement; others like Kidder that it was the appreciation of natural, real stratigraphy – the appreciation of what the levels showed in relation to history. For a most interesting account of the problems of metrical and natural stratigraphy it is recommended that you should read Willey and Sabloff, *A History of American Archaeology* (second edition 1980, 52ff.). This is the same fundamental problem that was met in India when Wheeler began to examine the results of his predecessors. The answer is a simple one. Metrical stratigraphy is recording: the appreciation of natural, or rather, humanly caused stratigraphy is archaeological interpretation.

In 1929 the famous aviator Colonel Charles A. Lindbergh began to appreciate the value of aerial photography for archaeology. He first photographed Pueblo sites in the American south-west. Professor Edgar L. Hewett described the Lindbergh photographs as the first successful application of aerial photography to archaeology in America. Alfred Kidder was quick to realize their value. 'Some of the photographs taken by Colonel and Mrs. Lindbergh', he said, 'show clearly the relation that existed in ancient times between water supply, land available for farming and easily defensible house sites.'

Later the same year the Lindberghs photographed the Mayan hinterland of Belize in what was called the Pan American Airways-Carnegie Institute Archaeological flights, which has been described as 'the first major exclusively archaeological enterprise of its kind in the Western Hemisphere' (Leo Deuel, *Flights into Yesterday*, 1969, 213).

5
New and Not-so-new Archaeology (1939–1980)

The Second World War broke out within a few weeks of one of the most sensational discoveries of modern archaeology – the finding of the
114
VI
Sutton Hoo Ship Burial in Suffolk with its remarkable collection of treasures. This cenotaph (no body has been identified) may have been that of the sixth-century King Redwald (599–635). Crawford devoted a whole issue of *Antiquity* to it and now it is being fully published by Rupert Bruce Mitford in three volumes.

For a while there was what has often been described as a phoney war and then, with the German invasion of Holland, Belgium and France, and after Dunkirk the real fears of an invasion in Britain, it looked to many as though Western European civilization and free unfettered liberal thinking about history and prehistory would be engulfed by the Nazi regime with its racist doctrines and its propagation of a Nordic-Aryan mythology.

Certainly a man like Gordon Childe, as well as many another, felt this was inevitable. In 1917 he had described the first Great World War as one 'which I believe to be destructive to civilization and true liberty'. Looking back in 1957 on the years of the second Great World War he said he thought of it as 'a bottomless cleft in which all traditions of culture were finally engulfed'. He had written to his great friend Robert Braidwood in 1945, at the end of the war, that 'the Old World outside the USSR is done for'.

But he was, fortunately for all of us, in and out of the USSR, wrong. His *Prehistoric Communities of the British Isles* came out in 1940 – then the best and most up-to-date survey of British prehistory. He now sat down to write *What Happened in History*, published in 1942: it was a primer for the public, though he wondered if ever there would be a public allowed to read impartial history and prehistory. He felt, as he wrote, that 'European Civilization – Capitalist and Socialist alike – was irrevocably heading for a Dark Age.'

The overall interpretation of history through archaeology set out in *What Happened in History* was a simple one. Man the Palaeolithic savage had developed agriculture once and once only in the area of south-west Asia called, by Breasted, the Fertile Crescent: this was the Neolithic Revolution which happened on the horns of the crescent, in Egypt and Mesopotamia. Then two Neolithic barbarian communities, in contact with each other, developed city life and literacy: this was the Urban Revolution. The literate cities of the Near East eventually gave

rise to the classical historical civilization of Greece and Rome, as also
the civilizations of the Indus Valley and China. Europe in the first and
second pre-Roman millennia was a pale reflection of the most ancient
Near East. All new ideas and inventions were diffused from the Near
East by invasions, trade and the spread of ideas.

I was the Local Secretary of Section H of the British Association for
the Advancement of Science at its meeting in Cambridge in 1938, when
Childe was its President. We met several times and discussed his
Presidential Address, which was called 'The Orient and Europe': he
had, of course, taken this title from Montelius and deliberately so. We
discussed it again after the war, a war that had not destroyed Western
civilization, and he repeated that the study of Europe in the Neolithic,
Bronze and Iron Ages was the story of 'the irradiation of European
barbarism by oriental civilization'.

This was in 1946: ten years later, when he came to write *The Dawn of
European Society*, he was changing his views. In *The Aryans* (1926), a
book which he wisely wished to forget in later life, he had emphasized
the native European contribution to European achievement, and in due

114 The richest cenotaph
ever discovered on British
soil: the Sutton Hoo Ship
Burial, seen here during
excavation in 1939.

115 Discovered by schoolboys in 1940, the cave of Lascaux in Dordogne has some of the most superb examples of Palaeolithic art ever found. Here a cow, painted in black and red wash, leaps over ponies, sketched predominantly in black.

course he began to appreciate, as many archaeologists did at the time, the message in Christopher Hawkes's *Prehistoric Foundations of Europe* (1940), namely, that though in Europe as elsewhere, irradiation from another source was important, it was not the only factor. Since then C14 dates have established early dates for many European cultural achievements previously thought to be irradiations from the most ancient East, and since the demonstration by Colin Renfrew, John Coles and others that C14 dating proves the beginnings of metallurgy and megalith building in Europe before any irradiation from the Aegean or the ancient East, we have moved into a post-Childe phase of archaeology.

Actually, in 1940, when Childe was writing *What Happened in History*, two exciting and important events occurred. On 12 September in that year, at the height of the Battle of Britain, four schoolboys discovered the painted and engraved Palaeolithic cave of Lascaux near Montignac in Dordogne: it has been called the number two to Altamira. In many ways, to my idea, it is the most superb and number one example of Upper Palaeolithic art. It is a European achievement: here in pre-Neolithic times was no irradiation from the Near East. The art of the Upper Palaeolithic in the caves of southern France or Cantabria remains an extraordinary European achievement. Those who think about the origins of art or the development of man's cultural life are bound to ask why these great works of art were produced, for the most part, in a limited area of south-west Europe.

The second question which all historians of archaeology must ask themselves is this. We now know of some two hundred painted and engraved caves dating from 20,000 to 8000 BC: they contain the representations of some two thousand animals. What proportion does this represent of the total artistic achievement of Upper Palaeolithic man? Fifty to a hundred years from now a future historian of archaeology may be recording a fresh series of astonishing discoveries: the new Gallery at Niaux, found as recently as 1970, is a dramatic demonstration of the incompleteness of our knowledge of Upper Palaeolithic art.

We have as yet no idea, and in my view never will have any idea, of the raison-d'être of this earliest and astonishingly naturalistic and moving art of our early ancestors. Sympathetic magic as Breuil said, an art gallery as others have supposed, a record of killed animals (a sort of Palaeolithic game book) as has also been suggested, or a complete symbolic representation of male and female symbols as A. Leroi Gourhan has, unconvincingly, argued – Upper Palaeolithic art points clearly to what should be a dictum in prehistoric archaeology: often alas, we do not know the answers.

But also in 1940, when Lascaux was discovered, Simpson was sending up his balloons in New York and discovering the existence of C14 as well as C12, and from his observations began the development of C14 dating, properly associated with Willard F. Libby of Chicago. 117

Science in Archaeology

Nothing has been more important to archaeology in the period from 1939 to the present day than the discovery of C14 or radiocarbon dating, announced by Libby in 1949. The antiquarian and geological revolutions of the early nineteenth century brought archaeology into existence: the radiocarbon dating revolution of the fifties and sixties of the twentieth century brought archaeological dating into a new phase of certainty. This new and revolutionary dating technique is based on the fact that all living matter contains minute traces of C14, a radioactive isotope of carbon. It is formed at high altitudes by the action of neutrons in atmospheric nitrogen, quickly becomes oxidized to carbon dioxide and ultimately mixed with the non-radioactive carbon dioxide of the atmosphere; it is therefore taken up by all plants in a fixed proportion to that of ordinary carbon (an atom of C14 for every million million atoms of the non-radioactive C12). When an organism dies, this proportion is no longer maintained: the radioactive C14 diminishes at a known rate. The Libby value for the half-life of C14 (when one half of the C14 will have disintegrated) was 5568 ± 30 years and our present instructions are to use this figure, although a new and more accurate value of the half-life appears to be 5730 ± 40 years and dates on the old half-life may be converted to those on the new half-life by multiplying by 103.

There are now well over eighty laboratories in the world making radiocarbon determinations and about 50,000 dates have been determined. The radiocarbon laboratories report their dates in years bp (before the present) and the year 1950 has been arbitrarily adopted to mean 'the present', and should be deducted from all bp dates to give ad/bc dates.

The practical limits of C14 dating were thought some years ago to have been reached at between 40,000 and 50,000 years ago; but now it seems likely that the technique can be extended much further backwards to as early as 80,000 years ago. The C14 dates determined in the 1950s and early 1960s caused considerable confusion among archaeologists. They proposed a much earlier chronology for barbarian Europe than had been set out by the cross-dating methods of Montelius, Childe and others. Some, like Milojčič, rejected them *in toto*; others were cautious, particularly in accepting early dates for the megalithic monuments of Malta and Brittany which made them earlier than the pyramids of Egypt and the ziggurats of Mesopotamia – indeed the earliest architecture in the world. Then the C14 dates for early protohistoric Egypt did not appear to agree with the dates produced by the accepted Egyptian chronology based on written records. As the Egyptian written records were apparently unassailable, it seemed cautious and right to suppose there was something wrong with C14 dating.

By a strange chance dendrochronology, which no one had very seriously considered in the second quarter of the twentieth century, was applied to checking C14 dates. The tree-ring chronology provided by *Pinus aristata*, the bristle-cone pine growing in eastern California, went back to 7,000 years ago and showed that the years produced by C14 determination were not, as had been thought, calendar years. It was suggested that the C14 in the earth's atmosphere was not constant, possibly due to changes in the earth's magnetic field. The variation between C14 years and calendar years has been worked out in a number of laboratories. No agreed calibration curve has yet been published, but the one reproduced here gives a generally accepted picture of the problem. It is now widely accepted practice that C14 dates which are in radiocarbon years should be cited as bp, ad, and bc; and that calibrated dates which are in calendar years should be cited as BP, AD and BC.

116 A generally accepted calibration curve for the conversion of C14 dates (denoted bp or 'before the present') to true calendar dates (BP), using the tree-ring chronology. It will be seen that C14 dates become increasingly too young before about 2400 BP.

117 (*Opposite*) Professor W. F. Libby (1908–80) in his geochronological laboratories at the University of California, Los Angeles.

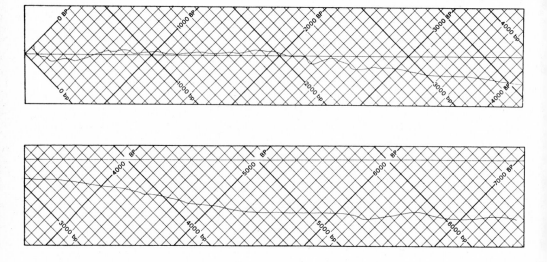

The technique of dating by thermoluminescence (TL) is almost as startling and novel as C14 and so is potassium-argon dating. TL dating is based on the emission of light, over and above ordinary red-hot glow, when a substance is heated, and this light represents the release of energy which has been stored as trapped electrons in the crystal lattice of the minerals. In most pottery there are mineral constituents which have the property of accumulating thermoluminescence. This dating technique has been developed in Oxford in the Research Laboratory for Archaeology and the History of Art and in the MASCA unit of the University Museum, Philadelphia and elsewhere. The journal *Archaeometry*, which is the Bulletin of the Oxford Research Laboratory, is a forum for discussion of thermoluminescence and other archaeometric matters.

Potassium-argon dating was developed at Berkeley, California, by Drs Evernden and Curtis and was designed to ascertain the age of volcanic materials and other igneous rocks, and of tektites, and hence, by association, the age of deposits in which they occur: it is based on the fact that potassium (K40) decays to argon (Ar40) at a constant rate.

These techniques, and many others, are fully described by Kenneth Oakley in his *Frameworks for Dating Fossil Man* (second edition 1970): and also in Don Brothwell and Eric Higgs (eds), *Science in Archaeology: a survey of progress and research* (second edition 1969) – an invaluable compendium which discusses all the various scientific techniques now used in archaeology, not only for dating but for the discovery of sites (including geophysical methods of prospecting), the geological identification of rocks, and analytical techniques such as electron micro-probing, neutron activation analysis, X-ray fluorescence spectrometry and many another. We recommend to our readers E. Pyddoke (ed.), *The Scientist and Archaeology* (1963), and the very clear and useful summary produced in 1970 by the Council for British Archaeology entitled *Handbook of Scientific Aids and Evidence for Archaeologists*.

In 1955 Carlo Lerici established the Milan Fondazione Politecnico and developed there an interesting technique by which a periscope with a camera which took photographs through 360 degrees was inserted into an unexcavated burial chamber. In 1956 he began using this method in the Etruscan necropolises of Cerveteri and Tarquinia, and his work there and at Vulci exceeded all reasonable expectations. The Lerici Foundation produces a journal called *Prospezioni Archeologiche* which deals with these matters.

Air photography has continued to be increasingly used. Just as the First World War showed archaeologists the potentialities of aerial reconnaissance, so the Second World War trained many archaeologists in air photo interpretation. John Bradford's *Ancient Landscapes: Studies in Field Archaeology* (1960) was based on his work as a military air photo interpreter in the Central Mediterranean. After the war the University of Cambridge created a Department of Aerial Photography, with its own aircraft and pilot and with J. K. St Joseph as its Curator. This department has made remarkable contributions to archaeology not only in Britain but in Ireland, Denmark and France. Insular historians of archaeology, remembering the pioneer achievements of

O. G. S. Crawford, Hamshaw Thomas and Major Allen have sometimes thought of archaeological air photographic reconnaissance as an English activity; we should also remember Colonel Barradez, whose work on the North African Roman *limes* was published in 1949 under the title of *Fossatum Africae: Investigations on the Organization of the Border of the Sahara in the Roman Period,* and the work of Roger Agache in the north of France. His *Détection aérienne de vestiges protohistoriques, Gallo-Romaines et Médiévaux* (1970) is as classic a work as *Fossatum Africae* or *Wessex from the Air.*

In 1925 Salomon Reinach wrote: 'The richest museum of the ancient world lies at the bottom of the Mediterranean . . . This museum is, however, still inaccessible.' In the period under review in this chapter it has become accessible, but we should not forget the early attempts at underwater archaeology. In 1446 the Italian architect Leon Battista Alberti tried to refloat the two Roman galleys at the bottom of Lake Nemi, fifteen-and-a-half miles south-east of Rome and in 1535 Francesco Demarchi organized diving with helmets to get to the ships.

Modern underwater archaeology has progressed thanks to the work, among others, of Jacques-Yves Cousteau in the Marseille area, George Bass and Peter Throckmorton in the East Mediterranean and Keith Muckelroy and others in Britain. When Bass was working in Turkey, with a University of Pennsylvania underwater team, he was equipped with a two-man submarine, the *Asherah,* which he described as 'not only the first submarine ever built for archaeology, but the first non-military submarine ever sold by the Electric Boat Company (of Groton, Connecticut) in its sixty-year history.' Those wishing to pursue the

118 Roger Agache, a distinguished French air photographer, captured ghostly chalk foundations in this view of a Gallo-Roman villa at Warfusée, Abancourt, in the department of the Somme, northern France.

119 The development of underwater archaeology has been one of the most important advances since the Second World War. Here a diver examines the cargo of a Greek merchantman wrecked near Kyrenia, Cyprus, in the fourth century BC. The grid-frame was used by the archaeologists to plan the amphorae and grain-mills found inside the hull.

development of underwater archaeology since the last war should read George Bass's *Archaeology under Water* (1966), Joan du Plat Taylor (ed.), *Marine Archaeology, Development during Sixty Years in the Mediterranean* (1965) and Keith Muckelroy's *Maritime Archaeology* (1978).

Sometimes all these scientific aids to archaeology seem astonishing to a straight old-fashioned archaeologist like the author of this book, trained in the macroscopic examination of artifacts and their taxonomy and typology. But it is only too true, as Frank Hole and Robert F. Heizer say in their *Introduction to Prehistoric Archaeology* (second edition 1969), that 'the two decades since 1950 will certainly become known historically as the age of technological innovation in archaeology'. And in the preface to their *Science in Archaeology* (1969) Brothwell and Higgs say: 'It will be many years before the impact of scientific applications in archaeology are fully appreciated ... the reorientation towards a more scientific attitude in archaeological research continues at a surprising pace.'

I do not share this view. I think that by now most archaeologists are fully aware of the contributions of science to their work and of the dangers of not employing all scientific aids to the fullest possible extent. The scientific revolution in archaeology has taken, and is still taking, place and archaeology is now a new discipline. But this does not mean, as some have easily slipped into thinking, that archaeology is now a science. We must be careful what we are talking about when we refer to science: sometimes it can mean knowledge, that is to say all knowledge of the varieties and achievements of man and nature; at other times it can mean only knowledge of nature, and this is what is meant by the natural sciences such as physics, chemistry, mineralogy, geology, botany, zoology and astronomy; and thirdly it can mean the historical and social sciences which study the knowledge we have about man in history and society. Some say that because the archaeologist is so vitally concerned with, and assisted by, the natural sciences he must be himself a natural scientist but this is not so: he is still studying man in society for the last two million years. He is still a historian, a human historian and not a natural historian.

There are many archaeologists, particularly in America, who say that archaeology is nothing unless it is anthropology. O. G. S. Crawford declared that archaeology was the past tense of anthropology and Lowie insisted that prehistory was simply the ethnography of extinct social groups. But what do these statements mean – apart from being bold and challenging?

They mean that the archaeologist should strive to get more out of the past than was provided by say Sophus Müller and Montelius, by de Mortillet and Breuil, by Pitt-Rivers and Burkitt – that our task is to write as detailed an account as we can of extinct societies, that we must bring to life the builders of Carnac and Stonehenge, the warriors of the Heuneberg and Maiden Castle. These are fine aims and we pay lip-service to them but so often we lack imagination – the sort of imagination which Cyril Fox and Mortimer Wheeler had in England and Wales – and confine ourselves to the artifacts.

Modern American Archaeology

It seems to me that the most important change in archaeology in the period under review is the emergence of American archaeology as a mature scientific discipline which keeps asking Old World archae-ologists whether they really know what they are at. O. G. S. Crawford was completely uninterested in American archaeology and *Antiquity* under his editorship had very few articles or news about America. Gordon Childe thought American archaeology was a sideline of no importance to the general history of man. In *What Happened in History* he said that pre-Columbian American archaeology was 'outside the main stream of history', by which, of course, he meant the stream of history in the Old World that started in the Most Ancient Near East and flowed through Palestine, Greece and Rome to medieval, renaissance and modern Europe. Mortimer Wheeler once said to me that American archaeology was 'peripheral and of no interest to anyone'; and after a pause added, 'it's barbaric'.

How misguided were those doyens of archaeology at that time! In writing this short history I find it incredible that the archaeologists working in Europe, concerned as they were with Acheulian axes, Swiss lake-dwellings, and Celtic hill-forts, and modelling the past in terms of the early civilizations of Egypt and Sumeria, were so complacent about America. The history of archaeology must show that while the fifteenth century was puzzled by Amerindians, the nineteenth and early twentieth centuries eschewed to their cost what was going on in America. Few European writers on archaeology seemed to have read or appreciated W. W. Taylor's *A Study of Archaeology* (1948), in which he urged what he called the conjunctive approach to archaeology, namely the total study of the culture of a period of time. Yet here was a way to a *new* archaeology, and it was called a new archaeology in the 1960s but without due credit to Taylor.

The contribution to American archaeology that most influenced the structure of that subject and the reconsideration by European archaeologists of their technological model was the work of Willey and Phillips with their historical-developmental interpretation of New World prehistory. Set out first in an article in 1955, it was clearly adumbrated in their book *Method and Theory in American Archaeology* (1958). Their scheme projected a model for the past of the New World which comprised five major stages as follows:

1 *Lithic*, Palaeo-Indian and other Early Man beginnings in the Americas;
2 *Archaic*, post-Pleistocene hunting-collecting adaptations;
3 *Formative*, the village agricultural threshold and the beginnings of sedentary life;
4 *Classic*, the beginnings of urban development; and
5 *Postclassic*, the imperialistic states.

This scheme for the past of early America has been widely used since, and the history of pre-Columbian America is now well established. In the last thirty years it has become clear that man first got to America across the Bering Straits from Asia at a date that may be somewhere between 15,000 and 20,000 years ago, or even earlier, and that food plants were being cultivated in at least four areas of America – the American south-west, southern Tamaulipas, the Tehuacan valley and Coastal Peru, with the possibility of a fifth in the South American tropical forest, at various dates between 5000 BC and 1000 BC. Fundamental to our understanding of American agricultural origins are R. S. MacNeish's excavations in the valley of Tehuacan, a dry valley in southern Mexico: the reports of the Tehuacan Archaeological-Botanical Project were published by the Peabody Foundation of Andover in 1961 and 1962.

From these native American food-producing communities there emerged the Middle American civilizations – the Olmec and the Maya – and the civilization of Peru. The Maya had been well known for some time: the Olmecs were a new, exciting and surprising civilization with their great stone heads and weird jaguar-figures. For a good account of the Olmecs see Michael D. Coe's *America's First Civilisation: Discovering the Olmec* (1968) and his *Mexico* (1962, revised edition

120 Earlier than the Maya, the Olmecs of the Mexican Gulf Coast produced giant basalt heads like this one from Tres Zapotes during the first millennium BC. Their civilization had a strong influence on the development of Middle American culture. Ht 2.27 m.

1976), in which he says, 'There is now not the slightest doubt that all later civilisations in Mesoamerica, whether Mexican or Mayan, ultimately rest on an Olmec base.'

For up-to-date summaries of modern knowledge of pre-Columbian America see G. R. Willey's magisterial treatment in *An Introduction to American Archaeology: 1. North and Middle America* (1966); *2. South America* (1972); for a less ambitious and more popular treatment G. H. S. Bushnell, *The First Americans: the Pre-Columbian Civilizations* (1968) and, for a very clear and up-to-date statement, Warwick M. Bray, Earl H. Swanson and Ian S. Farrington, *The New World* (1975).

As already mentioned, in the 1960s in America there came into existence what was consciously and deliberately called the 'new' archaeology. For an account of this I would refer the reader to S. R. and L. R. Binford, *New Perspectives in Archaeology* (1968); Mark P. Leone (ed.), *Contemporary Archaeology; A Guide to Theory and Contributions* (1972), and Willey and Sabloff, *A History of American Archaeology* (1974, second edition 1980). Let me quote what Willey and Sabloff see as the key points in the new archaeology:

> To begin with, it was the product of anthropological archaeology, of young archaeologists, who, as graduate students, had been partly trained by social anthropologists as well as archaeologists. Their central concern was the elucidation of cultural process. . . . Second, the new archaeology was (and is) pervaded with a great optimism about the possibilities of success in processual explanation and in arriving at laws of cultural dynamics. A third attitude held that archaeology, in its revelation of explanation of cultural process, could be made relevant not only to the rest of anthropology but to the problems of the modern world as well.

The evolution of the American new archaeology of the 1960s is an important part of the history of archaeology and we must devote some attention to it. How did it come into existence and why? In my *A Hundred and Fifty Years of Archaeology* (1975) I wrote:

> This new movement in America stems, of course, from the barrenness of the pre-Columbian record of archaeology; for centuries nothing happened of general interest to the student of world history – no Stonehenge, no Maltese temples. American archaeologists, dismayed by their archaeological record, have sought refuge in theory and methodology, and spend their time talking about 'the elucidation of cultural process' and the production of 'laws of cultural dynamics'.

That was a very severe judgment and I meant it to apply to North America. The archaeological record of the cities and temples of Central America and Peru has been the source of the greatest excitement for the last hundred and fifty years. It is pre-Columbian North America which is so unexciting and has driven archaeologists into the welcoming arms of anthropologists who are all, vainly in my view, hoping to adumbrate laws of human behaviour.

But was it all 'new', or 'very old hat' as many people have said? Binford himself says, 'we feel that archaeology in the 1960s is at a major point of evolutionary change'. But archaeologists have always been talking about evolutionary change and cultural process. The American archaeologists of this cult of the 1960s seem unaware of the history of archaeology and perhaps that is why this book was worth writing: let them read or re-read Thomsen and Worsaae and Montelius and Childe.

But particularly W. W. Taylor. In reviewing a collection of essays to which we have already referred, namely Binford and Binford, *New Perspectives in Archaeology*, Taylor says:

> A full discussion of a very similar overall approach to our discipline has been in print since 1948 (W. W. Taylor, *A Study of Archaeology*). The systematic view of culture has been a basic premise of American anthropology, including archaeology, certainly since Malinowski, if not since Boas, and as for Binford's other tenets, I can point to passages in *A Study of Archaeology* covering each of them, even of testing hypotheses. ... What the Binfords have produced in this book is not an exposition of the theory and practice of a new perspective but an explicit restatement of an old one (*Science*, 1969, 382–4).

Robert Braidwood's account of the development of the American 'new' archaeology is even more devastating. He writes:

> In the U.S. at least, the growth of the 'new' archaeology with all its scientism, will eventually be understood in part as a response to the growth of the National Science Foundation as a source for substantial financial support for archaeology in the anthropological tradition. It was important to behave and to talk like a scientist. Aid for fieldwork in the humanistic tradition has only come much more recently, with the development of the National Endowment for the Humanities. I feel certain, too, that in the U.S., the obstreperous spirit of many of the 'new' archaeologists reflected the unrest of the Vietnam years. These people belonged to the 'don't trust anybody over thirty' generation (they are, of course, themselves well beyond that now!). It was declared publicly at association meetings, for example, that 'nothing written before 1960 is worth reading' and, given the development of the movement's own new jargon, it was difficult for many of the 'new' archaeologists and their students to *understand* anything written before 1960.
>
> Those of us who were well over thirty in the critical years survived the movement's swaddling years with a combination of wry amusement and no great anticipation of monumental breakthroughs in contributions to knowledge. I do have a rueful feeling that at least some of the writings of the 'new archaeologists' may have brought confusion to students and younger colleagues beyond North America and western Europe (*Antiquity*, 1981, 24–25).

Of this I have no doubt; so many of the advocates and practitioners of the 'new' archaeology have used jargon often indistinguishable from gobbledygook. In Britain two distinguished archaeologists, one no longer, alas, with us, have been keen and influential propagators of the 'new' archaeology. One was David Clarke, a Cambridge don, whose early death in 1976 was a tremendous loss to the subject. His book *Analytical Archaeology* (first edition, 1968; second edition revised by Bob Chapman, 1978) was hailed by many as one of the most important ever published in modern archaeology. In it Clarke described the 'new' archaeology as 'an interpenetrating set of new methods, new observations, new paradigms, new philosophies and new ideologies within a new environment'. The other was Colin Renfrew, recently elected to the Disney Chair of Archaeology in Cambridge. In a stimulating paper entitled 'The Great Tradition versus the Great Divide', Renfrew declares his belief that 'Binford, with his associates, has made a greater contribution to archaeological thought than any worker in this century', but he does go on to say:

> The so-called 'New Archaeology' unfortunately has been treated in some quarters as a cult, and like any cult means many things to many people. Of course one man's cult is another man's heresy, and the developments in archaeological theory have been written off by many students of the Ancient World as a jargon-laden and woolly attempt to impose a mathematicist and scientistic straight-jacket on the humanism and liberal scholarship of the Great Tradition [of archaeology]. There is of course plenty of evidence to support such a view, and the New Archaeology, ten years after, is now a house with many mansions, not all of them brilliantly illuminated (*American Journal of Archaeology*, 1980, 293-95).

A historian of archaeology must record his own views honestly and I am certainly on the side of Braidwood and Taylor: by the end of this century I think we will see that the claims of David Clarke and Renfrew were extravagant and themselves displayed a lack of knowledge of the history of their subject. Nevertheless the stimulus given by the discussions of the 1960s has provided the inspiration for a lot of remarkable new work of lasting value: let us cite only David Clarke (ed.), *Models in Archaeology* (1972), Renfrew's *Before Civilisation* (1973), *The Emergence of Civilisation: the Cyclades and the Aegean in the Third Millennium B.C.* (1973), and a book of collected essays and papers entitled *Problems in European Prehistory* (1979).

My view is that after the turmoil and heart-searching discussion prompted by the 'new' archaeology, archaeology will return, strengthened and refreshed, to its proper role of writing the history of man in the fullest possible sense. Most of the wise and good historians have failed to find universal laws in the human past, and certainly nothing that will help the human future. The new archaeologists of the 1960s and their present followers in Britain and Scandinavia will become the disillusioned men of the 1980s and 1990s, realizing that man's past is something to be recorded, described, appreciated and understood, but that the hope of discovering laws of cultural dynamics in archaeology and anthropology is probably a vain one doomed to failure. I may be proved wrong, however; the history of archaeology is full of false assumptions and predictions.

Fact, Fiction and Fantasy

American archaeology in the period under review has given us theoretical issues to think about, but it has also shown us that it is not only in the nineteenth and early twentieth centuries that American archaeology has been bedevilled by cranks and crackpots who, rejecting the evidence for the independent development of food-producing cultures and of civilizations in the New World, want it to be colonized by Egyptians, the lost tribes of Israel, the Phoenicians, Greeks, Irish, Welsh, Atlanteans, inhabitants of Mu, or extraterrestrial persons in flying saucers – indeed anything that is going. For breathtakingly impudent and totally unreliable accounts of these follies, fantasy buffs and tasters should read Cyrus H. Gordon's *Before Columbus* (1971), von Sertima's *They came before Columbus: the African presence in Ancient America* (1976) and two books by Barry Fell, *America BC* (1977) and *Saga America* (1980). Fell was a Professor (not, praise be, of archaeology, but of Marine Biology) at Harvard; his two books are perhaps the most ridiculous, ludicrous examples of what, alas, flourishes on the wilder shores of archaeology – if we exclude the ignorant ravings of Erich von Däniken. The latter apart, the three writers we have cited are scholars with fixed ideas that have become delusions, as Elliot Smith put it long ago. But the Manchester School have nothing in their prejudices and follies to compare with the extravagances and ignorances of the Gordons, Sertimas and Fells. What is so sad is that the general reader, presented with these dotty books in bookstores, has no obvious way of distinguishing between fact and fantasy, fair assessment of the available evidence and folly.

In denigrating these strange, wayward and ill-informed writers, so well pilloried by Wauchope in his excellent myth-America debunking book, *Lost Tribes and Sunken Continents* (1962), we must not move into a position that denies the possibility of the actuality of trans-Atlantic and trans-Pacific voyages in pre-Columbian times. Heyerdahl demonstrated by his *Ra* expedition that it was possible to cross the Atlantic in a reed boat from east to west, having previously demonstrated by his famous *Kon-tiki* experiment that it was possible to cross the Pacific from east to west on a balsa raft. Modern experiments show possibilities: they do not demonstrate actualities. We still await positive proof that the people and civilizations of the Old World got to America. That they could have done so is beyond dispute: and the Phoenicians, who apparently circumnavigated Africa in the time of the Pharaoh Necho, could easily have crossed the south Atlantic to Brazil. Possibilities exist but proof depends on facts. The only facts for pre-Columbian trans-Atlantic contacts that we have at the moment are the Viking settlement at L'Anse-aux-Meadows in Newfoundland and recent discoveries, by the Canadian Arctic Institute, of Viking finds on Ellesmere Island and the recognition of a coin from Maine as being of genuine twelfth-century Viking manufacture.

These are facts, and no sensible archaeologist would deny the possibility that genuine Phoenician remains (Egyptian seems highly doubtful – they were not a great seafaring nation) could be found in Brazil or anywhere else in east-coast America. The difficulty in this, as in many issues in archaeology, is to distinguish fact from fantasy, supposition, however carefully argued, from wishful thinking. Cyrus Gordon, von Sertima and Fell are wishful thinkers uncritically jumping all guns as did the Elliot-Smith/Perry Manchester School. We highlight them because therein lies one of the dangers of popular archaeology.

Pacific contacts, in the reverse direction from the *Kon-tiki* expedition, have always been a possibility, and Meggers and others have argued for the presence of Japanese Jomon pottery in Ecuador. The archaeological record must be reviewed in terms of possibilities, probabilities and facts and not in terms of preconceived ideas.

Research in India and China, in parallel with America and elsewhere, has shown that in both areas, as in America, agriculture and civilization developed indigenously and independently of the Most Ancient Near East.

Human settlement from about two million years ago in eastern Asia and western Indonesia is now well attested. The origins of horticulture in south-east Asia and the subsequent development of Neolithic and Metal Age societies took place between 10,000 and 2,000 years ago. There was pottery in south-east Asia by 5000 BC; and well-developed Neolithic cultures with rice, cattle, pottery and polished stone implements by 3000 BC, and, it would seem, localized copper and bronze working in Thailand by the same time. It is now clear that plant domestication was developed in south-east Asia as early as in south-west Asia. For a good summary of modern views on the archaeology of south-east Asia and the Pacific see P. Bellwood, *The Polynesians* (1978) and *Man's Conquest of the Pacific: the prehistory of South-East Asia and Oceania* (1978): in this latter book the author declares (p. 198) that 'Archaeology has further to go in South-East Asia than anywhere else in the world.'

The development of scientific techniques of dating and the extension of prehistoric archaeology to a worldwide basis have made all archaeologists think again about the nature and reality of man's cultural development in prehistoric times. That man has been in existence for two or three million years is now well-established in East Africa: that man the hunter-gatherer changed to man the farmer and pastoralist in various parts of the world at around ten thousand years BC is also now generally accepted. What is likewise well established is that many of these peasant village communities gave rise to literate urban communities which we properly label civilizations. Archaeology is still working on the premise that there was a change from the savagery of the Palaeolithic to the barbarism of the Neolithic and to the urban civilization of the Bronze and Iron Ages. The question remains: were these changes ones that happened independently in various parts of the world, or did they originate in one place only, as Childe argued when he made his Neolithic and Urban Revolutions happen in the Most Ancient Near East? What does modern archaeology say about the perennial dispute between diffusion and independent invention? In my view it provides an answer which is different from the universal social and cultural evolution of Morgan, Engels, Marx and modern Russian archaeological thinking, and different from the diffusionism of Childe and Montelius (and most certainly different from the hyper-diffusionism of the Elliot Smith Manchester School).

Archaeology now seems to suggest that the change from man the hunter-gatherer to man the farmer and stockbreeder took place in many different parts of the world independently in the period 12,000–7000 BC, and that these farming and pastoral communities gave rise to the societies we describe as ancient civilizations independently in many different parts of the world. In my book *The First Civilizations: the Archaeology of their Origins* (1968) I said that it then seemed to me that civilization, what Gordon Childe called the Urban Revolution, and what I preferred to describe as the process of synoecism, had happened independently seven times in the world: four times in the Old World (namely, Egypt, Mesopotamia, India and China) and three times in the New World (the rise of the Olmecs, the Maya, and the classic civilization of central Peru). In the last ten years it has become clear that the roster of seven independent civilizations was too small a list and that there should be at least two additions: one the Aegean-Minoan civilization, and the other the civilization of south Russia.

To my way of thinking this all makes sense. We overconceptualized cultural origins for far too long and discussed issues like the origins of agriculture, megaliths and urbanism when we should have been describing the sequence of material culture change in different areas.

It is very difficult to get across the results of our new archaeology of the 1970s to the general public, on whom the professional archaeologist relies so much for encouragement, the occasional find, and political pressure on governments to preserve and study our internationally shared patrimony. Archaeology is, these days, very popular. Gone, fortunately, is the picture of archaeology as a subject dominated and practised by old men with long white beards like Flinders Petrie or eccentric retired army officers like General Pitt-Rivers. It is now a respectable and understood branch of historical science (or learning). The change in the climate of public thought can be exemplified in a simple way: in 1927 there were seven or eight posts in archaeology in British universities, now half a century later there are about three hundred posts. This is a dramatic, astonishing and continuing change.

There is, nowadays, no doubt about the academic worth of archaeology; but it is the general public as well as the specialized academic that needs to know the potentialities and results of current archaeological research.

This can be done in part by television and broadcasting, by lecturing, and by popular books and journals. There can be no doubt that the American archaeological/ethnographical television quiz programme *What in the World?* did a great deal to interest the public in these matters, as did the British derivative programme *Animal, Vegetable, Mineral?* which ran with such success for six years in the 1950s. These programmes on the BBC gave rise to serious archaeological documentaries such as *Buried Treasure* and the *Chronicle* series devised by Paul Johnstone which, after many years, continues successfully. The BBC has now an archaeological and historical unit and other television companies in Britain, France, Denmark and elsewhere are using the television screen for archaeological instruction.

121

The journal *Antiquity* is now over fifty years old. In Britain it has new, younger and vigorous contemporaries such as *Current Archaeology*, *World Archaeology* and *Popular Archaeology*. The USA has its own *Popular Archaeology* as well as *Archaeology*, *Early Man* and *Expedition*. France has *Archéologia* and *Initiation à la préhistoire*. Denmark produces that most famous and remarkable of all popular archaeological journals, *Skalk*, with a circulation of 50,000 – one person in a hundred in Denmark reads (or at least buys) *Skalk*.

But does all this, and the great and welcome increase in sound works of *haute vulgarisation*, mean that we are moving to a public well-educated in archaeology? Alas, only partly so. Archaeology is popular now, it is 'à la mode', but its popularity is shared by even more popular books on false archaeology. The good can apparently only grow with a parallel growth of the bad, which is sad. The truth is that when we go back to write the history of man before writing and have to rely entirely on non-written sources, the record is thin and the resultant story often unsatisfactory to the eager, interested general reader. We apply all the scientific techniques at our disposal, we meticulously collect and analyse new and old information, we do our best, but, even so, the questions so many people ask elude answers. Who painted the animals at Lascaux and why? Who planned and built Stonehenge and why? Why were the great Olmec heads and the statues of Easter Island and Corsica constructed?

In a conservative, but not defeatist view of archaeology (shared by the present writer), Stuart Piggott said: 'Archaeological evidence alone can inform us of only the broadest aspects of social structure or religious belief, and that in a tentative way. All the prehistorian can really perceive is the history of technology.'

It is not surprising that the difficulties of exposition, and the inherent limitations of the story that can be exposed, have driven many into the lush lunatic fringe of the subject. In Western Europe, though perhaps less than in America, there is a great cult of what is variously described as alternate archaeology, lunatic archaeology, or bullshit archaeology. Its practitioners are the people who believe in the lost tribes of Israel, Egyptians, Phoenicians, Atlantis, Mu, the ley hunters and pyramidiots, and the strange people who believe they can find the signs of the Zodiac in the hedgerows of the English countryside.

Latterly, with the encouragement of people like Erich von Däniken, 'archi-evhémériste' as Rehork has described him in his *Recherche Fascinante: L'Archéologie Moderne* (1971), visitors from outer space have been added to the already long catalogue of archaeological myths. Von Däniken, purveyor of more dangerous nonsense about ancient man than anyone (and I say this advisedly, remembering Elliot Smith, Fell, Donnelly, Bellamy and Velikovsky), has added astronaut archaeology to the already dubious semi-scholarship and semi-lunacy of astro-archaeology, and of course everything – the Tassili frescoes, the Nazca lines, and falsely interpreted Maya glyphs – have been pressed into the service of his chariot-riding gods.

It used to be said by my teachers, mentors and advisors that the lunatic fringes of archaeology were an amusing whimsy to be disregarded. This is not so: one of the tasks of archaeology and

archaeologists in the 1980s is to see that the lunatics are exposed and the truth as it appears to us at the moment is properly, cogently and frequently presented. The great, almost enormous, new body of archaeological information and scholarship must be made available to everyone. Archaeology is no longer a secret hobby or practice of a John Evans or a Boucher de Perthes. It is the source of our information from cultural and other fossils as to whether we are men or mice.

My view is that we are men and that a history of archaeology, compressed as it had to be, into the limits of this book, shows this. It demonstrates the great technological achievement of man in the past and the gradual change in our ideas about our own past.

Perhaps this is the most cogent reason for studying the history of archaeology, namely, that it is part of the history of ideas and therefore an essential element in our awareness of our appreciation of ourselves as historically evolving persons. As Stuart Piggott has wisely said,

> In studying the origins and development of historical disciplines, we are, in effect engaged in the investigation of the history of ideas: ideas about the past held by those who are now the objects of our own historical investigation, and the techniques they devised, deliberately or accidentally, to obtain and interpret the basic material from which history can be written (*Ruins in a Landscape*, 1976, 1).

121 Sir Mortimer Wheeler and Glyn Daniel examine an object on the BBC television quiz programme, *Animal, Vegetable, Mineral?*, which did much to popularize archaeology in Britain during the 1950s.

The Major Discoveries

But let us not end this chapter on a note of passion and polemic. Let us briefly record some of the remarkable discoveries and new interpretations that have occurred in the last forty years. We have already referred to Sutton Hoo in 1939 and Lascaux in 1940.

In 1942 Emile Gagnan and Jacques-Yves Cousteau developed the aqualung and initiated a new era in marine archaeology. In 1943 Seton Lloyd and Sayyad Fuad Safar began digging in Tell Hassuna and established a new understanding of the early Neolithic of the Near East. In that same year work for the extension of the airfield of Valley in Anglesey (north Wales) brought to light the Llyn Cerrig Bach hoard of Celtic objects and started Sir Cyril Fox off on new researches which eventually produced his *Pattern and Purpose* (1958).

This was the year in which Wheeler's *Maiden Castle* report, to which we have already referred, was published: that year there was already printing Paul Jacobsthahl's *Early Celtic Art*, which the Oxford University Press published in 1944 – a magisterial and epoch-making survey of barbarian art in the four pre-Christian centuries, which has had a lasting impact.

122 In 1944 in the bog of Tollund, near Viborg in Jutland, was found a body that has become celebrated because, as P. V. Glob has said in his evocative book, *Land of the Tollund Man* (1767), 'for the first time a human face has come down to us from prehistoric times unspoilt. No bust from Rome or Renaissance Italy, no painted portrait, nothing created by man for man's immortalization is so real as the face of this blackened body.' The head of Tollund man is preserved for all to see in the Museum of Silkeborg, twenty-five miles west of Aarhus. It is strangely moving: a face from the past – the face of a man who lived two thousand years ago and died by ritual hanging. To quote Glob again, 'One feels that one knows the man: knows who he is and can hear his voice. His lips are confident and there is a warmth of irony in the corners of his mouth: there is imperturbable humour in the smile of his eyes. He has just closed his eyes: one cannot believe him dead.'

In the late 1950s the BBC did a television programme on Tollund man and Sir Mortimer Wheeler and I were made to taste a meal based on the known contents of his stomach at the time of death – it was a tasteless mush of cultivated and wild grains and grasses. I thought at the time, and still think, how much a reflection on archaeology it is that we could reconstruct his last meal but of course will never know his name, why he was hanged, or his last thoughts. These are the continuing limitations of prehistoric archaeology, which we must always bear in mind.

In the first year after the war, in 1946, R. J. C. Atkinson, now Professor of Archaeology at University College, Cardiff, and famous for his excavations at Stonehenge and Silbury Hill, used electrical prospecting for archaeological purposes at Dorchester-on-Thames, and this was the beginning of all the scientific devices now used in archaeological prospecting.

The territory of the Lacandón Indians in south-east Mexico is, according to Ceram, 'a god-forsaken region visited by white men only

122 (*Opposite*) Tollund man, who died by ritual hanging in the first century BC and whose body was recovered miraculously preserved from a Danish peat bog two thousand years later.

IX

when they are seeking mahogany trees or chicle, the raw material for chewing gum' (*A Picture of History of Archaeology*, 1958, 327). In 1946 the United Fruit Company commissioned a film unit to make a documentary film entitled *The Maya in the Course of the Ages*. The Lacandón Indians are a dying group of the Maya: they are extremely primitive and have never been Christianized – indeed they seem to be the only Maya tribe virtually still in a pre-Hispanic state of culture. The unit photographer, Giles G. Healey, managed to establish good and friendly relations with the Indians and they eventually showed him their sacred mystery, the 'coloured walls' of Bonampak. Some Mayan frescoes were already known and showed gods and symbols. But the Bonampak walls revealed pictures of the daily life of the Maya in a rich and beautiful way.

The following year an Arab shepherd boy threw a pebble into a cave at Qumran on the shores of the Dead Sea; puzzled by the sound, he explored the cave and found what are now referred to as the Dead Sea Scrolls. That summer Mademoiselle G. Henri-Martin found remains of *Homo sapiens* at Fontéchevade in the Charente Atlantique, and Heyerdahl sailed his balsa raft, the *Kon-tiki* from Ecuador to Polynesia.

In 1949 Rudenko dug in the mounds at Pazyryk in the Altai region of Siberia. These fifth-century BC Scythian tombs – there are sixty or so of them – were first examined in 1929 by Gryaznov and Rudenko.

123 A sheet from the Dead Sea Scrolls, the Hebrew and Aramaic manuscripts of the first century AD discovered in a cave at Qumran in 1947. Nearly all the books of the canonical Old Testament are represented.

124 Sir Max Mallowan (1904–78) (left) on site at Nimrud, northern Iraq.

Rudenko's account of his excavations was first published in Russian in 1953. In 1970 a revised English translation appeared under the title *Frozen Tombs of Siberia: the Pazyryk Burials of Iron Age Horsemen.* These Scythian graves were wooden chambers at the bottom of deep shafts: the timber roofing had been removed by grave-robbers, rain water had seeped in on to the corpses and frozen, with the extraordinary results of preservation: clothing, leather, wood and felt have survived for two and a half thousand years, including embroidered Chinese silk, woven Persian stuffs, a wool-pile carpet and a tattooed man.

In 1949 Grahame Clark began his excavations at Star Carr in Yorkshire, one of the most interesting Mesolithic settlement sites; its publication in 1954 was a model of interdisciplinary archaeological scholarship. In this same year Max Mallowan began his excavations at Nimrud which were to reveal among other things fascinating finds of ivories, and Dorothy Garrod and Suzanne de Saint-Mathurin began their excavations of the rockshelter at Angles-sur-l'Anglin in the Charente which revealed new and remarkable treasures of Upper Palaeolithic art.

124
125

Also in 1949 Alberto Ruz, a Mexican archaeologist, began excavations in the Temple of Inscriptions at Palenque and found an eight-stepped pyramid. Inside the temple on the top platform was found a staircase and down sixty-six steps Ruz found a room with skeletons, pots and objects of jade. Beyond was a chamber thirty feet long by thirteen feet wide (nine by four metres); stucco reliefs decorated the walls, and in it was the grave of a Maya ruler aged between forty and fifty with jade ornaments, large earrings inscribed

125 Suzanne de Saint-Mathurin (left) and Dorothy Garrod in the La Quina laboratory studying a Palaeolithic engraving on a block of stone. Together they excavated the rockshelter of Angles-sur-l'Anglin, Charente, in the 1950s.

with Maya hieroglyphs, a diadem, a mosaic mask, two enormous pearls and rings on all ten fingers. After this remarkable discovery it could no longer be claimed that none of the Maya pyramids were funerary. Naturally Ruz's discovery at Palenque had encouraged those who have for so long seen the Maya pyramids as proof of Egypt in America.

In 1950 Brian Hope-Taylor followed up an air photograph discovery and excavated with brilliance an Anglo-Saxon site at Yeavering in Northumberland: the first Anglo-Saxon hall to be discovered and possibly the *Ad Gefrin* described by Bede in his *Ecclesiastical History*. His report, eventually published in 1979, is an exemplary model of what such a report should be and a landmark in twentieth-century archaeological publication.

1951 saw the publication of Louis Leakey's *Olduvai Gorge*, and the first radiocarbon dates appeared in the journal *Science*. The next year saw the beginning of Kathleen Kenyon's work at Jericho, which produced a remarkable sequence of cultures and the discovery of the astonishing plastered skulls. It was also in 1952 that Grahame Clark's *Prehistoric Europe: the Economic Basis* was published: a pioneer effort in turning prehistory away from the old Three Age/Four Age/Five Age paradigm towards studying the life and economy of early man.

126, 127 A pupil of Sir
Mortimer Wheeler,
Kathleen Kenyon
(1906–78) (*opposite, below*)
adopted the same military
style of field campaign
in her excavation of
prehistoric Jericho during
the 1950s. The great
fortifications at the site
(*left*) proved to have been
the earliest of any city in
the world.

128 In 1954 a dismantled ship of the pharaoh Cheops was discovered buried in a pit beside the Great Pyramid at Giza. Over 4,500 years old, it was the earliest vessel ever to come to light. Ahmed Youssef Moustafa, the Egyptian restorer, spent fourteen years carefully reconstructing the ship, and it now stands in a specially built museum next to the Great Pyramid.

129

1952 saw revolution in Egypt and the closing down of foreign archaeological schools – a most retrograde step: the French had been working in Egypt since the time of Napoleon with the greatest success and to the greatest benefit of those inside and outside Egypt interested in the ancient past of that most ancient civilization. The expulsion of Drioton was sad and bad. The following year the Egyptian archaeologists themselves found a Royal Ship of the pharaoh Cheops buried beside the Great Pyramid at Giza, now fully described in Nancy Jenkins, *The Boat beneath the Pyramid* (1980).

1953 was in many ways an *annus mirabilis* in the history of twentieth-century archaeology. Michael Ventris published his decipherment of Minoan Linear B. As a seventeen-year-old pupil at Stowe he had heard Arthur Evans, then aged eighty, lecture on this script which he had been trying to decipher for forty years. This young schoolboy was fascinated and set himself the task of succeeding where Arthur Evans had failed. Seventeen years later, when he was only thirty-four, he had succeeded, without the bilingual and trilingual clues that had helped Champollion and Rawlinson.

The same year saw the debunking of Piltdown Man. Kenneth Oakley had applied the fluorine test to the dating of fossil bones in 1948. Then this and other scientific tests were applied to the Piltdown remains. The Piltdown ape-man, Smith Woodward's 'first Englishman' that never was, was disposed of by the brilliant co-operative scientific analyses organized by Oakley, Weiner and Le Gros Clark. The final *coup de grâce* was given when C14 tests showed the bones to be modern. *Eoanthropus dawsoni* was no more, except as a forgery which had been too readily and eagerly accepted by responsible scientists. The exposure of this remarkable and successful fraud is well set out by J. S. Weiner in *The Piltdown Forgery* (1955), in which by implication, if

not explicitly, he suggests that the forgery was mainly the work of Dawson. Others have suggested other names: Millar, in *The Piltdown Men*, argues unconvincingly for Elliot Smith; Sollas and Teilhard de Chardin have been canvassed. Maybe the whole truth will never be known but the lesson of Piltdown has been learned, as the lesson of Moulin Quignon had been forgotten when the Piltdown 'remains' were being publicized. It should now be virtually impossible for any comparable forgery to be perpetrated. The history of archaeology is the history of the critical evaluation of evidence.

In the year of the debunking of Piltdown there was found in Burgundy by René Joffroy, a Professor in the Lycée at Châtillon-sur-Seine (who subsequently became Director of the Musée des Antiquités Nationales at Saint-Germain), the princess's burial at Vix, one of the most splendid of all archaeological finds. This is the waggon-grave of a late Hallstatt princess dating from perhaps 525 to 500 BC. She was wearing a superb solid gold diadem of possibly Graeco-Scythian manufacture and buried with her was a large bronze *krater* five feet three inches (a hundred and sixty centimetres) in height weighing over 457 pounds, the biggest metal vessel that has so far survived from antiquity.

During demolition work carried out in the City of London in 1954 the Temple of Mithras was uncovered and subsequently excavated by Professor W. F. Grimes: its discovery caused the greatest excitement among people who were being indirectly indoctrinated in archaeology by *Animal, Vegetable, Mineral?*, and enormous queues waited for hours to see these not very exciting remains which have now, largely due to public interest, been preserved. The Mithras incident showed that the past is alive to the ordinary people of the present and that they warmly share with professional archaeologists the interest in and care for our

129 Michael Ventris (1922–56), who deciphered the Linear B script.

international patrimony, slowly but surely revealed by archaeology. Roman London is well described in Peter Marsden's book of the same title (1980).

While we were all still reeling from the Piltdown exposure *Figaro* and *The Times* of London published in 1956 the news of the discovery in Dordogne of 'the richest find of Palaeolithic art'. This was the cave of Rouffignac in the classic Les Eyzies area which has appropriated to itself, and, let us admit, not inappropriately, the title of 'capitale de la préhistoire'. This cave, known for centuries, is now revealed as full of engravings and paintings of animals which were not noticed by anyone, including the Abbé Breuil who spent a day there in 1915 (admittedly helping a friend look for butterflies). Martel, the great authority on French caves, saw no art there in his repeated visits from 1890 to 1930. Some of us have expressed our doubts and suspicions: the establishment world of Palaeolithic studies has accepted Rouffignac. I suspect that most of it is a forgery and when someone revises this book in fifty years time the proof of the falseness of Rouffignac will then be as clear as the proof of the falseness of Piltdown is now.

The next few years saw work in many fascinating and highly important sites: Lerici began his periscope prospecting of Etruscan tombs, Emery began work at Buhen on the border between Egypt and the Sudan, the Etruscan site of Spina was discovered in northern Italy, so was the astonishing hoard of Tartessian jewellery at El Carambolo near Seville, and the St Ninian's hoard in the Shetlands. James Mellaart visited Izmir and says he was shown the so-called Dorak treasure, which no one else had seen before or has seen since (for an account of this strange *cause célèbre* see Pearson and Connor, *The Dorak Treasure*, 1970).

In 1959 UNESCO took note of the plans of the Egyptian Government to flood the Nile Valley and build a new high dam at Aswan and mounted a campaign to salvage Nubia. This was the first example of international co-operation in an archaeological venture and it was highly successful. The final and most dramatic moment was when the great figures in the temples of Abu Simbel were cut out and   130
moved bodily up. But one wonders now whether this great inundation and the creation of Lake Nasser were necessary.

In the same year that UNESCO was beginning its great campaign to save the monuments of Nubia from extinction, Michel Fleury discovered the tomb of Queen Arnegunde at St Denis north of Paris, and Mary Leakey found a human skull in Bed 1 at Olduvai Gorge in Tanzania, which was dated to a million and three quarters years old: since then older human or semi-human finds have been made in various parts of East Africa, but this was our first indication of the very great antiquity of man.

The circumstances surrounding the remarkable Olduvai discovery need to be recorded in a history of archaeology. Louis Leakey was ill, lying on his bed at the base camp. Mary Leakey was working in the dry sands at the lowest geological levels of the Gorge. On 17 July 1959 she spotted bone fragments eroding out of the sloping wall of the Gorge. Let us put the rest of the story in the words of Brian Fagan's *Quest for the Past* (1978):

130 (*Opposite*) The building of the High Dam at Aswan and the creation of Lake Nasser would have involved the submergence of the temple of Abu Simbel. Combined archaeological operations under UNESCO removed the temple to a higher site. Here a colossal head of Ramesses II is being lifted up.

131 Louis Leakey (1903–72) displays fossil remains from Olduvai Gorge at a press conference in Washington in 1964. After nearly three decades of patient work, he and his wife had discovered man's earliest human-like ancestors then known, about one-and-three-quarter million years old.

Electrified, she carefully scraped away the clinging soil from two large teeth. They were unquestionably those of a human-like fossil, the first to be found in Olduvai Gorge. Mary jumped in the Land Rover and tore up to camp. 'I've got him, I've got him', she cried as she burst into the tent. His illness forgotten, Louis leaped into his clothes and together, husband and wife rattled down the track to the site. With great care, they examined the teeth and prised away more soil. There could be no doubt: Mary Leakey had uncovered a fossil skull of tremendous antiquity. A search that had begun twenty-eight years before was finally crowned with success.

131   The success was the discovery of *Zinjanthropus boisei*: 'Dear Boy' as he was known in the Leakey family, and Nutcracker Man as he was known to the world.

In that same year Pierre-Roland Giot published C14 dates for megalithic monuments in Brittany and showed that they were older than the pyramids of Egypt or the ziggurats of Mesopotamia – were in fact, just as we subsequently found the Maltese temples were, among the oldest architecture in the world. Archaeology was revolutionizing itself, and its picture of man in time, in the 1950s and 1960s.

The 1960s saw Yadin's excavations at Masada in Israel; Hole and Flannery beginning their work at Ali Kosh in Iran; Atkinson and Piggott digging at Stonehenge, Silbury Hill, West Kennet and Wayland's Smithy; the discovery of Lepinski Vir in Yugoslavia and its excavations by Trifunović and Srejović; and Michael Coe's excavation of the ceremonial Olmec sites at San Lorenzo in southern Veracruz.

132

It was these years that turned archaeology from being a subject confined to prehistory and the protohistoric civilizations of Egypt, Mesopotamia, Palestine, Greece and Rome to a humanistic discipline that dealt with the material remains of man at all times and in all places.

Prehistory was now world prehistory and the story of archaeology in America, Africa, south-east Asia, Australia and Polynesia was to be set side by side with the story of archaeology in Europe and the Near East that had been established in the nineteenth century and the beginning of the twentieth century. This world-widening of perspective is well shown in Grahame Clark's *World Prehistory* (first published 1961, third edition 1977), Chester S. Chard's *Man in Prehistory* (second edition 1975) and Brian Fagan's *People of the Earth* (second edition 1977) and his *World Prehistory: A Brief Introduction* (1979).

This chapter brings us up to the year 1980, a hundred years after Flinders Petrie began his work in Egypt, Pitt-Rivers his excavations in Cranborne Chase and de Sautuola published the Altamira paintings. The last ten years have shown that archaeology is more vigorously and usefully pursued than ever and that new and important discoveries continue to be made in all parts of the world.

In 1939 in an article in *Antiquity* entitled 'Volcanic Destruction of Minoan Crete' (1939, 425–39) Spiridon Marinatos, then Head of the Greek Archaeological Service, put forward the theory that the eruption or explosion of Thera and its side effects caused disastrous destruction in Crete. This theory was elaborated by Sir Denys Page in a paper

132 Restoration of one of the trilithons at Stonehenge in 1958. Richard Atkinson and Stuart Piggott established the first accurate building sequence for the monument through their excavations at the site in the 1950s and early 1960s.

133, 134 The Late Bronze Age frescoes discovered by Marinatos at Akrotiri on the island of Thera have added a new dimension to our knowledge of Minoan painting. One wall of a reconstructed room (*above*) shows the Theran landscape before the volcanic eruption which destroyed the site in about 1500 BC. Swallows dart among lilies and coloured rocks. Another painting (*opposite*) depicts a square-rigged pleasure boat.

published by the Society for Hellenic Studies in 1970, entitled 'The Santorini Volcano and the destruction of Minoan Crete'. Archaeologists remain split on this issue, which goes on being discussed in books and conferences. Marinatos's excavations at Akrotiri on Thera, with the remarkable frescoes there, have been published in a series of volumes in Athens from 1967 to 1976, and a one-volume account by Christos Doumas is due to appear shortly. Marinatos himself was killed when his Theran excavations collapsed under him, and he died in the arms of Sir Denys Page.

In 1972 there was discovered accidentally near the Lake of Varna close to the Black Sea coast of north-east Bulgaria a Copper Age cemetery: excavation of the cemetery by Ivan S. Ivanov of the Varna Museum revealed a large quantity of gold objects, the so-called Varna treasure, described by Colin Renfrew as 'the earliest major assemblage of gold artifacts to be unearthed anywhere in the world . . . an event of some note, comparable in significance with Schliemann's find of the Great Treasure of Troy more than a century ago.' (*Antiquity*, 1978, 199.) The finds at Varna are at least fifteen hundred years older than Troy II: they emphasize the fact of the early and autonomous development of metallurgy in south-east Europe.

Also in 1972 Richard Leakey, continuing the pioneering work in East Africa of his father Louis Leakey, announced the discovery of a skull of the genus *Homo* which dates back to more than two-and-a-half million years. The location on Lake Turkana where he found the skull has subsequently proved a fertile hunting ground for other equally ancient hominid remains.

In 1975 the discovery of some twenty thousand tablets, written in cuneiform, in a vast palace archive at Tell Mardikh (ancient Ebla) in Syria caused a sensation almost comparable with the discoveries at Lascaux and Sutton Hoo and of Tutankhamun's tomb. The head of the excavation was Professor Paolo Matthiae and the epigrapher Professor Giovanni Pettinato, both of Rome. Here was a lost civilization with a language hitherto unknown. For an account of these finds see Chaim Bermant and Michael Weitzman, *Ebla: An Archaeological Enigma* (1979) and Paolo Matthiae, *Ebla* (1980).

Hardly had the Ebla discoveries left the headlines than Malonis Andronikos, Professor of Archaeology at the University of Thessalonika, revealed in 1977 the finding of the tomb of Alexander the Great's father, Philip II of Macedon, at Vergina in northern Greece. Funerary objects of gold, silver and bronze suggested this was a royal burial, but it was five tiny ivory heads, with likenesses of Philip and Alexander, that seemed to indicate whose the burial was.

And so the list of new finds continues, and on a worldwide scale. R. S. MacNeish has recently made public his discovery of over sixty new sites in Belize which seem to push back Mayan origins several thousand years. And it is fitting that I should conclude with perhaps the most spectacular find of all – the vast terracotta army of the Chinese emperor Huang Ti, buried a mile from his tomb at Mount Li near the Yellow River in the third century BC to protect him in the afterlife. A new awareness of the importance of China will be a key development in archaeology in the decades ahead.

X

6
The Great Themes

The five preceding chapters, which form the body of this book, have chronicled, albeit in summary and selective fashion, the history of archaeology from its beginnings to the end of the third quarter of the twentieth century. It is a story full of excitement and of exciting personalities, a story based on the determination of individuals such as Schliemann at Troy and Howard Carter in the Valley of the Kings, a story of purpose in excavation and fieldwork but a story also of the strange way in which discoveries of great importance were made by chance – the Rosetta Stone, the Gallehus horns, the megalithic tombs of Cocherel in 1685 and New Grange in 1699, the Tell-el-Amarna tablets and the Dead Sea Scrolls, and Lascaux in 1940.

In bringing this book to a close let us think back to the main elements in the story: the principal themes in the history of archaeology. Here they are briefly summarized.

1 The Birth of Archaeology
This was the realization that legends, myths, folk-memory, the Bible and classical writers were not a sure or real source for our knowledge of the ancient past of man, that Dr Johnson was wrong when he said we had to rely on ancient writers, and that the artifacts of man from medieval castle to Roman villa, stone circle and Old Stone Age chipped hand-axe were the real sources of our knowledge of ancient man.

2 The Acceptance of Stone Artifacts
The next step forward was the recognition that stone implements were not made by fairies or elves but were fashioned by man. Mercati believed this, although his *Metallotheca* was not published until the eighteenth century: so did Sir William Dugdale, Sir Robert Sibbald, Edward Lhwyd, Lafitau, Mahudel, Goguet and Bishop Lyttelton. John Frere's letter of 1797 showed that he had no doubts.

3 The Technological Model
The appreciation that stone implements were man-made enabled the setting up of a technological model of the past. This was explicit in the writings of Goguet and Vedel-Simonsen but was first made manifest to the general public by the opening of the Copenhagen Museum in 1819 arranged by C. J. Thomsen on the basis of the three-age system.

4 The Discovery of the Monuments

Archaeology came into its own when antiquarians, travellers and eventually specialized persons began to record the surface monuments from antiquity. Such were Stuart and Revett in Athens, Wood and Dawkins in Asia Minor and the Near East, Carsten Niebuhr in Persepolis, Aubrey, Lhwyd and Stukeley in Britain, and the work of the French savants which resulted in the *Description de L'Egypte*.

5 The Development of Modern Geology

The appreciation of the stratification of rocks and the acceptance of the principle of uniformitarianism and of the new geology, as set out in Lyell's *Principles of Geology*, showed that man's antiquity went far further back than 'the present world' of 4004 BC. Geology not only showed the great antiquity of man but helped archaeologists to understand stratigraphy (see below).

6 Darwinism and Organic Evolution

The publication of *The Origin of Species* in 1859, in the same year as the antiquity of man was accepted in the Royal Society and the Society of Antiquaries, showed that evidence of early man in the form of his tools and skeletal remains was not only acceptable but necessary, and suggested that organic evolution might imply supraorganic or cultural evolution.

7 Excavation

Excavation began in the megaliths of Denmark in the sixteenth and seventeenth centuries and in Pompeii and Herculaneum in the eighteenth century, culminating in the work of Fiorelli and his *Scuola di Pompeii*. It moved to a careful and rigid discipline through the work of men like Curtius, Pitt-Rivers, Flinders Petrie, Wheeler and Schaeffer.

8 Stratigraphy

The appreciation and understanding of archaeological stratigraphy was a fundamental of archaeological excavation. It inherited this from stratigraphical geology but was based on the early observations of Worsaae in Denmark and Thomas Jefferson in Virginia. The stratigraphy of tells was understood first by Flinders Petrie at Tell-el-Hesi, Schliemann at Troy, and Pumpelly and Schmidt at Anau.

9 Lost Civilizations

Fieldwork and excavation have revealed civilizations hitherto entirely unknown from written sources. These have included, for example, the Sumerians in Mesopotamia, the Harappan civilization of the Indian subcontinent, the Shang civilization of China, and the Olmec civilization of Central America.

10 Decipherment

One of the most exciting aspects of the history of archaeology has been the decipherment of hitherto unknown forms of writing, from runic and ogham writing in Europe to Egyptian hieroglyphs by Champollion, the cuneiform of Mesopotamia by Grotefend and Rawlinson, Hittite by Hrozny, Linear B by Ventris and Chadwick, and here of course we must mention the discovery of the Ras Shamra alphabet.

11 Chronology
The sure basis of archaeology rests on accurate dating. Cross-dating with written sources was developed by Flinders Petrie, Montelius and Childe. Non-archaeological dating began with De Geer's varve-counting and Douglas's dendrochronology (already being used by the Reverend Manasseh Cutler and Thomas Jefferson in the eighteenth century). The development of C14, TL and Potassium-Argon dating since the Second World War has revolutionized prehistoric archaeology.

12 The Study of the Environment
The archaeology of the Swiss lake-dwellings in the 1860s was accompanied by the study of their flora and fauna; and Anau was a pioneer example of the study of ecofacts. Environmental and ecological studies have been developed as an essential part of archaeological research particularly in England (cf. the work of Zeuner, Grahame Clark, Eric Higgs) and elsewhere (e.g. Karl Butser's *Environment and Archaeology*, 1964).

13 Ethnographic Parallels
It was the discovery of Stone Age communities in the New World that persuaded Mercati and others to postulate a Stone Age. Père Lafitau and Goguet valued ethnographic parallels, so did Lubbock and Pitt-Rivers. W. J. Sollas, *Ancient Hunters and their Modern Representatives* (1911), was a classic example of the use of ethnographic parallels, although too deterministic in approach. Recently Colin Renfrew in *Before Civilization* has been using Polynesian societies as a possible guide to the interpretation of the prehistoric European societies who built megalithic monuments. In American archaeology the Maya and North American Indians survive as living exemplars of the archaeological record. This is perhaps why American archaeologists are so insistent that archaeology is anthropology. The present and the pre-Columbian past are closely interwoven in a way that does not occur in Europe and the Near East. But the study of folk-culture in northern Europe, pioneered in Scandinavia, provides a living ethnographic parallel of great value to archaeology.

14 The Non-technological Model
There was always a non-technological model of the past based on the Scottish primitivists and extending through Monboddo to Daniel Wilson. Sven Nilsson in Sweden developed this as did Tylor in England and Lewis Morgan in America. Morgan's ideas went through Engels to Marx and are the basis of the Marxist view of prehistory.

15 World Prehistory
Prehistoric archaeology began in Scandinavia, Britain, France and Switzerland, protohistoric archaeology in Asia Minor, Egypt and Mesopotamia. Gradually archaeological researches spread all over the

world, literally from China to Peru, from Greenland's icy mountains to India's coral strand. There is now, as we have said, even a nation-state named after the great archaeological site of Zimbabwe. In three areas, America, the Indian subcontinent and China, archaeological researches have become of paramount importance to our general understanding of man's antiquity because here we can observe the process of the cultivation of crops and synoecism developing apparently independent of contact with other comparable areas.

16 Independent Invention v. Diffusion

From the beginnings of systematic archaeology in the early nineteenth century its practitioners have been concerned with the explanation of cultural change, and thoughtful Danish scholars discussed the sempiternal opposed views of independent invention and diffusion. The excesses of the independent invention thesis can be seen in a rigid Marxist view of the past. The excesses of the diffusionist thesis are well shown by the Elliot Smith/Perry Manchester School. Montelius and Childe preached a modified form of diffusionism. By today it seems we must recognize both explanations of culture change as necessary and real. Certainly the Neolithic and Urban Revolutions of Childe occurred independently in many parts of the world.

17 Scientific Techniques

The twentieth century has seen the development of scientific techniques to assist the archaeologist in reconnaissance, prospecting, excavation and the handling of his data – a long story from the beginnings of geochronology and air photography to statistics and computer analysis.

18 Historical Archaeology

Just as the nineteenth-century archaeology of Europe has exploded and expanded into world prehistory, so has its prehistoric and protohistoric basis developed into the study of historical archaeology, first that of the Anglo-Saxons, Merovingians and Vikings, and then that of medieval and later Europe. The archaeology of the European colonies in North America has been a particularly fruitful field (cf. Noel Hume, *Historical Archaeology*, 1968).

19 The Critical Evaluation of Evidence

This has become of increasing importance in the development of archaeology and it is by such critical examination that we can assess the value and the limitations of the archaeological evidence. It is also by this critical appraisal that we view the forgeries and problems of authenticity in archaeology from Moulin Quignon and Piltdown to Glozel and Rouffignac. It is the duty of archaeologists to set out their critical conclusions, not only to their scholarly colleagues but also to the general public. *Haute vulgarisation* is an essential of archaeology: the history of archaeology shows only too clearly that without good, authoritative popularization the interested public will move away to what they call alternate archaeology and linger longingly in the lunatic fringes of the wilder shores of archaeology. From Queen Moo through

Atlantis to the lost tribes and non-existent space-men there is a powerful fascination in, and an almost religious feeling for, the simplistic, however fantastic, explanation of the past. The success of the Manchester School and the large sales of von Däniken's fantasies are clear warnings of the dangers facing serious archaeology.

20 The Ethics of Archaeology

Archaeology began in looting: the search for works of art for private or national collections. Belzoni, Rassam, Mariette and Layard were all concerned with finding treasures. Gradually this has changed to careful excavation and now to deliberately planned excavation to solve particular problems. Problem-orientated archaeology has eventually succeeded tomb robbing. Many ethical problems remain: whether material like the Elgin marbles should be returned to their original home, how and in what state of reconstruction and restoration should excavations be left, whether important sites should be totally excavated or parts left for posterity, the conflicting claims of rescue and research archaeology and so on.

These seem to me the twenty main themes that emerge from a study of the history of archaeology. Others may regard other themes as more important. To many it is still the great antiquity of man that seems the most dramatic lesson of the history of archaeology and as we write more claims are coming in of very ancient human beings and hominids in East Africa. Few people today would say with Sir Thomas Browne, 'time we may comprehend'.

But to me it is not the great age of man that is the excitement of archaeology but the variety and splendour of his ancient achievement. It was not surprising that archaeology and the world took so long to accept Upper Palaeolithic art: the Venus of Brassempouy, the cave paintings of Niaux, Altamira and Lascaux are still surprising, though now as illustrations in books on the history of art as commonplace as those of Queen Nefertiti and the Venus de Milo. They, and the art of the Celts, Scythians and Vikings, are among the most rewarding excitements that have resulted from studying the development of archaeology. So is an appraisal of the technical achievements of ancient man from the pyramids, the Maltese temples and Stonehenge to the Olmec heads and Inca cities. It is the unfolding achievement of man, an achievement which is part of the patrimony of us all, that makes the study of our awareness of this past so interesting and so relevant.

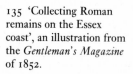

135 'Collecting Roman remains on the Essex coast', an illustration from the *Gentleman's Magazine* of 1852.

Further Reading

The bibliography of my *A Hundred and Fifty Years of Archaeology* provides a long and comprehensive list of books. Here is a shorter list classified by subject.

1 General Histories

BIBBY, GEOFFREY *The Testimony of the Spade*, New York 1956 and London 1957.
CERAM, C. W. *Gods, Graves and Scholars*, New York 1951 and London 1952.
——*A Picture History of Archaeology*, London 1958.
DANIEL, G. E. *The Idea of Prehistory*, London and Baltimore 1962.
——*A Hundred and Fifty Years of Archaeology*, London and Cambridge, Mass., 1975.
——(ed.) *Towards a History of Archaeology*, London and New York 1981.
DAUX, GEORGES *Les étapes de l'archéologie*, Paris 1942.
EYDOUX, H.-P. *History of Archaeological Discoveries*, London 1966.
FAGAN, BRIAN M. *Quest for the Past: Great Discoveries in Archaeology*, Reading, Mass., and London 1978.
GARNETT, HENRY *Treasures of Yesterday*, London and New York 1964.

2 Archaeology in the Context of Anthropology

BREW, J. O. (ed.) *One Hundred Years of Anthropology*, Cambridge, Mass., 1968.
CASSON, STANLEY *The Discovery of Man*, London and New York 1939.
HARRIS, MARVIN *The Rise of Anthropological Theory: a History of Theories of Culture*, London and New York 1968.
LOWIE, R. H. *The History of Ethnological Theory*, New York 1937 and London 1938.
PENNIMAN, T. K. *A Hundred Years of Anthropology*, revised edition, London 1952.

3 Antiquaries and Antiquarian Thought

KENDRICK, SIR THOMAS *The Druids*, London 1927.
——*British Antiquity*, London 1950.
PIGGOTT, STUART *William Stukeley*, Oxford 1950.
——*The Druids*, London and New York 1968.
——*Ruins in a Landscape*, Edinburgh and New York 1976.

WALTERS, H. B. *The English Antiquaries of the Sixteenth, Seventeenth and Eighteenth Centuries*, London 1934.

4 Near Eastern and Egyptian Archaeology

BAIKIE, J. *A Century of Excavation in the Land of the Pharaohs*, London and New York 1924.
BAINES, JOHN AND JAROMIR MALEK *Atlas of Ancient Egypt*, Oxford 1980.
BRATTON, F. GLADSTONE *A History of Egyptian Archaeology*, London 1967.
CAIGER, S. L. *Bible and Spade*, Oxford 1936.
FAGAN, BRIAN M. *The Rape of the Nile: Tomb Robbers, Tourists and Archaeologists in Egypt*, New York and London 1975.
——*Return to Babylon: Travellers, Archaeologists and Monuments in Mesopotamia*, New York 1979.
GREENER, L. *The Discovery of Egypt*, London and New York 1966.
LLOYD, SETON *Foundations in the Dust*, London 1947 (revised edition, London and New York 1980).
MACALISTER, R. A. S. *A Century of Excavation in Palestine*, London and New York 1925.
OATES, JOAN *Babylon*, London and New York 1979.
WORTHAM, J. D. *The Genesis of British Egyptology: 1549–1906*, Oklahoma 1971.

5 European Archaeology

EGGERS, J. H. *Einführung in die Vorgeschichte*, Munich 1959.
KLINDT-JENSEN, OLE *A History of Scandinavian Archaeology*, London 1975 and New York 1976.
LAMING-EMPERAIRE A. *Origines de l'archéologie préhistorique en France*, Paris 1964.
RODDEN, J. *A History of British Archaeology* (forthcoming).

6 American Archaeology

CERAM, C. W. *The First American: a Story of North American Archaeology*, New York 1971, London 1976.
FAGAN, BRIAN M. *Elusive Treasure*, New York 1977.
VON HAGEN, VICTOR *Search for the Maya; the Story of Stephenson and Catherwood*, New York 1975.
WILLEY, G. R. AND J. A. SABLOFF, *A History of American Archaeology*, London and San Francisco 1974 (second edition, San Francisco 1980).

7 Collections of Extracts from Writers

CERAM, C. W. *The World of Archaeology*, London 1966 (US: *Hands on the Past*, New York 1966).
DANIEL, G. E. *The Origins and Growth of Archaeology*, Harmondsworth and Baltimore 1967.
HAWKES, JACQUETTA *The World of the Past*, London and New York 1963.

HEIZER, R. F. *Man's Discovery of his Past: Literary Landmarks in Archaeology*, second edition, Englewood Cliffs, N. J. 1969.

SILVERBERG, ROBERT *Great Adventures in Archaeology*, New York 1964 and London 1966.

WAUCHOPE, ROBERT *They Found the Buried Cities: Exploration and Excavation in the American Tropics*, Chicago and London 1965.

8 Biographies of Archaeologists

COLE, SONIA *Leakey's Luck*, London and New York 1975.

DUFF, URSULA G. *The Life-work of Lord Avebury*, London 1924.

POOLE, L. AND G. *One Passion, Two Loves: the Schliemanns of Troy*, New York 1966 and London 1967.

RAWLINSON, G. *A Memoir of Major-General Sir H. C. Rawlinson*, London 1898.

THOMPSON, M. W. *General Pitt-Rivers*, Bradford-on-Avon and New Jersey 1977.

9 Autobiographies of Archaeologists

CRAWFORD, O. G. S. *Said and Done*, London and New York 1955.

LAYARD, A. H. *Autobiography and Letters*, London and New York 1903.

LEAKEY, L. S. B. *White African*, London 1937.

MALLOWAN, SIR MAX *Mallowan's Memoirs*, London 1977.

MURRAY, MARGARET *My First Hundred Years*, London 1963.

PETRIE, SIR FLINDERS *Seventy Years in Archaeology*, London 1931 and New York 1932.

THOMPSON, J. ERIC S. *Maya Archaeologist*, London and Oklahoma 1963.

WHEELER, SIR MORTIMER *Still Digging*, London and New York 1955.

WOOLLEY, SIR LEONARD *Spadework*, London and New York 1953.

List of Illustrations

Colour Illustrations

Monochrome Illustrations

Index

Numerals in italics refer to
numbered illustrations

Raglan, Lord, Sumerocentric hyperdiffusionist 150
Ramesses II, colossal carving of head of *130*
Ramsay, Sir A. C., on stone tools 53–4
Rao, S. R., at Lothal 172
Rassam, Hormuzd, in Mesopotamia 77–8, 120; *74*
Rawlinson, Henry, in Mesopotamia 79, 121; *53*; and cuneiform 80
Reinach, Salomon 100; quoted 114, 185
Reiss, Wilhelm, in Peru 142
Renaissance, the 15
Renfrew, Colin 180; on 'new' archaeology 192
Revett, Nicholas, in Athens and Ionia 15, 16
Rhŷs, Sir John, on early Britain 115
Rich, Claudius J., in Mesopotamia 72–3
Richborough, Roman city 26
Rigollet, Dr, at Saint-Acheul 53
Rivière, Émile, and cave art 98–9, 101
Rogers, Samuel, poem *Italy* by 35
Roman remains: on Essex coast *135*; in Isle of Wight 116–17; *see also* classical archaeology
Rosetta Stone 24; *8*; decipherment of 64, 66
Rouffignac cave 207
Royal Antiquaries: Denmark 31; England, to Henry VIII 25; Sweden 30, 32
Rudenko, S. I., at Pazyryk 200–1
Ruz, Alberto, in Mexico 201–2
rune-stones, runic inscriptions 30, 31

Sacken, Baron von, on Hallstatt 89
Sacy, Sylvestre de, and demotic script 65
Sahni, Daya Ram, at Harappa 173
St Joseph, J. K., air photographer 184
Saint-Mathurin, S. de 201; *125*
St Ninian's hoard, Shetland 207
Samothrace, excavations in 124, 161
Sandys, George (1578–1644) 22
Sarzec, Ernest de, and Sumerians 121–2
Sautuola, Marcellino de, at Altamira 98
savants, with Napoleon in Egypt 24, 64; *40*
Saville, M. H., in Honduras 142
Sayce, A. H. 152; and Hittites 137
Schaaffhausen, H., and Neanderthal man 54–5
Schaeffer, Claude, at Ugarit 161
Schliemann, Heinrich 107, 125–7, 129, 130, 148, 152; *78*
Schliemann, Sophia 125; *81*
Schmerling, P. C., in Belgium (1833) 48, 62
Schmidt, E. F., at Alishar Hüyük 159
Schmidt, Hubert, at Anau 134
Schoolcraft, H. R., and American mounds 92
Schuchhardt, H., *Alteuropa* by (1921) 162
scientific techniques, in archaeology 147, 181–7, 215
Scythians 88; frozen tombs of 200–1; goldwork of *VII*, *VIII*
Seba, Albert (1665–1736) 43
Sedgwick, Adam, geologist 50
Seler, Edward and Maya language and art 143
Sempler, W. T., and Troy 158; *101*
Sertima, I. von 193
Sèvres, Marcel de, on ancient man 48
Shakespeare, on the age of the earth 34
Sharpe, Lieut. P. H., air photographer 147; *95*
ship burials *see* Gokstad, Oseberg, Sutton Hoo
Sialk, excavation of 156–7
Sibbald, Sir Robert (1641–1722) 36
Simonsen, L. S. Vedel, on three-age model 58
Sippar (Abu Habbah) 120
skeletons, human: coloured red 49, 101
Sloane, Sir Hans (1660–1753) 46
Smith, Sir Cecil, in Greece 129–30
Smith, C. R., *Inventorum Sepulchrale* by 90
Smith, C. Piazzi, and pyramids 117
Smith, George, on Ashur-banipal 119
Smith, Sir Grafton Eliot, Egyptocentric hyperdiffusionist 115, 144, 149
Smith, William 'Strata' 51
Smithson, James, and Smithsonian Institution 92
Snake Goddess, Minoan statuette of *85*
societies, learned: in Europe (17th century) 46; in India 95, 96; in Russia 88; in USA 42, 90–1, 92
Solutrean period 64
Sphinx, at Giza *42*
Spinden, H. J., on Maya art 143
Spon, Jacques (1747–85) 13–14
Squier, E. G., in Mississippi valley 91
Star Carr, Yorkshire, Mesolithic site 201
Stein, Sir Aurel, in Central Asia 157–8
Stephens, J. L., in Mesoamerica 93–4, 142; *61*
Stiles, Ezra, President of Yale 40
Stone Age: divided into Palaeolithic and Neolithic 62; Mesolithic period inserted 102; *see also* three-age model
Stonehenge 26, 27, 117, 198, 209; *15*, *132*
stone tools: associated with bones of extinct animals 36, 38, 49, 52, 53, and with human bones 38; recognition of, as artifacts 35–6, 212
Stow, John (1525?–1605) 46
stratification 51; false and true *107*
stratigraphy, archaeological 60, 86, 213; in excavations 123, 126, 129, 140; metrical, and humanly caused (Kidder) 177
Stuart, James, in Athens and Ionia 15, 16
Stübel, Alphonse, in Peru 152
Stukeley, William (1687–1765) 29
Suhm, P. F., and three-age model 56
Sumerians 121, 155; tablets in language of 122
Sumerocentric hyperdiffusionist doctrine 150
Susa, excavation at 134; *87*